"This superb introduction to free will is highly accessible without paying the price in over-simplification. The debate format does a wonderful job of highlighting the pros and cons of Kane's and Sartorio's competing positions on free will. Ideal for an undergraduate course on free will."

Alfred R. Mele, *Florida State University, USA*

"This is an outstanding book by two of the very top philosophers working on free will and moral responsibility. They are each perfect representatives of the best recent developments of two important positions: libertarianism and compatibilism. The book is clear and lively, and it is a perfect text for an undergraduate course on these topics. Highly recommended!"

John Martin Fischer, *University of California, Riverside, USA*

Do We Have Free Will?

In this little but profound volume, Robert Kane and Carolina Sartorio debate a perennial question: *Do We Have Free Will?*

Kane introduces and defends libertarianism about free will: free will is incompatible with determinism; we are free; we are not determined. Sartorio introduces and defends compatibilism about free will: free will is compatible with determinism; we can be free even while our actions are determined through and through. Simplifying tricky terminology and complicated concepts for readers new to the debate, the authors also cover the latest developments on a controversial topic that gets us entangled in questions about blameworthiness and responsibility, coercion and control and much more.

Each author first presents their own side, and then they interact through two rounds of objections and replies. Pedagogical features include standard form arguments, section summaries, bolded key terms and principles, a glossary and annotated reading lists. Short, lively and accessible, the debate showcases diverse and cutting-edge work on free will. As per Saul Smilansky's foreword, Kane and Sartorio "present the readers with two things at once: an introduction to the traditional free will problem and a demonstration of what a great yet very much alive and relevant philosophical problem is like".

Key Features

- Covers major concepts, views and arguments about free will in an engaging format.
- Accessible style and pedagogical features for students and general readers.
- Cutting-edge contributions by preeminent scholars on free will.

Robert Kane is University Distinguished Professor of Philosophy and Law Emeritus at the University of Texas at Austin, USA. He is the author of *Free Will and Values* (1985), *Through the Moral Maze* (1993), *The Significance of Free Will* (1996), *A Contemporary Introduction to Free Will* (2005), *Ethics and the Quest for Wisdom* (2010); editor of *The Oxford Handbook of Free Will* (2002, 2011); and author of more than 80 journal articles.

Carolina Sartorio is Professor of Philosophy at the University of Arizona, USA. Her research expertise focuses on issues in causation, agency, free will and moral responsibility. She is the author of numerous leading research articles in these areas and the book *Causation and Free Will* (2016).

Saul Smilansky is Professor of Philosophy at the University of Haifa, Israel.

Little Debates About Big Questions

Tyron Goldschmidt
Fellow of the Rutgers Center for Philosophy of Religion, USA

Dustin Crummett
Ludwig Maximilian University of Munich, Germany

About the series:

Philosophy asks questions about the fundamental nature of reality, our place in the world, and what we should do. Some of these questions are perennial: for example, *Do we have free will? What is morality?* Some are much newer: for example, *How far should free speech on campus extend? Are race, sex and gender social constructs?* But all of these are among the big questions in philosophy and they remain controversial.

Each book in the *Little Debates About Big Questions* series features two professors on opposite sides of a big question. Each author presents their own side, and the authors then exchange objections and replies. Short, lively, and accessible, these debates showcase diverse and deep answers. Pedagogical features include standard form arguments, section summaries, bolded key terms and principles, glossaries, and annotated reading lists.

The debate format is an ideal way to learn about controversial topics. Whereas the usual essay or book risks overlooking objections against its own proposition or misrepresenting the opposite side, in a debate each side can make their case at equal length, and then present objections the other side must consider. Debates have a more conversational and fun style too, and we selected particularly talented philosophers—in substance and style—for these kinds of encounters.

Debates can be combative—sometimes even descending into anger and animosity. But debates can also be cooperative. While our authors disagree strongly, they work together to help each other and the reader get clearer on the ideas, arguments, and objections. This is intellectual progress, and a much-needed model for civil and constructive disagreement.

The substance and style of the debates will captivate interested readers new to the questions. But there's enough to interest experts too. The debates will be especially useful for courses in philosophy and related subjects—whether as primary or secondary readings—and a few debates can be combined to make up the reading for an entire course.

We thank the authors for their help in constructing this series. We are honored to showcase their work. They are all preeminent scholars or rising-stars in their fields, and through these debates they share what's been discovered with a wider audience. This is a paradigm for public philosophy, and will impress upon students, scholars, and other interested readers the enduring importance of debating the big questions.

For more information about this series, please visit: https://www.routledge.com/Little-Debates-about-Big-Questions/book-series/LDABQ

Do We Have Free Will?

A Debate

Robert Kane and Carolina Sartorio

With a Foreword by Saul Smilansky

Routledge
Taylor & Francis Group

NEW YORK AND LONDON

First published 2022
by Routledge
605 Third Avenue, New York, NY 10158

and by Routledge
2 Park Square, Milton Park, Abingdon, Oxon OX14 4RN

Routledge is an imprint of the Taylor & Francis Group, an informa business

British Library Cataloguing-in-Publication Data
A catalogue record for this book is available from the British Library

Library of Congress Cataloging-in-Publication Data
Names: Kane, Robert, 1938– author. | Sartorio, Carolina, author.
Title: Do we have free will?: a debate/Robert Kane and Carolina
   Sartorio; with a foreword by Saul Smilansky.
Description: New York, NY: Routledge, 2022.
Series: Little debates about big questions | Includes bibliographical
   references and index.
Identifiers: LCCN 2021014463 (print) | LCCN 2021014464 (ebook)
   Subjects: LCSH: Free will and determinism. Classification: LCC
   BJ1461 .K3654 2022 (print) | LCC BJ1461 (ebook) | DDC
   123/.5—dc23
LC record available at https://lccn.loc.gov/2021014463
LC ebook record available at https://lccn.loc.gov/2021014464

ISBN: 978-0-367-25833-7 (hbk)
ISBN: 978-0-367-25832-0 (pbk)
ISBN: 978-1-003-21217-1 (ebk)

DOI: 10.4324/9781003212171

Typeset in Sabon
by Apex CoVantage, LLC

Contents

Foreword

The free will problem is indisputably one of the great, live problems of philosophy. It has been known for at least two thousand years, yet the last two generations saw a golden period for the free will debate, and more progress seems to have been made during those years than in the previous two millennia. The progress, in understanding and sophistication, is so considerable that arguably there is little need to read anything written on the problem before the 1960s.

Some of the great problems of philosophy may no longer be alive for many people. The question of whether God exists seems to be so in many West European countries, following Darwin and mass secularization. Other classical philosophical problems, such as those about the nature of time or about universals, have not been solved but are not obviously relevant to everyday, "real" life, except for a few professional philosophers. The free will problem is one of those great philosophical problems that are, at once, still *universally* in contention and *highly relevant* to people's everyday lives. The free will problem is a killer whale roaming the philosophical oceans, and trying to catch it by its tail captures the excitement and relevance of philosophy.

Since we deny many people their liberties for committing crimes and are likely to keep incarcerating criminals, it manifestly seems to matter a great deal whether we think that those people are nothing but helpless victims of the circumstances that created them, ultimately beyond their control, or free blameworthy agents deserving of punishment. Some forms of appreciation of others' efforts and achievements, as well as our own self-respect, admittedly do not require assumptions about free will: we value babies and appreciate people with innate talents, for example. Nevertheless,

moral appreciation, and the related reactive attitudes, such as gratitude and central forms of love, seem fundamentally dependent upon
ideas of free agency and moral responsibility. We believe that the
people being appreciated decided freely to do good and are hence
deserving of our appreciation—that they are praise*worthy*.

In this splendid dialogue introduction to the free will problem,
Robert Kane and Carolina Sartorio present the readers with two
things at once: an introduction to the traditional free will problem
and a demonstration of what a great yet very much alive and relevant philosophical problem is like.

In order to locate this book within the contemporary debate it
is helpful to understand the free will problem as a combination of
five questions (Smilansky 2017). The first two are the more familiar
ones—the *Classic Problem*—and the latter three have emerged as
central in the last two generations—we might call these the *Modern
Additions*. The questions are as follows:

1. **Is there libertarian free will?** Do we have free will, in a sense
    that transcends necessitation by our environment and genes
    and the whole past history of the universe? Here we would get
    entangled in further questions of the nature of the necessitation
    (aka *determinism*), whether indeterminism would give us the
    right sort of control and so on. On the one side, libertarians
    think there is free will and that it is libertarian. On the other
    side, compatibilists think there is free will but that it is not of
    this libertarian sort. In contrast to both, denialists (aka *hard
    determinists*) think there is no free will whatsoever. If these
    terms seem hard, don't worry—Kane and Sartorio will set you
    straight. The first question is metaphysical; that is, about what
    kind of stuff there is in the world.
2. **If libertarian free will does not exist, do we still have free will
    and moral responsibility and related notions such as desert?**
    This is the compatibility question: are free will and moral
    responsibility compatible with determinism or, more accu-
    rately, are they compatible with the absence of libertarian free
    will, irrespective of determinism? Compatibilism and denialism
    are opponents on the compatibility question. This question is
    mostly ethical.
3. **If we have no free will and moral responsibility in light of
    the absence of libertarian free will, or if free will and moral
    responsibility are at least seriously weakened by the absence of**

libertarian free will, is this good or bad? In other words, are we better off without (or with much less) valid attribution of free will and moral responsibility, so that we ought to welcome the absence of libertarian free will, or are we worse off? This question is ethical, more broadly value-related and psychological.

4. Can common beliefs, attitudes and practices concerning free will, moral responsibility, desert and so on change and, if so, how radical can this change be and what forms can it take? This question is mostly psychological, sociological and historical.

5. What can and should we do about the replies to Questions 1–4? Descriptive questions that concern the nature of folk belief and moral questions such as whether the continuation of widespread false belief can be tolerated are included as subquestions.

In this book, Kane and Sartorio mostly consider the first two questions, that make up the Classic Problem. Kane is a libertarian and Sartorio is a compatibilist. Both accept the widely shared assumption that free will and moral responsibility go together. Most of the interest in free will derives from the implications for moral responsibility and related notions, although not all does (for example, concern about the meaning of life need not be related to morality). And the notion of free will that is nearly always the focus of debate in the free will problem is the sort of free will that is required for moral responsibility. Yet beyond this agreement, they disagree about most aspects of the free will problem.

Kane introduces and defends both the motivation behind and the actual likelihood of our having a form of free will based upon the denial of determinism. If everything is determined, he argues, we do not have the fair opportunity to avoid doing the things that we do, which is a requirement for moral responsibility and all that depends upon it. A real freedom to do otherwise has to be within our grasp if we are to have the required sense of control. Sartorio, by contrast, argues that indeterminism would not introduce more control and hence would not further our free will and moral responsibility.

A helpful way to understand their striking disagreement about free will and moral responsibility would be to think about it as a matter of how high one aims. Kane puts the bar high: in order to have free will, we need to be able to form ourselves in a way that requires a transcendence of determination. He presents and defends his own well-known and sophisticated brand of libertarian free will. Kane's exposition is an excellent example of a detailed defence of a single, distinct view—in this case, a version of libertarian free will—which he sets out carefully in addition to replying to objections masterfully.

Sartorio understands free will very differently and in a way that sets the bar for freedom much lower. For her, free will is not some highly contentious capacity that requires the seeming magic of combining indeterminism and control. Rather, she argues, free will and moral responsibility emerge from the more pedestrian abilities and capacities of daily life. Nearly all people going about their lives, adequately responding to reasons and doing what they wish to do, are sufficiently free. Sartorio superbly spreads before the reader a broad gamut of possibilities, familiar from the compatibilist literature, for making sense of the compatibilist picture of free will and moral responsibility. She also points out the versions of compatibilism that seem to her more convincing.

Each of our authors contend that their favourite position follows from common sense views about free will. In a way that is typical for philosophy, both make a plausible case. Indeed, both wish to speak about our being the "real sources" of our choices and actions yet view what this means in radically different ways. Readers are likely to have their own intuitions here and be initially inclined to side either with Kane or with Sartorio. Yet open-minded readers—those who really wish to experience the challenge of struggling with one of the most important philosophical problems ever discovered—would do well to focus on the side of the debate that seems to them *unconvincing*. While in normal life we naturally welcome and focus upon confirmations of our pet intuitions and beliefs, deep and intellectually honest philosophical engagement requires the very opposite attitude. We need to welcome challenges to what seems to us most likely correct and attempt to sympathetically understand the opposite views, which are likely to seem to us highly implausible and, indeed, incredible.

At this stage we need to welcome another party into the Classic Problem, the denialists (or *hard determinists* or *free will skeptics*, as they are sometimes called). Like the libertarians, the denialists are incompatibilists; that is, they hold that free will and moral responsibility are not compatible with determinism (or absence of libertarian free will irrespective of determinism). Yet unlike the libertarians the denialists hold that there is no reason to think that we have the necessary form of libertarian free will and, indeed, they hold that determinism is very likely true. The denialists put the bar for free will and moral responsibility as high as the libertarians but deny that we can clear that bar. They have high standards but are pessimistic about the possibility of our ever meeting them.

These three positions—libertarianism, compatibilism and denialism—are, then, the three great alternatives on the Classic Problem. Libertarianism and compatibilism are the most popular views, and there is no better way to understand them than first reading Kane, then reading Sartorio, and then following their engaging debate in the rest of the book. For denialism, readers can explore, for example, the writings of Pereboom (2014) and Waller (2011).

As we already noted, the free will debate has gone beyond the Classic Problem and into what I called the Modern Additions—Questions 3–5. The motivation for this is diverse yet can be seen to emerge quite naturally from working through the Classic Problem. For example, if one opts for denialism, this immediately raises the question of whether living without belief in free will and moral responsibility would be good or bad (Question 3) and how much our beliefs, reactive emotions and practices can in fact change (Question 4). It is easy to see how a large spread of possibilities can emerge.

I can illustrate this through my own complex view of the free will problem: on the Classic Problem, I hold that Kane's view is not robust enough for what is required for a control-based notion of moral responsibility. Yet a robust libertarianism does not exist and arguably is even incoherent (see G. Strawson 1994). As to Question 2, I believe that we need to try and combine the limited but partly true insights of *both* compatibilism and denialism. That is the human condition—our being creatures who typically have a large measure of local compatibilist control, who ought to be treated as responsible agents, who are allowed to live out the consequences of our choices within a Community of Responsibility—but we are at the same time determined beings, operating as we were moulded, and this often generates severe injustice and great limitations in value and meaning.

Concerning Question 3, I argue that living without belief in free will and moral responsibility would be, all considered, morally, personally and socially highly destructive. Concerning Question 4, I claim that views which deny that there is a real risk of change (such as in P.F. Strawson's great paper "Freedom and Resentment" (see Watson 2003) are far too complacent (see Smilansky 2001). I therefore argue that we need to be careful, conservative and risk-averse in dealing with the highly dangerous free will problem. Due to the practical tension within the "dualistic" or compatibility–pluralist perspective and to the grim inherent implications of the realization of the absence of libertarian free will for matters such as desert-based justification, moral value and self-respect, I argue, concerning Question 5, that we need to (continue to) deceive ourselves on the free will problem. False belief in libertarian free will and overconfidence in the shallower compatibilist substitutes are largely *positive illusions* (Smilansky 2000, 2011, forthcoming). If my view is right, you, the reader, would do well to abandon reading this present volume and keep your distance from the free will problem altogether!

If you nevertheless decide to reject my advice and continue to pursue philosophical wisdom, you have come to the right place. *Do We Have Free Will?: A Debate* is an exposition of the Classic Problem concerning free will that at once acknowledges and respects the complexity of the issues and the sophistication of the professional philosophical debate while making everything as accessible as possible for the intelligent reader.

Saul Smilansky, 2021

References

Pereboom, Derk. 2014. *Free Will, Agency and Meaning in Life*. New York: Oxford University Press.

Smilansky, Saul. 2000. *Free Will and Illusion*. Oxford, UK: Oxford University Press.

Smilansky, Saul. 2001. "Free Will: From Nature to Illusion." *Proceedings of the Aristotelian Society* 101: 71–95.

Smilansky, Saul. 2011. "Free Will, Fundamental Dualism and the Centrality of Illusion." In Robert Kane (ed.), *The Oxford Handbook of Free Will*, 2nd ed., 425–41. New York: Oxford University Press.

Smilansky, Saul. 2017. "The Free Will Problem: Nonstandard Views." In Kevin Timpe, Meghan Griffith and Neil Levy (eds.), *The Routledge Companion to Free Will*, 136–46. New York: Routledge.

Smilansky, Saul. Forthcoming. "Illusionism." In Derk Pereboom and Dana Nelkin (eds.), *The Oxford Handbook of Moral Responsibility*. New York: Oxford University Press.

Strawson, Galen. 1994. "The Impossibility of Moral Responsibility." *Philosophical Studies* 75: 5–24.

Strawson, P.F. 2003. "Freedom and Resentment." In Gary Watson (ed.), *Free Will*, 72–93. Oxford, UK: Oxford University Press.

Waller, Bruce. 2011. *Against Moral Responsibility*. Cambridge, MA: MIT Press.

Opening Statements

Chapter 1

The Problem of Free Will
A Libertarian Perspective

Robert Kane

Contents

DOI: 10.4324/9781003212171-2

Introduction: An Ancient Problem with Modern Significance

> "There is a disputation that will continue till mankind is raised from the dead, between the necessitarians and the partisans of free will".

These are the words of 13th-century Sufi Muslim poet and philosopher Jalalu'ddin Rumi. The problem of free will and necessity or determinism of which he speaks has arisen in history whenever humans have reached a higher stage of self-consciousness about how profoundly the world may influence their behavior in ways unknown to them and they do not control. The rise of doctrines of determinism or necessity in the history of ideas is an indication that this higher stage of self-consciousness has been reached. People have wondered at various times whether their actions might be determined by Fate or by God; by the laws of physics or the laws of logic; by evolution, genes or environment, unconscious motives, upbringing, psychological or social conditioning or, with the latest scientific threats from the neurosciences, by the activity of the neurons of their brains of which they are not conscious.

There is a core idea running through all of these historical doctrines of determinism or necessity, whether they are religious, secular or scientific, that shows why many people have felt that they are a threat to free will. This core idea may be stated as follows:

> **Determinism**: given the past at any time and the laws governing the universe, there is only one possible future. Whatever happens is therefore inevitable, it cannot but occur, given the past and laws.

Free Will, by contrast, implies (i) an open future, with multiple possible paths into the future, and that (ii) it is sometimes "up to us" which of these possible paths we will take.

Such a picture of an open future that free will seems to require is often illustrated by an image made famous in a short story of the well-known South American writer, Jorge Luis Borges. It is the image of a "garden of forking paths" illustrated in Figure 1.1. At each juncture there are forking paths into the future. If we believe that our choices about which of these paths we will take at such times are *free* choices, we must believe that both options are "open" to us while we are deliberating. We could choose different paths into the future at various points in our lives, and it would be "up to us" and no one and nothing else which of these paths will be taken.

I believe that such a picture of different possible paths into the future, at least at some times in our lives, is essential to our understanding of free will. Such a picture is also important, we might even say, to what it means to be a person and to live a human life. Yet determinism, if true, would seem to threaten this picture, because it implies that there really is, at all times, only one possible path into the future, not many. We may *believe* there are multiple paths available to us, but in reality, if determinism is true, only one of them would be possible.

I. Modern Debates and Views

Like Rumi and many other thinkers of the past, I had always believed that there was some kind of conflict lurking here that was very deep and could not be easily dismissed by facile arguments. Yet I was also aware that many philosophers and scientists, especially in the modern era, have argued that doctrines of determinism pose

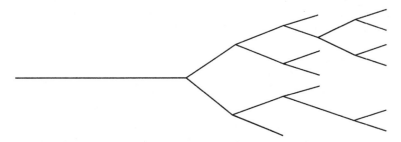

Figure 1.1 A Garden of Forking Paths

no real threat to free will, or at least to any free will "worth wanting". These thinkers are usually called *compatibilists.*

> **Compatibilists** about free will believe that free will is compatible with determinism, so that we can have all of the free will that is possible and worth wanting, even if determinism should be universally true.

Even in a determined world, these compatibilists argue, we would want to distinguish persons who are free from such things as physical restraint, addiction or neurosis, coercion, compulsion, covert control by others or political oppression, from persons who are not free from these things, and we could affirm that these freedoms might exist and would be preferable to their opposites *even in a determined world.* In addition, these modern compatibilists commonly argue that requiring that free actions must be *un*determined would not do anything to enhance our freedom but rather would reduce our freedom to mere chance or luck or mystery.

In modern debates about free will, compatibilist views of these kinds are opposed by

> **Incompatibilists:** those who deny that every kind of freedom "worth wanting" is compatible with determinism.

I will be defending such an incompatibilist view in this debate. Though many kinds of freedom may be compatible with determinism, as the preceding paragraph suggests, I believe that there is one important kind of freedom—traditionally called the "freedom of the will"—that is also worth wanting but is not compatible with determinism.

Freedom of will of this incompatibilist kind satisfies the two conditions mentioned earlier that seem to be threatened by determinism; that is, (i) at least at some points in our lives we face a genuinely open future, with forking paths into that future, either of which we may choose, and (ii) at these crucial times, it is "up to us", and no one and nothing else, which of these possible paths into the future will be taken. We determine our future at such times and the kinds of persons we will become. Those who believe that there is an important kind of freedom of will that we can possess satisfying these conditions that is not compatible with determinism are usually called *libertarians* about free will in contemporary debates (from the Latin *liber* meaning "free").[1]

> **Libertarians about free will** believe that there is an important kind of freedom of will that we can possess that is *incompatible* with determinism and satisfies the following conditions: (i) at some points in our lives we face a genuinely open future, with forking paths into that future, either of which we may choose, and (ii) at these crucial times, it is "up to us", and no one and nothing else, which of these possible paths into the future will be chosen.

I will be defending such a libertarian and incompatibilist view of free will in this debate. Many thinkers believe that a free will of the kind libertarians defend—a free will that is not compatible with determinism—is not even possible or intelligible. It is not a kind of freedom, they argue, we *could* have. This worry has a long history and is related to an ancient dilemma: If free will is not compatible with determinism, it does not seem to be compatible with *indeterminism* either. Arguments have been made since the time of the ancient Stoics that *undetermined* events would occur spontaneously and hence could not be controlled by agents in the way that free and responsible actions would require.

If, for example, a choice occurred by virtue of some undetermined quantum events in one's brain, it would seem to be a fluke or accident rather than a responsible choice. Undetermined events occurring in brains or bodies, it is commonly argued, would not seem to enhance our freedom and control over, and hence responsibility for, actions but rather to diminish freedom, control and responsibility. Arguments such as these and many others have led to often-repeated charges throughout history that undetermined choices or actions, such as a libertarian free will would require, would be "arbitrary", "random", "irrational", "uncontrolled", "mere matters of luck" or "chance" and hence could not be free and responsible actions at all.

---

1. Libertarianism *about free will* should not be confused with political and economic doctrines of libertarianism. Libertarians about free will can, and do, hold differing views on political and economic matters.

In response, libertarians about free will throughout history have often appealed to special and unusual forms of agency or causation to explain undetermined free actions, and their opponents have cried magic or mystery. Indeterminism might provide "causal gaps" in nature, libertarians frequently reasoned, but that was only a negative condition for free will. Some special form of agency or causation was needed that went beyond familiar modes of causation in the natural order to "fill" those causal gaps in nature left by indeterminism. And thus we had historical appeals to "extra factors," such as noumenal selves outside space and time (e.g., Immanuel Kant), or immaterial minds (e.g., Rene Descartes) or uncaused causes, nonevent agent causes or prime movers unmoved that might account for an otherwise undetermined free will.

Tempting ways to think, to be sure. But such traditional ways of thinking have also prompted charges by compatibilists and free will skeptics and many other modern critics of libertarian free will. These critics argue that one cannot make sense of an undetermined free will without appealing to magical or mysterious forms of agency that have no place in the modern scientific picture of the world and of human beings.

Friedrich Nietzsche summed up this prevailing modern skepticism in his inimitable prose when he said that such a traditional notion of freedom of the will that would underwrite an ultimate responsibility for our actions and require that one somehow be an undetermined "cause of oneself" was "the best self-contradiction that has been conceived so far" by the human mind (1989, §17.8).

I agree that a traditional idea of free will that would require its being incompatible with determinism is likely to appear utterly mysterious and unintelligible in a modern context unless we learn to think about it in new ways. Hence my long struggle in attempting to defend and make sense of such an idea of free will without reducing it to mere chance, on the one hand, *or* to mystery, on the other. Yet the struggle seemed worth the effort. For, like many another issue of modernity, the question is whether *something* of this traditional idea of free will in what Nietzsche called "the superlative metaphysical sense" can be retrieved from the dissolving acids of modern science and secular learning. Or would it become, along with other aspects of our self-image, yet another victim of the "disenchantments" of modernity?

Yet I came to realize that any retrieval of this idea of free will that would require its being incompatible with determinism would be no simple matter, if it were possible at all. Such a retrieval would require answering not one question but a whole host of questions. And it would require rethinking the relations of many different and related notions: agency, choice, mind, action, selfhood, will, control, responsibility, power and many others.[2] I will be addressing many of these questions and topics here, beginning with the following central question in contemporary debates about free will.

2. The Compatibility Question: Alternative Possibilities and Ultimate Responsibility

Why might one believe that there is an important kind of free will worth wanting that is not compatible with determinism? The first step in answering this question is recognizing that, as this so-called Compatibility Question is usually formulated in many modern discussions of free will—"Is *freedom* compatible or incompatible with determinism?"—the question is too simple. For, as noted in the previous section, *there are many meanings of "freedom"* (as one would expect from such a much-disputed and debated term), and many of these meanings *are* compatible with determinism. Even in a determined world, as noted, we would want to distinguish persons who are *free* from such things as physical restraint, addiction, coercion and political oppression from persons not free from these things. And we should acknowledge that these freedoms *are* significant ("worth wanting")—having them would be preferable to their opposites—even in a determined world.

Those of us who are libertarians about free will (who believe in a free will that is incompatible with determinism) should, I contend, concede this point to compatibilists: Many freedoms worth wanting are compatible with determinism.

> What **libertarians about free will** should insist upon is that *there is at least one kind of freedom that is also worth wanting and is not compatible with determinism.* This further freedom is **Freedom of Will**, which I define as: "**the power to be the ultimate source and sustainer to some degree of one's own ends or purposes.**"

2.   I have addressed these issues in Kane (1985, 1996, 2005, 2011c, 2014), among other writings.

To understand what this notion of free will amounts to, return to the two features mentioned earlier that have historically led persons to believe that free will is threatened by determinism. We believe we have free will when we view ourselves as agents capable of influencing the world in various ways. Open alternatives seem to lie before us (a "garden of forking paths" in the earlier image). We reason and deliberate among them and choose. We feel that (i) it is "up to us" what we choose and how we act, and this means we "could have chosen or acted otherwise" or that we had "alternative possibilities". This "up-to-us-ness" also suggests that (ii) the ultimate sources of our actions lie to some degree in us and not entirely outside us in factors beyond our control.

Most modern debates about whether such a free will is or is not compatible with determinism have tended to focus on the first of these two requirements. This first of these requirements might be called

> **The Condition of Alternative Possibilities (or AP):** Free agents must have "alternative possibilities" or "open alternatives" for choice or action, which implies that the agents "could have chosen or acted otherwise".

But arguments about whether or not this much-discussed Condition of Alternative Possibilities (AP) is compatible with determinism have led to contentious debates in modern philosophy. These debates in turn have tended to stalemate over differing interpretations of what it means to say that agents have alternative possibilities or that agents "could have done otherwise" than they actually did or that they had the "power" or "ability" at a given time to act and to act otherwise.

I believe that these contentious debates about the meaning of such expressions as "could have done otherwise" and the resulting stalemates about the role of this Alternative Possibilities condition or AP in modern debates about free will are symptoms of a deeper problem. The deeper problem is that focusing on alternative possibilities alone is too thin a basis on which to rest the case for the incompatibility of free will and determinism.

It is not that alternative possibilities and the power to do otherwise are unimportant for free will—far from it. They are very important, and we will return shortly to consider why. It is rather that other considerations must also be brought into the picture in arguing for the incompatibility of free will and determinism if we are to fully understand historical and contemporary debates about free will. *The Compatibility Question concerning free will and determinism cannot be resolved by focusing on alternative possibilities or the power to do otherwise alone.* Realizing this, I have argued that one must revisit the long history of debates about free will to see where else to look. When doing so, one finds that there is another historical condition fueling incompatibilist intuitions that to my mind is even more important than the alternative possibilities condition. This other condition is related to the second of the two requirements for the "up-to-us-ness" of freedom of will mentioned—namely, that "the ultimate sources of our actions must lie to some degree in us and not entirely outside us in factors beyond our control". I call this further condition:

The Condition of Ultimate Responsibility (or UR): The basic idea is this: *To be ultimately responsible for an action, an agent must be responsible to some degree for anything that is a sufficient reason (a sufficient condition, cause or motive) for the action occurring.*

If, for example, a choice were to issue from, and can be sufficiently explained by, an agent's character and motives (together with background conditions) at the time, then to be ultimately responsible for the choice the agent must be at least in part responsible by virtue of choices or actions voluntarily performed in the past for *having* the character and motives he or she now has. Compare Aristotle's claim that if a man is responsible for wicked acts that flow from his character he must at some time in the past have been responsible for forming the wicked character from which these acts flow.

This condition of ultimate responsibility accounts for the "ultimate" in the original definition of free will given earlier: "the power of agents to be the *ultimate* sources and sustainers to some degree of their own ends or purposes".

In the Introduction, the problem of free will is introduced in historical perspective, with key terms such as determinism and free will defined. In section 1, contemporary debates about free will are discussed, and some of the main positions, such as compatibilism, incompatibilism and libertarianism are defined. In section 2, the Compatibility Question, one of the central questions about free will, was introduced: Is free will compatible or incompatible with determinism? Two crucial conditions were then discussed that have led many persons to believe that free will is not compatible with determinism: the Condition of Alternative Possibilities (AP) and the Condition of Ultimate Responsibility (UR).

3. Self-forming Actions

Importantly, such a condition of ultimate responsibility or UR does not require that we could have done otherwise (AP) for *every* act done "of our own free wills". This UR condition thus partially vindicates compatibilists and others who insist that we can be held morally responsible for many acts even when we could not have done otherwise than perform them. But the vindication is only partial. For this ultimate responsibility or UR condition *does* require that we could have done otherwise with respect to *some* acts in our past life histories by which we *formed* or *shaped* our present characters, motives and purposes (that is, our wills). I call these character and will-forming actions:

> Self-forming Actions (SFAs): those acts by which we form and re-form our wills (our characters, motives and purposes) and for which we could have done otherwise, which must occur at some times in our lives, if we are to be ultimately responsible for having the wills we have and hence for being the kinds of persons we become.

To bring out the importance of these self-forming actions or SFAs, consider a familiar line of argument purporting to show that moral responsibility does not require alternative possibilities or the power to do otherwise *at all*, a line of argument illustrated by compatibilist Daniel Dennett's much-discussed example of Martin Luther (1984: 131–33). When finally breaking with the Church at Rome, Luther said, "Here I stand, I can do no other". Suppose, says Dennett, that Luther was literally right about himself at that moment.

Given his character and motives, he literally could not then have done otherwise. Does this mean that he was not morally responsible? Not at all, Dennett says. In saying, "I can do no other," Luther was not disowning responsibility for his act but taking full responsibility for it. Thus, compatibilist Dennett concludes that "could have done otherwise" and hence alternative possibilities (AP) are *not* required for free will in a sense demanded by moral responsibility.

In response, I argue that incompatibilists about free will may, and indeed should, grant that Luther could have been responsible for this act, *even ultimately responsible in the sense of UR*, though he could not have done otherwise *then and there*, and even if his act was determined by his existing will at that moment. But this would be so, incompatibilists should argue, to the extent that Luther was responsible for his present *motives and character* (his will) by virtue of some earlier struggles and self-forming choices (SFAs) that *brought him to this point where he could do no other*.

Acting of "Our *Own* Free Will": Often we act from a will already formed, but it is "our *own* free will" by virtue of the fact that we formed it by other choices or actions in the past (*self-forming choices or actions* or SFAs) for which we could have done otherwise. If this were not so, *there is nothing we could have ever done differently in our entire lifetimes to make ourselves different than we are*—a consequence, I believe, that is incompatible with our being (at least to some degree) ultimately responsible for being the way we are.

---

4. Freedom of Action and Freedom of Will: AP and UR

Focusing on this condition of ultimate responsibility or UR tells us something else of importance about the traditional problem of free will. It tells us why it is a problem about the freedom *of the will* and not just about the freedom *of action* and why these freedoms must be distinguished if the Compatibility Question and other questions about free will are to be adequately addressed.

There has been a tendency in the modern era of philosophy, beginning with Thomas Hobbes and John Locke in the 17th century, and coming to fruition in the 20th century, to reduce the problem of free will to a problem of free action. I believe that such a reduction oversimplifies the problem.

> *Free will is not just about free action*, though it involves free action. Free will is about *Self-formation*, about *the formation of our "wills"or how we got to be the kinds of persons we are*, with the characters, motives and purposes we now have. Were we ultimately responsible to some degree for having the wills (characters, motives and purposes) we do have, or can the sources of our wills be completely traced back to something over which we had no control, such as Fate or the decrees of God, heredity and environment, social conditioning or hidden controllers and so on? Therein, I believe, lies the core of the traditional problem of "free *will*".

John Locke famously said in the 17th century that the so-called problem of free will that had so exercised medieval and earlier philosophers was really a problem about *free agency*, or the freedom *of the agent*, and not about the freedom *of the will* (1975). Like other thinkers of the modern era, Locke was skeptical of medieval references to the "will" in general that often made it out to be a mysterious inner homunculus or power capable of influencing actions and events in ways not countenanced, Locke believed, by the new emerging sciences of his day.

Many moderns down to the present time have followed Locke in this skepticism. They argue, as did Ludwig Wittgenstein (1953) and Gilbert Ryle (1949) in the mid-20th century, that references to the *will* and *acts of will* were outdated remnants of premodern modes of thought and should go the way of witches and phlogiston. Even some modern libertarians and incompatibilists about free will have joined compatibilists in arguing that the historical "problem of free will" is really about the freedom of agency and hence about the freedom of action and not about the freedom of the will.

I believe this is a mistake. It is *not* wrong, to be sure, to say as Locke does, that the traditional problem of free will is really a problem about *free agency*. But it *is* wrong to say it is not therefore *also* about the freedom of the will. For, as described in these paragraphs, *freedom of will is an important aspect of free agency* and, moreover, *free will is that particular aspect of free agency that has been the subject of historical debates about whether it is or is not compatible with determinism.*

For if the case for the incompatibility of free will and determinism cannot be made by appealing to the condition of alternative possibilities or AP alone, the case can be made if UR is added. I have thus argued that UR should be moved to center stage in free will debates. To be ultimately responsible for an action in the sense required by UR, an agent must be responsible to some degree for anything that is a sufficient reason (cause or motive) for the action occurring. And this implies, as noted, that if a choice or action can be sufficiently explained by an agent's present character, motives and purposes, then to be ultimately responsible for the choice or action the agent must be at least in part responsible by virtue of choices or actions voluntarily performed in the past for having the character, motives and purposes he or she now has. But this being the case, an impossible infinite regress of past choices or actions would be required unless *some* choices or actions in the agent's life history (self-forming actions or SFAs) did *not* have *sufficient* causes or motives (and hence were not determined).

Yet if one could arrive at the incompatibility of free will and determinism from this condition of ultimate responsibility or UR alone in this manner, one might wonder whether appeals to alternative possibilities or AP are needed at all for free will. Some recent philosophers who are impressed by arguments of the above kind for incompatibilism (they are sometimes called "source incompatibilists") have suggested that appeals to alternative possibilities and the power to do otherwise are not needed at all for free will.

I believe this is also a mistake. *Both conditions—Ultimate Responsibility or UR and Alternative Possibilities or AP—are needed for free will.* But the reasons why both conditions (UR and AP) are needed are more subtle than is generally realized, and understanding them requires further steps in rethinking the Compatibility Question.

5. Plurality Conditions and Plural Voluntary Control

The first of these further steps concerns what I call *plurality conditions* for free will. When we wonder about whether the wills of agents are free, it is not merely whether they could have done otherwise that concerns us, *even if the doing otherwise is undetermined*. What interests us is whether agents could have done otherwise *voluntarily* (or *willingly*), *intentionally* and *rationally*. Or, to put it more generally, we are interested in whether agents could have acted voluntarily, intentionally and rationally *in more than one way*, rather than in only one way, and in other ways merely by accident or mistake, unintentionally, involuntarily or irrationally. I call such conditions

> **Plurality Conditions** for free will (Kane 1996: 107–11): the power of agents to act voluntarily, intentionally and rationally *in more than one way*, rather than in only one way, and in other ways merely by accident or mistake, unintentionally, involuntarily, inadvertently or irrationally.

Such conditions seem to be deeply embedded in our intuitions about free choice and action. Most of us naturally assume that freedom and responsibility would be deficient if it were always the case that we could *only* do otherwise by *accident* or *mistake, unintentionally, involuntarily* or *irrationally*.

To illustrate, imagine a world in which there is a considerable amount of genuine indeterminism or chance in human affairs as well as in nature. In this world, people set out to do things— kill prime ministers, press buttons on machines, punch computer keys, hit targets, etc.—usually succeeding, but sometimes failing by mistake or accident. Suppose an assassin, who usually hits his targets, is aiming to kill a prime minister from a distance with a high-powered rifle, when some undetermined events in his nervous system lead to a wavering of his arm and he misses his target. Or suppose I approach a coffee machine meaning to push the button for black coffee when, due to an undetermined brain cross, I accidentally press the button for coffee with cream.

Now imagine further that *all* actions in this world in the lifetimes of agents, whether the agents succeed in their purposes or not, are such that their reasons, motives and purposes for wanting and trying to act as they do are always preset or settled by prior circumstances of heredity, environment, social conditioning and other formative circumstances. Whether the assassin misses the prime minister or not, his *intention* to kill is already *settled* prior to his attempt by his past formative circumstances. Whether I succeed in pressing the button for coffee without cream, my wanting to do so because of my dislike of cream is already *settled* by my formative circumstances. And so it is, we are to assume, for all persons and all of their actions in this imagined world.

I would argue that persons in such a world lack free *will*, even though it may often be the case that they have (i) *alternative possibilities* and that their actions are (ii) *undetermined*, because they can sometimes do otherwise than they do in a manner that is undetermined but only inadvertently or unintentionally, by mistake or accident, as in the case of the assassin or my pressing the wrong button on the coffee machine—and this is a limited kind of freedom at best. What they cannot do is *will* otherwise than they do. Their reasons, motives and purposes have been already "set one way" before, and when they act, so that if they act otherwise, it will *not* be "*in accordance with their wills*" but rather by chance or accident.

What this shows is that when we wonder about whether the *wills* of agents are free, it is not only whether they could have done otherwise that concerns us, even if their doing otherwise is undetermined. What interests us is whether they could have done otherwise *voluntarily* (in accordance with their wills), *intentionally* (knowingly rather than inadvertently and on purpose rather than accidentally) and *rationally* (having reasons for so acting and acting for those reasons). Or, to put it more generally, we are interested in whether they could at some times have acted voluntarily, intentionally and rationally *in more than one way*, rather than in only one way, and in other ways merely by accident or mistake, unintentionally, inadvertently or irrationally.

We thus arrive at an answer to the question of why these "plurality conditions" are so deeply embedded in our intuitions about free choice and action. We naturally assume that freedom and responsibility would be deficient, if it were always the case that we could *only* do otherwise by accident or mistake, unintentionally, involuntarily or irrationally—in short, *unwillingly*. To have freedom of will, we must not only be able to do otherwise, we must be able to do otherwise *willingly* or *at will*. If free *will* involves more than alternative possibilities and indeterminism, these plurality conditions appear to be among the significant additional requirements.

Reflecting on these plurality conditions tells us something else of importance about free will, because satisfying such plurality conditions implies that agents must be able to exercise a certain kind of control over some of their actions, which I refer to as

Plural Voluntary Control (PVC): Agents have *plural voluntary control* over a set of options (e.g., choices or actions) when (i) they are able to bring about *either* of the options *voluntarily* (without being coerced or compelled or otherwise controlled by other agents), *intentionally* (knowingly and on purpose, rather than merely by accident or mistake) and *rationally* (for *reasons* that they then and there wish to act upon) and (ii) *whichever* option they do bring about by exercising such plural voluntary control will have been brought about by them voluntarily, intentionally and rationally in these senses.

These conditions can be summed up by saying, as we sometimes do, that the agents can act or choose either way "*at will*" or, alternatively, that it is "*up to them*" which way they will choose or act when they choose or act.

6. Will-Setting and Self-formation

Focusing in this way on plurality conditions and plural voluntary control also leads to a further important and often neglected topic in free will debates that I call "*will-setting*" (Kane 1996: 113–15). In the imagined scenario of the previous section, all of the motives and purposes of agents in every situation are already "preset" or "set one way" *before* they act. The assassin's desires and purposes are set on killing the prime minister, not on missing or killing an aide. My desires and purposes are set on pressing the button for black coffee and not any other button. In such cases, where the motives and purposes of agents are already "set one way" *before* they act, we may say that their actions are "will-settled".

> Actions are **Will-Settled** when the wills of agents, their motives and purposes are already "set one way" on doing something *before* they act

By contrast,

> Actions are **Will-Setting** when the wills of agents, their motives and purposes are *not* already "preset" or "set one way" *before* they act. Rather, the agents set their wills one way or another *in the performance of the actions themselves.*

Choices or decisions, which are self-forming actions or SFAs, in the sense defined here, are "will-setting" in this sense. The agents' wills are not already set one way before they choose but they set their wills, one way or the other, voluntarily, intentionally and rationally *in the act of choosing itself*. Such self-forming actions would thus satisfy the plurality conditions.

The imagined world in which all of the motives and purposes of agents are already set one way whenever they act thus provides a clue to the deep connection between will-setting, ultimate responsibility, free will and the plurality conditions. If we are to be to some degree ultimate determiners of our own wills, as ultimate responsibility requires, some actions in our lifetimes (self-forming actions or SFAs) must be will-setting in the above sense and hence must satisfy the plurality conditions.

But these self-forming actions will then satisfy the condition of alternative possibilities or AP as well, because if one can do or do otherwise, voluntarily, intentionally and rationally either way, it follows that one can do or do otherwise. One has alternative possibilities. AP would therefore be necessary for free will after all, *at least sometimes in our lives when we engage in self-formation*.

In section 3, the idea of self-forming actions (SFAs), which I argue are crucial to free will, was introduced and explained. In section 4, two notions of freedom—freedom of action and freedom of will— were distinguished; and it was argued that these notions of freedom must be distinguished if the Compatibility Question and other questions about free will are to be adequately addressed. In section 5, two further conditions crucial for free will were discussed: plurality conditions and plural voluntary control; and in section 6, these two conditions were related to two other notions crucial for free will: will-setting and self-formation.

7. The Compatibility Question Revisited: Free Will and Moral Responsibility

Focusing on both ultimate responsibility or UR and alternative possibilities or AP when discussing the Compatibility Question, rather than merely on alternative possibilities or AP alone, has another significant consequence. It shows why issues about free will have been so deeply entangled throughout history with issues about *moral responsibility* for actions. This entanglement is no accident. It has to do with the very meaning of freedom *of will* (which involves both ultimate responsibility or UR and alternative possibilities or AP). Reflecting on this entanglement of free will and moral responsibility leads to further arguments relating to whether freedom of will is or is not compatible with determinism—arguments having to do with our ordinary practices of holding persons responsible for their actions in everyday moral and legal contexts.

Many contemporary compatibilists and other philosophers have been influenced on these topics by a seminal 1962 article by British philosopher P.F. Strawson. In this influential article, titled "Freedom and Resentment," Strawson focused on our ordinary practices of holding persons morally responsible and on what he called the

> **Reactive Attitudes:** attitudes toward persons usually associated with ordinary practices of holding persons morally responsible, including attitudes such as blame, resentment, indignation, guilt, moral approval and moral praise.

Strawson argued that our ordinary practices of holding people responsible, including these reactive attitudes, were basic to our human form of life and could be wholly "insulated" from traditional abstract philosophical and scientific concerns about free will and determinism. To believe, he argued, that our ordinary practices of holding persons responsible in everyday life and the reactive attitudes related to them would have to be qualified in some ways—or even possibly abandoned—if we found that all of their actions were determined by prior causes was to "overintellectualize" the issues.

This "insulation thesis" (as it has sometimes been called) is a controversial feature of Strawson's article, and it has had numerous proponents and critics. Interestingly, one of the most prominent of the critics was Strawson's son, Galen Strawson, who, in his 1986 book *Freedom and Belief*, took issue with his father's contention in "Freedom and Resentment" that ordinary practices of blaming and other reactive attitudes *could* be entirely "insulated" from metaphysical concerns about determinism.

Against this contention, Galen Strawson argued that "the roots of the incompatibilist intuition" (that free will is incompatible with determinism) "lie deep" in our ordinary practices and in the reactive attitudes associated with those practices. These ordinary practices and the reactive attitudes associated with them, he argued, "enshrine the incompatibilist intuition," rather than being "insulated" from that intuition (1986: 89).

I agree with Galen Strawson on this issue, though my reasons are not all the same as his. Like him, I believe that our ordinary practices of holding persons morally responsible and related questions about blameworthiness and the reactive attitudes cannot be *entirely* insulated from philosophical worries about free will and determinism that have engaged philosophers for centuries. This genie cannot be kept in the bottle, annoying as he may be. There are a number of ways to show this that I will now explore.

8. Fair Opportunity to Avoid Wrongdoing: Hart and Others

The first way focuses on ordinary practices of ascribing responsibility, culpability and blame in courts of law and other legal contexts. A widely cited condition among legal theorists for such ascriptions was stated by the influential British legal theorist H.L.A. Hart (1968). It may be called

> The Fair Opportunity Condition: is a necessary condition for ascribing responsibility and culpability to agents in legal contexts according to which the agents must have had a "fair opportunity to avoid wrongdoing" or, more generally, a "fair opportunity to have done otherwise" than they have done.

In an important recent article, David Brink and Dana Nelkin (2013) argue persuasively that this "fair opportunity" criterion of Hart is not only crucial for understanding legal and criminal responsibility but crucial as well for understanding moral responsibility in general, in an accountability sense that would justify blame, sanction and punishment. Hart's "fair opportunity" condition, the requirement that responsible agents have a fair opportunity to avoid wrongdoing, Brink and Nelkin argue, is thus a crucial part of the "architecture" of ordinary practices of ascribing moral as well as legal responsibility (2013: 284).

If this is the case, as I believe it is, it has implications concerning whether our ordinary practices of ascribing responsibility can *be* insulated from traditional philosophical debates about free will and determinism. Appeals to Hart's "fair opportunity" criterion for assigning responsibility in ordinary legal and moral practices land one squarely in the center of traditional philosophical debates that have concerned incompatibilists about whether causal determinism rules out the freedom to do otherwise and whether and to what degree the freedom to do otherwise is required for moral responsibility.

To show this, it is instructive to consider the following: If causal determinism were true, anything you might have done differently in the course of your life to make yourself different than you are would have been *causally impossible* in the following sense:

> **Causal Impossibility:** An event *E* occurring at a time *t* is *causally impossible* just in case the following is true: "If the past prior to *t* is as it is in the actual world and the laws of nature are as they are in the actual world, then *E* cannot possibly occur at *t*".

If causal determinism were true, *anything you might have done differently in the course of your life* to make yourself different than you are at any time—your character, your motives, your dispositions, your intentions, the quality of your will—would have been causally impossible in this sense, because, as we have seen earlier, causal determinism implies that given the past and the laws governing the universe at any time, there is only one causally possible future. And *if an agent's avoiding wrongdoing was causally impossible in this sense, it would certainly appear that the agent lacked a "fair opportunity" to avoid doing it.*

An important qualification, however, must immediately be added here—a qualification that is crucial not only for understanding Hart's fair opportunity criterion but also for understanding ascriptions of responsibility in ordinary moral contexts generally. The qualification is that the causal impossibility of avoiding wrongdoing *in certain particular circumstances* will not always imply that agents are excused from moral responsibility *in those circumstances.* It implies this only on certain conditions.

For example, if it could be shown that it was causally impossible for a drunk driver to have avoided hitting a pedestrian on a dark and rainy night, given all the circumstances at the moment of the accident, that fact alone will not excuse the driver of responsibility.

One must also ask whether the driver was responsible by virtue of earlier actions or omissions for the existence of some of those crucial circumstances that made it now causally impossible for him to have avoided the accident, such as his prior decisions to drink and then drive. In other words, the causal impossibility of avoiding doing something *now* (e.g., avoiding the accident when it occurred) will not excuse an agent of responsibility, if some of the crucial circumstances that made it now causally impossible to avoid doing it were the results of actions or omissions by the agent in the past, *which the agent had a "fair opportunity to avoid" when they occurred.* And this last phrase is crucial. For the problem is that if determinism is true, there would be no actions or omissions in an agent's past that were not causally impossible for the agent to have avoided doing when *they* occurred.

9. Reactive Attitudes, Criminal Trials and Transference of Responsibility

Another significant way of highlighting problems with the thesis that issues about responsibility and the reactive attitudes can be insulated from philosophical concerns about determinism has been discussed by several other writers. It was discussed recently, for example, by Shaun Nichols in his book *Bound: Essays on Free Will and Responsibility* (2015). Nichols' book focuses on the implications of new research in empirical psychology and experimental philosophy for traditional philosophical debates about free will and moral responsibility. The passages of interest here in his book are where Nichols discusses Galen Strawson's claim, mentioned earlier, that our ordinary practices of holding responsible, and the reactive attitudes related to them, "enshrine" incompatibilist intuitions about freedom and responsibility rather than being entirely "insulated" from such intuitions.

In discussing what he takes to be important arguments supporting this claim of Galen Strawson's, Nichols introduces two examples that play a pivotal role in his discussion. One of these examples is from Gary Watson's (1987) well-known and much-discussed account of the ruthless murderer, Robert Harris, on death row in California for multiple murders. The other example Nichols considers in his book is taken from my own writing about the trial of a young man who assaulted and raped a teenage girl. The examples have similar import. But I will focus on my example because it brings out some key points that Watson does not emphasize. As Nichols points out, my example is roughly based on experience, triggered by the trial of the young man accused of the assault and rape.

My initial reactions attending the trial of this young man were anger and resentment against him, because we knew the family of the teenage girl who was his victim and who lived in our neighborhood. But as I listened daily to the testimony of how the young man came to have the mean character and perverse motives he did have—a sordid story of parental rejection, sexual abuse, bad role models and other such factors (not entirely unlike Watson's case of Robert Harris)—some of my resentment toward the young man decreased and was directed toward other persons who abused and influenced him.

But—and here is a key point—I wasn't yet ready to shift all the blame away from the young man himself. I resisted this "transference of responsibility" entirely to others and wondered whether some residual responsibility and blame might not belong to the young man himself. My question became: Was his behavior *all* a matter of bad parenting, neglect and abuse and like factors, or did he have any crucial role to play in choosing it?

We know that parenting and society, genetic makeup and upbringing have a profound influence on what we become and what we are. But were these influences entirely *determining* or did they "leave anything over" for the young man to be responsible for? Note that

---

The question of whether the young man was merely a victim of bad circumstances or had some residual responsibility for being the way he is—the question, that is, of **whether he became the person he is to any degree** *of his own free will*—**seems to depend on whether these other factors were or were not** *entirely* **determining**. It seems to depend, in other words, on whether or not it was *ever causally possible for the young man to have resisted the influences of his genetics and upbringing* and to have acted differently at some points in his life to make himself different than he now is. And if determinism was true, acting differently than he actually did at *any* time in his lifetime would have been *causally impossible*.

One might argue here that my particular reactions at this trial to the young man—the fact that my reactive attitudes of resentment and blame toward him were mitigated to some degree and transferred to others when I learned about his sad history—were the reactions of a "philosopher" and not the reactions of ordinary folk. But this was far from being the case. My wife and I sat in this courtroom with friends and other neighbors of the young girl's family, none of whom were philosophers. They were firemen, businesswomen, store owners, high school football coaches, teachers and many others, and all had reactions similar to ours. Keep in mind that, like us, they all resisted mightily transferring responsibility entirely away from the young man. But their reactive attitudes, including retributive ones, were nonetheless mitigated to some degree and influenced by hearing the sordid stories of his history.

Moreover, if there *were* any persons in that courtroom whose retributive attitudes were not in any way influenced by listening to the history of the young man (as I am sure there were), then I would not want to see those persons anywhere near a jury deciding the fate of persons I cared about or any other persons whatever, because they would not be capable of responding in ways I believe would be *fair* to those they judge. They would not be capable of responding fairly if they were not capable of appreciating that, to the extent that the young man's sad history made it *causally impossible* for him to have turned out differently, to that extent he would not have had a *"fair opportunity to avoid wrongdoing."*

10. Transference of Responsibility and Compatibility Questions

It is worth reflecting further on this interesting notion of "transference of responsibility". We are inclined to do this to some degree to other persons who may have influenced agents to be the way they are and act as they do, to the extent that we believe that the influences of these others *were difficult for the agents to have resisted when they occurred*. In such cases we are inclined to "transfer" at least some of the responsibility and blame to those others who so strongly influenced the agents (parents, caregivers, role models, abusers and so on) and to mitigate the responsibility of the agents accordingly. In some extreme cases, such as Watson's Robert Harris or the young man of my example, we might possibly conclude that the influences were so strong that resisting them to any degree was not causally possible. We could be wrong about this. Such judgments are fallible and should be made with great caution. But the crucial point is that *such judgments are relevant to our ordinary practices of holding agents responsible and blameworthy*, including who should be held responsible and to what degree.

Moreover, as noted, such judgments seem to depend on whether or not it was ever causally possible for the agents to have resisted the influences of their environment and upbringing and to have acted differently at some points in their lives to make themselves different than they are. And if determinism were true, this would never have been causally possible.

There are further interesting and relevant implications of this notion of transference of responsibility for free will debates. Many compatibilists—Daniel Dennett (1984) being a prominent example—are willing to concede that this transference of responsibility and related reactive attitudes, such as blame and resentment, to other persons who may have abused or otherwise exerted powerful influences over agents is indeed a normal feature of our ordinary practices of holding persons responsible. But these compatibilists go on to argue, as does Dennett, that such transference is only reasonable if the responsibility, blame, resentment, etc., is transferred to some other *persons*. If the influences on the agent's behavior and quality of will are due to natural causes alone and no other persons can be implicated, these compatibilists say, then it is not reasonable to transfer responsibility and other reactive attitudes, such as blame and resentment, to nature. After all, nature is not a person.

This is true enough as far as it goes and should be admitted by incompatibilists. It is an important fact about this transference phenomenon that transference of moral and legal responsibility must be to other *persons* and cannot be to natural causes alone. Indeed, this fact is related to something important about the reactive attitudes, such as resentment, indignation and blame, in general, namely, that they are appropriately directed only at beings who are themselves capable of *responsible agency*. But rather than providing a decisive argument for compatibilism, further reflection on this significant fact can take us in an opposing direction.

To see why, return for a moment to the young man at trial. Because he seems to have acted voluntarily and intentionally from a perverse and vicious will, our reactive attitudes of blame and resentment were initially focused entirely on him. But when we heard more about his past we wondered whether some of the blame at least should be transferred to the sexually abusive father and others who may have enabled the father. But now suppose we learn that the abusive father was as he was because *he* was sexually abused by his father and so on back indefinitely. Perhaps it was all in some bad genes. Or suppose the young man having the perverse will from which he acted was all a matter of determining genetic mutations in his fetal development for which we cannot blame the father *or* any other persons.

Suppose further that, as evidence unveiled in the courtroom made clear, the young man's acting from his perverse will in this incident satisfied familiar compatibilist conditions for free and responsible agency: he acted voluntarily, without being coerced or forced by others; he acted intentionally, knowing exactly what he was doing and doing it on purpose; he was reasons-responsive in the sense that he was calculating and would have altered his behavior appropriately, if his beliefs, desires and circumstances had been different in various ways. Nor was he acting compulsively, as in Harry Frankfurt's description of the unwilling addict, who wanted to resist the desire to take a drug but could not resist taking it anyway (1971). To the contrary, this young man had, in Frankfurt's terms, "the will he wanted to have" (1971: 15) and he was wholehearted and not ambivalent in his commitment to act in accordance with the will he had, perverse though it might be.

It was indeed the evidence of all this, coming to light in the proceedings, that led most of those present in the courtroom to our initial attitudes of resentment and moral anger toward the young man. Most of us, to be sure, transferred these reactive attitudes to some degree to others when we learned more about the sordid details of his upbringing. But we are now imagining a different situation. We are now supposing that the young man having the perverse will from which he acted was a matter of determining genetic mutations in his fetal development for which we cannot blame an abusive father or any other persons. So we cannot blame any other *persons* for the young man having the perverse will he does have. Yet it seems that we can't blame *nature* either, which is not a person. And this prompts the following reflections.

Imagine two young men, possessing exactly the same wills and motives as this young man and satisfying all of the same compatibilist criteria for responsibility (uncoerced, reasons-responsive, etc.). Yet one of these young men was determined to be so by the actions of other persons, like the abusive father; the other young man was determined to be so by natural, impersonal causes alone (such as mutations in his genetic development). The first young man is not fully responsible, we might say, to the degree that the actions of other persons made him this way. The responsibility transfers at least in part to those others.

But should we then say the second young man *is* fully responsible because no other persons, but only natural causes, made him the way he is—in other words, because *we cannot find anyone else to blame* in his case?

Such reasoning seems not only perverse but completely unfair to the second young man, because the question that begs to be answered *in both cases* is whether it was ever *causally possible* for either young man to have resisted the circumstances that influenced him and to have made himself different than he turned out to be, whether those influencing circumstances were the result of the actions of other agents or the results of natural causes alone. And if these circumstances were *determining* either way, it would not have been causally possible for *either* young man to resist them. Neither of the young men would have had a "fair opportunity" to have turned out otherwise.

---

11. Two Dimensions of Responsibility

Reflections such as these suggest that if full justice is to be done to our understanding of moral and legal responsibility and to our practices of holding persons responsible, two dimensions of responsibility must be distinguished. Both dimensions, I would argue, are necessary for a fully adequate account of these practices, and neither dimension alone is sufficient. The first dimension is responsibility for *expressing the will* (the character, motives and purposes) *one has in action* and doing so *voluntarily* and *intentionally*.

The second dimension of responsibility is another matter. It is not responsibility for expressing in action the true quality of will one has or the real self one is but responsibility for *having* the quality of will one *expresses* and *being* the kind of self one *is*. The distinction, put succinctly, is between the

> **First Dimension of Responsibility:** responsibility for *expressing* in action the will one *has*.
> **Second Dimension of Responsibility:** responsibility for *having* the will one *expresses* in action.

To be responsible in this second dimension it must be that at least some time in one's life, when one acts responsibly and hence voluntarily and intentionally in the first dimension, it was also possible for one to have voluntarily and intentionally *done otherwise*, not by being forced or by accident but in a manner that would also have expressed the true quality of one's will and the self that one was at the time. To be responsible in this second dimension, in other words, it cannot be at all times in one's life that only one possible action is determined by, and expressive of, one's *already existing will*. Some choices or actions in one's life must be, as explained earlier, *will-setting* and not already *will-settled*; that is, *self-forming actions*.

In section 7, the issue of why questions about moral and legal responsibility are often intertwined with issues about free will and determinism was explained. In section 8, this discussion was continued by considering practices of ascribing responsibility and blame in courts of law and other legal and moral contexts. The important legal condition of Fair Opportunity to Avoid Wrongdoing poses problems, it was argued, for claims that free will is compatible with determinism. Further issues about responsibility and free will in criminal trials on matters of retribution and punishment were then discussed in sections 9 and 10. Finally, these discussions were concluded in section 11, where two dimensions of responsibility in moral and legal contexts were distinguished and related to issues about free will.

12. Compatibilist Responses (I): Conditional Analyses

Compatibilists are not without further responses to the preceding arguments concerning free will and moral responsibility.

Historically, compatibilists have in fact pursued a number of different strategies we have not yet discussed to show that freedom and moral responsibility are compatible with determinism. The most common strategy attempting to show this employed by compatibilists in the modern era—from Hobbes and Locke in the 17th century to David Hume and John Stuart Mill in the 18th and 19th centuries, and well into the 20th century, is often called the "classical compatibilist" strategy. It involves conceding that moral responsibility *does* require the freedom or power to do otherwise *in some sense*. But then this classical compatibilism involves defending *conditional* or *hypothetical* interpretations of the freedom or power to do otherwise, according to which that power turns out to be compatible with determinism.

According to such **classical compatibilist strategies**, what we mean when we say that agents were "free or had the power to do otherwise" or "could have done otherwise" is that the agents *"would or might have done otherwise, if* the past (or the laws of nature) had been different in some way".

If, for example, persons had had different beliefs or desires, had reasoned or chosen differently or were in different circumstances, they would or might have acted differently. And saying persons would or might have acted differently, if the past or laws had been different in some way, these compatibilists then argue, is consistent with saying that the agents acting as they did was determined, given the past and the laws as they actually were.

I believe that this standard compatibilist strategy is deeply flawed. Immanuel Kant, as is well-known, called it a "wretched subterfuge" and William James a "quagmire of evasion", and I think they were right. A number of cogent objections have been made against such conditional interpretations of the freedom to do otherwise since the mid-20th century, and even many compatibilists today express doubts about such analyses. I believe they do so with good reason.

It may be true that persons would or might have done otherwise, if the past or the laws had been different in some way. But the difficulty is that the actual past when they do act was not different in some way; it was as it was. Likewise, the actual laws were not different; they were as they were. *Our freedom and responsibility must be exercised in the world that actually is, not in some hypothetical or merely possible world that might have been but never actually was.* And if determinism is true of this actual world in which we live and act, then acting otherwise than we do *in the circumstances we actually find ourselves* would always be causally impossible. It is not excusing to be told that persons would or might have acted otherwise in some merely hypothetical or possible worlds that never actually existed, if their acting otherwise in the actual world in which they do live and act was causally impossible.

Imagine a 16th-century incarnation of a modern classical compatibilist who took it upon himself to correct Luther when Luther said, "Here I stand. I can do no other". "You were mistaken, sir", this classical compatibilist might have said to Luther. "For all we mean when we say, 'I can now do other' is simply that in some possible worlds in which the past or the laws were different in some ways from the actual past and laws—in which, for example, you had had different beliefs or reasons or purposes—you would or might have done otherwise. And this may well have been true of you sir, this classical compatibilist might have said to Luther, at the time you said, 'Here I stand. I can do no other'. So, you see, you were mistaken at that time to say that you 'could not have done otherwise' at that moment".

Luther would likely have replied, "Get thee gone, sophist! What I meant when I said, 'I can do no other' is that in the *actual world where I found myself at that moment* with all the beliefs, reasons and purposes I had actually acquired in my long difficult journey to that point, my doing otherwise would have been impossible. What is it to me that I would or might have done otherwise in some merely possible world that did not actually exist at the time? Moreover, it was to some important degree the result *of my own past choices and actions* that the actual world that did exist and in which I acted at that moment was one in which I could not then have done other. For I had brought myself to that point in great part by my own past actions and choices. What you are claiming, therefore, not only distorts what I was saying; it devalues and insults my own contribution to making that actual world in which I was acting at that moment the kind of world in which I could not then have voluntarily and rationally done otherwise".

13. Compatibilist Responses (II): Frankfurt-Style Examples

Most traditional arguments for compatibilism, like the classical compatibilist one just considered, have conceded that the power to do otherwise *is* required for moral responsibility but have argued that this power, properly understood, is compatible with determinism. But a different and more radical strategy has become especially popular in contemporary philosophy among compatibilists. It is to argue more directly that the power to do otherwise is not required *at all* for moral responsibility. The most widely discussed and sophisticated versions of this compatibilist strategy in recent philosophy involve appealing to so-called Frankfurt-style examples (FSEs), named for Harry Frankfurt, who formulated the first of these influential examples in 1969.

Frankfurt's aim in formulating the first of these examples was to refute a principle he called

> The Principle of Alternative Possibilities (PAP): Agents are morally responsible for their actions, only if they could have avoided performing them or could have done otherwise when they performed them.

To refute this principle, Frankfurt imagined the following scenario:

> A controller, Black, has direct control over the brain of another man, Jones, and wants to allow Jones to do only what Black wants him to do. Black prefers, however, to allow Jones to act on his own whenever possible and so will only intervene if Jones is about to do something that he, Black, does not want.

Given this scenario, Frankfurt asks us to consider situations in which Jones is about to do what the controller Black wants, so that Black does not intervene. In such situations, Frankfurt argues, Jones could be morally responsible for acting as he does, because he would have acted on his own, from his own motives and for his own reasons, and nothing and no one (including Black) would have interfered with or prevented him from doing what he chose to do.

Yet Jones in such situations, Frankfurt argues, could not have done otherwise, for if he had given any indication of doing otherwise, the controller Black would have prevented him from doing so. Thus, this Principle of Alternative Possibilities or PAP, Frankfurt concluded, is false: It is *not* true that agents can be morally responsible for what they have done *only if* they could have done otherwise, because such Frankfurt controlled agents could be responsible for what they have done, if they did it on their own and the controller did not intervene, even though the agents could not have done otherwise, because the controller would have intervened and not let them do otherwise.

Now the first thing to be said about this line of argument is that it should not surprise us at this point that this Principle of Alternative Possibilities (PAP) of Frankfurt's is false. We have already seen from the discussion of the Luther example and other examples that agents can be morally responsible for actions that flow from their wills at the time they acted and such that they could *not* have done otherwise *at that time*. One can be responsible for "will-settled" actions like Luther's "Here I stand," even if one could not have done otherwise than perform them when they were performed. In other words, *we don't need to appeal to unusual examples involving Frankfurt-style controllers to establish that Frankfurt's principle PAP is false.*

But not all of our actions in our lifetimes could be determined or already will-settled in this way when we act, if *we* are ever to be responsible for our wills being set the way they are when we act. For this to be the case, we would have to, at some times in our lives, be capable of not merely "will-settled" but also "will-setting" or "self-forming" choices or actions (SFAs) that were not determined by our existing wills when we performed them and were such that we could have willingly done otherwise when we performed them. In other words, *some*, even many, morally responsible actions in the course of our lives may be such that, at the time we performed them, we could not then and there have *willingly* done otherwise, like Luther's act. But it does not follow that *all* of our morally responsible actions could be like this, if we are ever to be morally responsible to any degree for the state or quality of our wills.

So such examples do show that Frankfurt's principle PAP is false: It is *not* true that agents can be morally responsible for their actions *only if* they could have avoided performing them or could have done otherwise *when* they performed them. Frankfurt-style examples show this as well, and so he and others are right in saying that these examples show that Frankfurt's Principle of Alternative Possibilities is false. But such Frankfurt-style examples fail to show the falsity of a more complex principle required for free will that might be stated as follows and that may be called

> **Will-Setting Condition:** Agents are ultimately responsible for having the wills (characters, motives and purposes) they express in action, only if at some times in their lives they had the power to willingly (voluntarily and intentionally) perform certain ("will-setting" or "self-forming") actions (SFAs) that they also had the power to have willingly avoided performing.

These results have more general implications for Frankfurt-style examples. It can be shown that if all actions were under the control of Frankfurt controllers or mechanisms as in such examples, there could be no such self-forming choices or actions (SFAs) and hence no will-setting of the kind required for agents to be responsible for having the wills they do have.

This is the case because, in all Frankfurt-style examples, including all of the more sophisticated versions proposed since Frankfurt's original one, the one thing the Frankfurt controllers can never allow is the following: Frankfurt controllers can never allow the agents an opportunity to bring to completion "will-setting" or "self-forming" actions such that the agents are able to willingly perform the actions and are also able to willingly do otherwise. The controllers must always intervene in some way to prevent such will-setting actions from occurring so that *they* themselves, *the controllers and not the agents*, can *ensure* that the agents always do what the controllers want them to do. The essence of a will-setting or self-forming action is that *the agent, and no one or nothing else*, can determine how such a will-setting action will turn out when it is performed.

These sections responded to compatibilist arguments against claims that free will and responsibility are threatened by determinism. Section 12 dealt with classical compatibilist arguments to the effect that the power to do otherwise required for free will is merely a conditional power and is compatible with determinism. Section 13 dealt with other influential compatibilist arguments, based on so-called Frankfurt-style examples, which deny that moral responsibility requires the power to do otherwise at all and conclude that moral responsibility is therefore compatible with determinism. These sections attempt to answer both of these common kinds of compatibilist arguments.

14. The Intelligibility Question

We arrive finally at the most common and powerful objection made against libertarian views of free will that require its being incompatible with determinism. This objection has been made in various forms throughout history and continues to be commonly made and widely accepted in the present age. It is the objection that a libertarian and incompatibilist free will requiring ultimate responsibility is not even *intelligible* or *possible*. It is *not* something we *could* have anyway.

The culprit here is not determinism but indeterminism. As noted in section 1, this objection is related to an ancient dilemma: If free will is not compatible with determinism, it does not seem to be compatible with *indeterminism* either. Arguments have been made since ancient times, as noted earlier, that undetermined events would occur spontaneously and hence could not be controlled by agents in the way that free and responsible actions would require. If a choice occurred by virtue of some undetermined events in one's brain, it would seem a fluke or accident rather than a responsible choice. Undetermined events occurring in brains or bodies, it is commonly argued, would not seem to enhance freedom or control over or responsibility for actions but rather to diminish freedom, control and responsibility.

In response to such arguments, as also noted, libertarians about free will have often appealed throughout history to special and unusual forms of agency or causation to explain undetermined free actions. Libertarians have appealed to noumenal selves outside space and time, to immaterial minds, uncaused causes, nonevent agent causes and the like to account for an otherwise undetermined free will. And their critics have responded in turn that these appeals reinforce the critics' objection that one cannot make sense of an undetermined free will without appealing to unusual forms of agency that have no place in the modern scientific picture of the world and of human beings. These debates thus lead us to another central question concerning libertarian free will that must now be considered. It may be called

The Intelligibility Question: Is a libertarian free will requiring ultimate responsibility even *intelligible* or *possible*? Can one make sense of such a free will requiring indeterminism without reducing free will to mere *chance*, on the one hand, *or* to *mystery*, on the other, and can such a free will be reconciled with modern scientific views of the cosmos and of human beings?

15. Indeterminism: Empirical and Philosophical Questions

In approaching these questions, let us first be clear that it is an empirical and scientific question whether any indeterminism *is* there in nature in ways appropriate for free will—in the brain, for example. No purely philosophical theory alone can settle the matter. As the Epicurean philosophers said centuries ago, if the atoms don't "swerve" in undetermined ways and in the right places, there would be no room in nature for free will. Christoph Koch is a distinguished neuroscientist and a tough-minded one at that. He argues that "there is no evidence that any components of the nervous system—a warm and wet tissue strongly coupled to its environment—display quantum entanglement" (2009: 40).

But Koch goes on to say that "what cannot be ruled out", however, "is that tiny quantum fluctuations deep in the brain are amplified by deterministic chaos" so that they might have nonnegligible nondetermined effects on neural processing and thereby affect human decision making (Koch 2009: 40). Koch does not endorse this idea but says it cannot be ruled out, given what is currently known about the brain. And such a role for indeterminism is all that would be needed for the view to be presented here.

In the most recent edition of *The Oxford Handbook of Free Will* (2011), Robert Bishop agrees with Koch and cites a number of other neuroscientists and philosophers who have made similar suggestions. If minute quantum indeterminacies occurred at the intraneural or synaptic levels of the brain, affecting the timing of firing of individual neurons, Bishop argues, these indeterminacies, however minute, could be amplified, due to sensitivity to initial conditions, so that they had nonnegligible effects on neural processing in the form of neural noise. Bishop goes on to point out that one need not even appeal only to chaos to get these effects. As he notes, "The exquisite sensitivity needed for ... the amplification of quantum effects is a general feature of nonlinear dynamics and is present whenever nonlinear effects are likely to make significant contributions to the dynamics of a system" (2011: 91). And it is generally agreed, Bishop adds, that nonlinear dynamics is pervasive in the functioning of human brains.

A growing number of other scientists, not mentioned by Bishop, have also made suggestions about the possible role of indeterminism in the brain in recent years, including, interestingly, its potential evolutionary significance. They include neuroscientist Peter Ulric Tse, who has made detailed and highly original suggestions about these topics in a recent book (2013), as well as neuroscientists Paul Glimcher (2005) and Michael Shadlin (2014), biologists Bjorn Brembs (2011) and Martin Heisenberg (2013), astrophysicist Robert Doyle (2011), physicists G.F.R. Ellis (2009) and John Polkinghorne (2009) and psychologist Dean Simonton (2004), among many others.[3] It remains an open scientific question, of course, whether indeterminism does function in the neural processing of the brain. But rather than being dismissed out of hand, as in the past, this possibility is now regarded as a serious one by these and other scientists.

Yet our question at present is a philosophical one that has boggled people's minds since the time of the ancient Stoics and Epicureans: What could one *do* with indeterminism, assuming that it was there in nature in the right places, to make sense of free will as something other than mere chance or randomness and without appealing to mystery? If minute quantum indeterminacies in the firings of individual neurons were amplified so that they introduced some indeterminism into the larger scale processing in deliberation and decision making, how could this help to make sense of free choice as something other than mere chance? This is the Intelligibility

---

3. For example, Satinover (2001), Vasiri and Plenio (2010), Rolls (2012), Stapp (2007), Hameroff and Penrose (1996).

Question, just defined, about an incompatibilist free will that we must now address.

16. Initial Pieces: Self-formation, Efforts, Willpower, Volitional Streams

Let us begin by recalling that indeterminism does not have to be involved in all actions done "of our own free wills". It need be involved only in those choices or acts by which we make ourselves into the kinds of persons we are, with the wills we have. These are the "will-setting" or "self-forming" actions or SFAs of earlier sections.

I believe that these self-forming actions or SFAs would occur at those difficult times in life when we are torn between competing visions of what we should do or become, and they would be more common in everyday life than one may think. Perhaps we are torn between doing the moral thing or acting from ambition or between present desires and long-term goals, or we are faced with difficult tasks for which we have aversions or have to exert willpower to keep prior commitments and resolutions rather than break them.

In all such cases and many others, we are faced with competing motivations and have to strive or make an effort or exert willpower to overcome the temptation to do something else we also strongly want. At such times, the tension and uncertainty we feel about what to do, I suggest, would be reflected in some indeterminacy in our neural processes themselves—in the form of amplified background neural indeterminacy as described in the previous section—neural indeterminacy that is "stirred up", one might say, by the conflicts in our wills.

> The uncertainty and inner tension we feel at such soul-searching moments of self-formation would thereby be reflected in some indeterminacy in our neural processes themselves. The experienced uncertainty would correspond physically to the opening of a window of opportunity that temporarily screens off complete determination by the past.

A further step would then involve noting that in such cases of self-formation, where we are faced with competing motivations, whichever choice is made will require an effort of will or exercise of willpower to overcome the temptations to make the alternative choice. I thus postulate, in such cases, that different goal-directed cognitive processes (*volitional streams*, we might call them) would be involved in the brain, corresponding to these exertions of effort or willpower. These cognitive processes or efforts would have different goals corresponding to the different choices that might be made (e.g., a moral choice or a self-interested choice). But, importantly, it is not being claimed that these efforts or exercises of willpower aimed at different choices would be occurring at the same time during deliberation. Nor would they be occurring throughout the entire deliberation. Rather, different efforts or exertions of willpower may be initiated at different times depending on the course of the agent's reasoning.

To illustrate, consider a familiar example of van Inwagen's of a would-be thief—call him John—who is deliberating about whether or not to steal from a church poor box (1983). Suppose that John is deeply torn because, on the one hand, he is desperately in need of money and knows that no one is usually in the church on weekday afternoons, so he can likely steal the money without being caught. On the other hand, he has moral qualms about doing so because he knows that the money in the poor box is used to help other people who are in need, some of whom may need it as much as, or more than, he does.

We might then imagine that in the course of John's deliberation, various thoughts, experiences and memories come to mind and various preferences, desires and possibilities are assessed and weighed, so that his considered reasons incline him to choose to steal the money rather than not to steal it. Of crucial importance, however, if this is a self-forming choice situation in the sense described in prior sections, we must say that the reasons motivating the choice to steal the money merely *incline* John to make that choice at this time rather than the alternative choice. These reasons do not determine he will do so.

To use a traditional expression of Leibniz, his reasons "incline without necessitating". If a choice is thus to be made in accord with these inclinations, effort would have to be made or willpower exerted to overcome the resistance in his will. This resistance would be coming from his motives to make the contrary choice, which motives also remain important to him.

This is where indeterminism would enter the picture as well. In the manner described earlier in this section, this conflict in John's will would "stir up" indeterminism in the effort to make the choice to which he is currently inclined (to steal from the poor box), making it uncertain that the effort will succeed in attaining its goal. If the effort to choose to steal from the poor box in terms of his presently inclining reasons does succeed, despite this indeterminism, the choice to steal to which John is presently inclined would be made and the deliberation would terminate.

Note that if this should happen, the choice to steal, *despite being undetermined*, would have been made *by John* purposefully and in accordance with his will, because it would have been the result of a goal-directed effort of will to make just this choice at this time rather than an alternative choice. Moreover, the choice would have been made for the reasons inclining him toward that choice rather than the alternative at the time. Thus, it wouldn't have been a mere accident that the choice occurred, even though its occurrence was undetermined. The choice would have been brought about voluntarily and on purpose, as a result of the goal-directed effort of the agent.

What would happen, however, if, due to the indeterminism involved, the effort to choose to steal did *not* succeed at that time and the choice had not been made? Many critics of a free will requiring indeterminism assume that if a choice is undetermined, the agent would be able to make a different choice—for example, to steal *or* not to steal—given exactly the same deliberation leading up to moment of choice, including exactly the same desires, beliefs, thoughts, inclinations and prior reasoning. And given this assumption, it would follow, these critics argue, that if John had failed to choose to steal from the poor box at the time he did choose, due to the indeterminism involved, he would instead have chosen *not* to steal from the poor box at that time instead. And this seems problematic, these critics argue, given that his deliberation would have been exactly the same leading up to the choice. What would explain the difference in choice except possibly chance?

But this commonly made assumption need not be made, nor is it made, in the account of self-forming choices being given here. It is not assumed, nor need it be assumed on this account, that if a choice is undetermined the agent might make different choices—for example, to steal or not to steal—given exactly the same deliberation, including exactly the same desires, beliefs and reasoning, leading up to the choice. All that follows from the assumption that a self-forming choice or SFA is undetermined is that the effort to make it may succeed *or may fail* at a given time in overcoming the resistance in the will to making it. And from this, it does not follow that if the effort fails, an alternative choice would be made at that same time. *Failure would rather be a signal to the agent not to choose too quickly in terms of the presently inclining reasons. Failure would say in effect: Think more about this.* The resistant motives for the alternative choice (for example, John's motives for *not* stealing from a poor box) *still matter to you and these resistant motives should not be dismissed too readily.* These resistant motives are the causal source of the indeterminism in the effort to choose to steal in the first place, making it uncertain that the effort will succeed here and now. The stronger these resistant motives are, the greater the probability the effort may fail, due to the indeterminism to which the resistant motives give rise.

In other words, a distinction needs to be made between John's *not choosing to steal* at a time and his choosing *not to steal* at that time. What is assumed, if John fails in his effort to choose to steal from the poor box at a time, due to the indeterminism involved, is not that he would have made the contrary choice not to steal at that same time but rather that no choice at all would have been made at that time. The deliberation would continue until a potential reassessment of the motivating reasons that inclined to one choice or the other led to another later effort to make the choice to steal or a potential reassessment led to a later effort to make the choice not to steal. Or the deliberation might terminate without any decision being made.

John, we may imagine, if he fails to overcome the resistance in his will to making the choice to steal at a time, might reconsider his motivating reasons. Then, moved by his moral qualms about stealing money from a poor box used to help other people, he may be inclined seconds or minutes later to choose *not* to steal and make an effort to choose in accord with that inclination. The success of this further effort would also be undetermined, but if it succeeded nonetheless, the choice not to steal would be made. Or John may find on reconsidering that he really needs the money and makes a further effort at a later time to overcome his moral qualms. This effort may in turn fail as well, but if it succeeds despite the indeterminism, he would make the choice to steal at this later time. Or the deliberation may terminate without any decision being made. John may leave the church planning to think more about it, perhaps berating himself for his indecisiveness.

Note that in any of these possible scenarios, if John does succeed at a time in an effort to make one or another of the choices to which he is inclined at that time, he will have brought about the choice made and will have done so voluntarily and intentionally and for the motivating reasons that inclined him toward that choice at that time, because he would have succeeded in an effort whose goal was to make that very choice for those inclining (though not necessitating) reasons, and this would be the case even though the choice was undetermined.

> Indeterminism would have been involved in the effort, but it would not be the cause of the choice, if the effort succeeds. The effort would have succeeded, despite the indeterminism and not because of it. The cause of the choice would have been the agent, whose effort or exercise of willpower brought about the choice.

Note also that the indeterminism that is ingredient in the agent's effort to make the choice to which the agent is then inclined *is not an accidental feature of the situation.* It does not just "happen" to be present. The presence of the indeterminism is rather a consequence of the conflict in the agent's will and of the resistant motives that are a feature of that conflict—resistant motives that have to be overcome by effort, whichever choice is made. The stronger these resistant motives are, the greater the degree of indeterminism stirred up and the greater the probability of failure of the effort.

> The idea is thus to think of the indeterminism involved in self-forming choices not as a cause acting on its own but as an ingredient in larger goal-directed activities of the agent in which the indeterminism functions as a hindrance

or interfering element in the attainment of their goals. The choices that result would then be achievements brought about by the goal-directed activities (the efforts of will or exercises of willpower) of the agent, which might have failed because they were undetermined but one or the other of which might succeed in its goal.

Moreover, if such processes aimed at different goals may occur at different times in the course of deliberation (in the conflicted circumstances of a self-forming choice), *whichever choice may be successfully made will have been brought about by the agent's volitional striving* (the effort) to make that particular choice rather than the other at that time, despite the possibility of failure due to the indeterminism.

17. Indeterminism and Responsibility

Another significant consequence of thinking of indeterminism in this way is the following: When indeterminism functions in this manner as an obstacle to the success of goal-directed activities, the *indeterminism does not undermine responsibility, if the activities succeed in attaining their goals* despite the indeterminism.

Consider the example introduced earlier of an assassin trying to kill a prime minister from a distance with a high-powered rifle when, owing to a nervous twitch in his arm, he fails to hit his target. Or consider another example of a husband arguing with his wife, who in anger swings his arm down on her favorite glass tabletop intending to break it. In each of these cases we could imagine that an element of genuine chance or indeterminism is involved. We might imagine that the nervous twitches in the arms of the assassin that lead to missing his target or the reduced momentum in the swing of the husband's arm that might lead to his failing to break the tabletop are the result of undetermined quantum events in their brains or nerve pathways.

Due to this indeterminism in their nerve pathways, they might fail to do what they were intending and trying to do. But suppose that, despite the indeterminism, the assassin *succeeds* in his goal of killing the prime minister and the husband in breaking the tabletop. In such cases, both the assassin and the husband would be fully responsible for their actions, because both would have succeeded in doing what they were intending and trying, and making efforts to do, despite the indeterminism involved.

It would be a poor excuse for the assassin to plead in the courtroom that he was not guilty of killing the prime minister because due to the indeterminism in his nerve pathways it was undetermined, and hence a matter of chance, that he succeeded in hitting his target. It would be equally absurd for the husband to offer the excuse to his wife that, because it was undetermined that his arm swing would break the tabletop, the breaking of the tabletop was a matter of chance *and so he was not responsible*. His wife would not be impressed—and for good reason.

There was indeed a "chance" these agents would fail in doing what they were trying or making efforts to do. But if they succeeded, nonetheless, chance would not have been the *cause* of the prime minister's death or the table breaking. *They*, the agents, would have been the causes, by virtue of the fact that they would have succeeded in doing what they were intending and trying, and making efforts, to do.

> *When indeterminism thus functions as an obstacle to the success of goal-directed activities, the indeterminism does not preclude responsibility if the activities succeed in attaining their goals nonetheless.*

This would be the case for self-forming choices or SFAs as well but with an important difference. *Whichever choice the agents should make* in the course of a deliberation in a self-forming choice situation, the agents would have succeeded in doing what they were making an effort to do at that time, despite the indeterminism involved in their neural processing.

If John, for example, chooses to steal from the poor box at any time during his deliberation, it will be due to the success of his effort to make that choice at that time, thereby overcoming the resistance in his will to doing so. And if he chooses not to steal from the poor box at any other time in the deliberation, it will be due to the success of his effort to make that other choice not to steal at that time, thereby overcoming the resistance in his will to doing so.

Whichever choice is thus made in such self-forming choice situations, the indeterminism involved would not be a cause acting on its own but an ingredient in a larger goal-directed cognitive activity of the agent that would have succeeded in attaining its goal, despite the indeterminism and not because of it. The agents would be responsible for the choices made because they would have succeeded in doing what they were intending and trying to do, and this would be the case whichever choice should be made in the course of their deliberation.

To sum up, I have been arguing that self-forming actions or SFAs occur at those difficult times in life when we are torn between competing visions of what we should do or become. *On such occasions of self-formation, agents are, as is often said, "of two minds". Yet they are not two separate persons. They are not dissociated from either of their conflicted states of mind.*

Consider a young woman who is about to graduate with honors from a law school and who is deliberating about which of two attractive job offers to accept. One offer is with a large corporate law firm in a big city; the other a smaller, up-and-coming, but less prestigious, firm in a smaller city near where she grew up. She is torn because each firm has features that are deeply attractive to her. On the one hand, people at the smaller firm are friendlier and there is more of a chance of attaining an eventual partnership. The smaller firm is also near to where she grew up and hence to her family and many friends. On the other hand, she is extremely ambitious and the chance to be part of this very prestigious firm in a large city is very attractive to her, despite the difficulties it may involve. She is a small-town person with big-time ambitions.

The young woman of this example is a complex creature, torn inside by different visions of who she is and what she wants to be, as we all are from time to time. But this is the kind of complexity needed for genuine self-formation and hence for free will rather than merely freedom of action. And when agents, like this young woman, decide in such circumstances and the indeterminate efforts they are making become determinate choices, they make one set of competing reasons or motives prevail over the others then and there by deciding. They thereby voluntarily and purposefully commit themselves to a particular pathway into the future, and this will be so whichever choice they should succeed in making, despite the indeterminism involved.

Section 14 introduces another important question about free will, the "Intelligibility Question": Is a libertarian free will requiring indeterminism intelligible or possible at all? Many thinkers have argued that an undetermined free will is not intelligible because undetermined events occur by chance and hence could not be controlled by agents, as free and responsible actions must be. Section 15 discusses the empirical and scientific issues surrounding this question concerning whether indeterminism is or is not present in nature in ways that free will would require. Finally, sections 16 and 17 explain, in detail, ways in which this difficult Intelligibility Question might be answered by libertarians about free will.

18. Initial Questions and Objections: Indeterminism and Chance

Many questions and potential objections naturally arise about this view as so far presented. Addressing them will allow us to bring out more features of the view, which is far from complete. Many of the most obvious objections people have to views of free will requiring indeterminism, including the view presented here, rest on intuitions they have that if choices are undetermined, they *must* happen merely by chance—and so must be "random", "capricious", "uncontrolled", "irrational" and all the other things usually charged. Such intuitions are deeply rooted. But if we are going to understand free will, I think we have to break habits of thought supporting such intuitions and learn to think in new ways.

The first step would be to question the intuitive connection in people's minds between "indeterminism's being involved in something" and "it's happening merely as a matter of chance or luck".

"Chance" and "luck" are terms of ordinary language that imply "something's being out of one's control". So, using them already begs certain questions and may mislead us. Whereas

---

"Indeterminism" is a technical term that merely rules out deterministic causation, not causation altogether. Indeterminism is consistent with probabilistic forms of causation, where outcomes are caused but not inevitably. It is thus a mistake—one of the most common mistakes in the long history of debates about free will—to assume that "undetermined" must mean or imply "uncaused".

Another common source of misunderstanding is the following: Suppose that our young law graduate does decide to join the larger firm in the big city. If her decision is undetermined up to the moment when it occurs, one may have the image of her first making the effort to overcome the still strong motives to do otherwise (to join the smaller firm) and then at the last instant "chance takes over" and decides the issue for her.

But this image is misleading. On the view presented, one cannot separate the indeterminism and the effort, so that *first* the effort occurs *followed by* chance or luck. Rather, the efforts or exertions of willpower are temporally extended goal-directed processes of the agent and the indeterminism is an ingredient in these larger processes, not something separate that occurs *after* or *before* them. The neural networks that realize the efforts in the brain are circulating impulses and there is some indeterminacy assumed in the timings of firings of individual neurons in these circulating impulses. But these processes as a whole are her efforts and they persist right up to the moment when the decision is made.

There is no point at which her effort stops and chance "takes over". She decides as a causal result of her effort, even though she might have failed due to the indeterminism ingredient in the effort. Likewise, the husband breaks the table as a causal result of his effort, even though he might have failed because of the indeterminacy. This is why his excuse "chance broke the table, not *me*" is so lame when he succeeds.

19. Further Questions and Objections: Phenomenology and Rationality[4]

Yet another frequently made objection is that we are not introspectively or consciously aware of making efforts and performing multiple cognitive tasks in self-forming choice situations. But it is not being claimed that agents must always be introspectively aware of making such efforts or exertions of willpower (though sometimes they might be when they are very conflicted). And, importantly, as emphasized earlier, it is not being claimed that these efforts or exercises of willpower aimed at different choices would be occurring at the same time during deliberation. Nor will they be occurring throughout the entire deliberation. Rather different efforts or exercises of willpower may be initiated at different times depending on the course of the agent's reasoning.

What persons are introspectively aware of in self-forming choice situations is that they are trying to decide about which of competing options to choose and either choice is difficult because there are resistant motives pulling them in different directions, some of which will have to be overcome, whichever choice is made. In such introspective conditions, I am theorizing that what is going on underneath is complex processing in the brain that may involve, at various times in the course of deliberation, one or another goal-directed cognitive process whose goal is making a specific choice and thereby overcoming resistance in the will to making that choice.

There is a more general point here that I have often emphasized: *Introspective evidence cannot give us the whole story about free will.* Stay on the conscious surface and libertarian free will is likely to appear obscure or mysterious, *as it so often has in history.* What is needed is a theory about what might be going on behind the scenes when we exercise such a free will, not merely a description of what we immediately experience. There is, in fact, a growing body of

---

4.   Objections addressed in this section and subsequent ones have been made in various forms by many critics of these features of libertarian views of free will, including Pereboom (2001), Clarke (2003), Mele (2006), Haji (2009), Fischer (2006), Levy (2011), Vargas (2009), Caruso (2012), Double (1996), Waller (1990), among others. Other attempts to answer such objections have been made by defenders of libertarian views, including O'Connor (2000), Balaguer (2010), Franklin (2018), Lemos (2018), Speak (2004), Ekstrom (2000), Steward (2012), Griffith (2010), Timpe (2008), Pink (2011), Mawson (2011), Widerker (1995), Doyle (2011).

empirical evidence showing that in complex cognitive processes such as practical reasoning, much of the processing that is going on occurs unconsciously.[5] Moreover, some of what occurs unconsciously may involve effort making or exercises of willpower; for example, to access memories or associations or considerations that may have a bearing on a decision, to overcome temptations to suppress other information we may not want to think about, to resist strong inclinations, to avoid rationalizations or self-deception and so on.

Another common objection is that it is irrational to make efforts to do incompatible things. I agree that it would be irrational if the efforts to make incompatible choices (say, to steal or not to steal) were being made at the same time, given exactly the same reasoning up to that time. But this is not what is being assumed here in the case of self-forming choices. Rather, one or another of these efforts or exercises of willpower may be initiated at different times, depending on the trajectory of the agent's reasoning up to that time.

In particular, one such effort may be initiated when, in the course of deliberation, the agent's considered reasons at that point incline (without necessitating) the agent to make one of the choices rather than another. It is not irrational to make an effort to make a choice in such situations in terms of one's presently inclining reasons, though it would be irrational to also make an effort to make an opposing choice at *this same* time, given these same inclining reasons.

It is important in this regard to recognize the uniqueness of such self-forming choice situations. Our normal intuitions about efforts are formed in everyday situations in which our wills are already "set one way" on doing something, where obstacles and resistance have to be overcome if we are to succeed in doing it. We want to open a door that is jammed, so we have to make an effort to open it. Such ordinary situations are what were earlier called "will-settled" situations where our wills are already set or settled on doing what we are making efforts to do. I am making an effort to open a jammed closet door to get what is inside. There is no resistance in my will to doing so, and no reasons to do otherwise: I need what is in the closet for my day's activities. The resistance that has to be overcome by effort thus has an external source, in the conditions of the door and door frame. The resistance is not coming from my own will.

---

5. See, for example, Nichols (2015), Balaguer (2010), Jedlicka (2014), Usher (2006), Miller and Cohen (2001), Glimcher (2005), Shadlin (2014), Brembs (2011).

By contrast, self-forming choices or SFAs, as we have seen, are "will-setting", not already "will-settled." Our wills are *not* already settled on doing what we are making efforts to do. The resistance that has to be overcome by effort is thus not coming from an external source. It is coming from our own wills. We "set" our wills one way or the other only in the act of choosing itself, when an effort we are making succeeds in overcoming the resistance in our will to making the choice in question.

This feature of will-setting choices—that the resistance to making them is coming from our own will, not from an external source—is related in turn to the fact that the reasons motivating the efforts to make such will-setting or self-forming choices merely "incline" without necessitating. The reasons motivating an opposing choice still matter to the agent and must be overcome by effort if the choice to which the agent is presently inclined is to be made. It is thus rational to make an effort in such circumstances in terms of one's presently inclining reasons if the resistance in one's will is to be overcome. What would *not* be rational would be to make an effort to make a contrary choice at this same time, given these same inclining reasons.

It would also be irrational to make no effort at all to overcome the resistance in one's will to making the choice to which one is inclined but rather to leave the outcome to "chance" and "hope" that the choice to which one is inclined "wins" out.

Self-forming choices are not a matter of certain motivations "winning out" over others "on their own". Rather, self-forming choices involve the agent bringing it about that one set of motivations wins out over another by the agent making an effort to do so and succeeding in that effort.

Because most efforts in everyday life, such as the effort to open the jammed closet door, are made in will-settled situations where our wills are already set on doing what we are trying or making efforts to do, we tend to assimilate all effort-making to such situations. We thereby fail to consider the uniqueness of *will-setting*, which is of a piece, in my view, with the uniqueness of **free will**.

20. Micro vs. Macro Control

Another common line of reasoning lying behind many objections to an undetermined free will is the following: Is it not the case, one might ask, on the view proposed that whether agents succeed in making a choice A in the circumstances of a self-forming choice (i) depends on whether certain neurons involved in their cognitive processing fire or not (perhaps within a certain time frame) and is it not the case that (ii) whether or not these neurons fire is undetermined and hence a matter of chance and hence that (iii) the agent does not have control over whether or not they fire? But if these claims are true, it seems to follow that the choice merely "happened" as a result of the chance firings of these neurons and so (iv) the agent would not have had control over whether the choice of A was made or failed to be made and (v) hence the agent would not be responsible for making the choice.

For many persons, this line of reasoning clinches the matter. It looks like the outcome *must* be merely a matter of chance or luck after all. Yet they reason too hastily, because the really astonishing thing is that, even though agents do not have control over whether or not the undetermined neurons involved in their cognitive processing fire or not, it does not follow that the agents do not have sufficient control to be responsible for the choices ultimately made.

This does not follow when the following three things are also true: (i) the choosing of A rather than B (or B rather than A, whichever occurs) was something the agent was striving or trying to bring about at the time, (ii) the indeterminism in the neuron firings involved in this striving or trying was a hindrance or obstacle to the achievement of that goal and (iii) the agent's striving or trying nonetheless succeeded in achieving the goal despite the hindering effects of the indeterminism.

Consider the husband swinging his arm down on the table. It is also true in his case that (i) whether or not his endeavoring or trying to break the tabletop succeeds "depends" on whether certain neurons in his nervous system fire or do not fire. It is also true in his case that (ii) whether these neurons fire or not is undetermined and hence a matter of chance and is (iii) not under his control. Yet, even though we can say all this, it does not follow that (iv) the husband did not break the tabletop and that (v) he is not responsible for breaking the tabletop, *if* his endeavoring or trying to do so succeeds. And, importantly, each of these things would be true in the case of a self-forming choice, whichever choice was made. Astonishing indeed! Yet this is the kind of surprising result one gets when indeterminism or chance plays an interfering or hindering role in larger goal-directed activities of agents that may succeed or fail.

It would be good to meditate on this: We tend to reason that if an action (whether an overt action of breaking a table or a mental act of making a choice) depends on whether certain neurons fire or not (in the arm or in the brain), then the agent must be able to make those neurons fire or not, if the agent is to be responsible for the action. In other words, we think we have to crawl down to the place where the indeterminism originates in the individual neurons and make them go one way or the other.

We think we have to become originators at the micro level and "tip the balance" that chance leaves untipped if we (and not chance) are to be responsible for the outcome. And we realize that we cannot do that. But we do not have to. It's the wrong place to look. We do not have to micromanage our individual neurons one by one to perform purposive actions and we do not have such *micro control* over our neurons even when we perform ordinary free actions such as swinging an arm down on a table.

What is needed when we perform purposive activities, mental or physical, is *macro control* of processes involving many neurons—processes that may succeed in achieving their goals despite the interfering or hindering effects of some recalcitrant neurons.

We do not have micro control over each individual neuron or muscle that might be involved in our purposive activities. But that does not prevent us from having macro control over these purposive activities themselves (whether they are mental activities such as practical reasoning or physical activities such as arm-swingings) and being responsible when those purposive activities attain their goals.

---

21. Control and Responsibility

But if indeterminism does not take away control altogether, does it not at least *diminish* the control agents have over their actions? Is it not the case that the assassin's control over whether the official is killed (his ability to realize his purposes or what he is trying to do) is lessened by the undetermined impulses in his arm—and so also for the husband and his breaking the table? Their control is indeed lessened. But a further surprising thing worth noting is that *diminished control in such circumstances does not entail diminished responsibility* when agents *succeed* in doing what they are trying or making efforts to do. The assassin is not less guilty of killing the official if he did not have complete control over whether he would succeed because of the indeterminism, nor is the husband less guilty of breaking the table if he succeeds, despite the indeterminism involved.

Suppose there were three assassins, each of whom killed an official. Suppose one of them (an older assassin contemplating retirement) had a 50% chance of succeeding because of the indeterministic wavering of his arm, another had an 80% chance and the third (a young stud) had nearly a 100% chance. Is one of these assassins less guilty than the others *if they all succeed*? It would be absurd to say that one assassin deserves 100 years in jail, the other 80 years, and the third 50 years. The diminished control in the assassins who had an 80% or a 50% chance does not translate into diminished responsibility when they succeed.

There is an important further lesson here about free will in general. We should concede that indeterminism, wherever it occurs, does diminish control over what we are trying to do and is a hindrance or obstacle to the realization of our purposes. But recall the case of the young law graduate mentioned earlier. The indeterminism that is admittedly diminishing her control over the choice she may be trying to make (to join one law firm or another) is coming from her own will. It is coming from the motives she has for making the opposing choice (to join the competing firm).

In each case, the indeterminism is functioning as a hindrance or obstacle to her realizing one of her purposes—a hindrance or obstacle in the form of resistance within her will that has to be overcome by effort. If there were no such hindrance—if there were no resistance in her will—she might indeed in a sense have "complete control" over one of her options. There would be no competing motives standing in the way of her choosing it and therefore no interfering indeterminism. But then she also would not be free to *rationally* and *voluntarily* choose the other purpose (to choose otherwise), because she would have no good competing reasons to do so. Thus,

By being a hindrance to the realization of some of our purposes, indeterminism opens up the genuine possibility of pursuing other purposes—of choosing or doing otherwise in accordance with, rather than against, our wills. To be genuinely self-forming agents (creators of ourselves)—to have free will—there must at times in life be obstacles and hindrances in our wills of this sort that we must overcome. Free will is a gift, but it also involves struggle—and achievement.

These sections answer some objections to the libertarian view of free will sketched in sections 16 and 17 and in the process further develop that view. Section 18 addressed objections that libertarian free choices would occur merely by chance or luck. Section 19 addressed objections about whether we experience our free choices introspectively or consciously and whether it is rational to make efforts to do incompatible things. Section 20 addressed questions about what kind of control we exercise over self-forming choices (whether micro or macro control). And section 21 considered whether or not indeterminism diminishes control and whether its doing so would undermine rather than enhance free will.

22. Agency, Complexity, Disappearing Agents

Another question that has had a hypnotic effect on modern free will debates, reflecting deeply rooted intuitions, is the following: Do we not have to postulate an additional kind of "agent causation" over and above causation by states and events to fully capture libertarian free choices, given that such choices must be undetermined by prior states and events? There is a residual fear underlying questions of this kind that the "agent," will somehow "disappear" from the scene if we describe its capacities and their exercise, including free will, in terms of causation by states and events alone involving the agent. I believe this fear is ultimately misguided.

A continuing substance (e.g., an agent) does not disappear from the ontological stage because we describe its continuing existence—its life, if it is a living thing—including its capacities and their exercise, in terms of states, events and processes involving it. One needs more reason than this *to think that agents do not cause things, only events cause things.* Human agents are continuing substances with both mental and physical properties. But it is not inconsistent to say this and to say that the *lives* of agents, their capacities and the *exercise* of those capacities, including free will, must be spelled out in terms of states, processes and events involving them. In short,

> One does not have to choose between agent (or substance) causation and event causation in describing freedom of choice and action. One can affirm both.

In the case of self-forming choices or SFAs, for example, it is true to say both that "the agent's deliberative activity, including her effort, caused or brought about the choice" and to say that "the agent caused or brought about the choice." Indeed, the first claim *entails* the second. Such event descriptions are not meant to deny that agents cause their free choices and free actions. Rather, the event descriptions spell out in more detail *how* and *why* the agents did so. There is thus no reason to worry that the "agent" will somehow "disappear" from the scene if we describe its capacities and their exercise, including free will, in terms of causation by states and events involving the agent.

Relevant here to explaining the role of agents in the causation of action is a peculiarly modern scientific way of understanding this role that has roots in ancient views, such as that of Aristotle.

Agents, according to this modern conception with ancient roots, are to be conceived as *information-responsive complex dynamical systems.* "An agent's causing an action" is to be understood as "an agent, conceived as such an information-responsive complex dynamical system, exercising *teleological guidance control,* over some of its own processes".

Complex dynamical systems are understood in this context in the manner of "dynamical systems theory". Such systems (now known to be ubiquitous in nature and which include living things) are systems in which emergent capacities arise as a result of greater complexity. When the emergent capacities arise, the systems as a whole impose novel constraints on the behavior of their parts.

> Such complex systems exhibit **Teleological Guidance Control (TGC)** when they tend through feedback loops and error correction mechanisms to converge on a goal (called an attractor) in the face of perturbations.

Such control, as neuroscientist Marius Usher argues (2006), *is necessary for any voluntary activity* and he interprets it in terms of dynamic systems theory, as I would as well. Neuroscientists E. Miller and J. Cohen (2001) argue that such cognitive (guidance) control in human agents stems from the active maintenance of patterns of activity in the prefrontal cortex that represent goals and the means to achieve them. These patterns provide signals to other brain structures, they argue, whose net effect is to guide the flow of activity along neural pathways that establish the proper mappings between inputs, internal states and outputs.

An important consequence of understanding the agent causation involved in free agency and free will in this way is that the causal role of the agent in intentional actions of the kind needed for free agency and will is not *reducible* to causation by mental states of the agent alone, such as beliefs, desires and intentions. That would leave out the added role of the agent, qua complex dynamical system, exercising teleological guidance control over the processes *linking* mental states to actions. In the absence of this *systemic control* by the agent over the *manner* in which the mental states cause the resulting events, the causation by mental states might be "deviant" and the outcomes would not be intentional actions of the agent.

A further significant consequence of understanding causation of free actions in this way, as Usher points out, is that, though the teleological guidance control (TGC) of the kind required is compatible with determinism, it is also compatible with indeterminism. A complex dynamical system can exhibit teleological guidance control, tending through feedback loops and error correction to converge on a goal, even when, due to presence of indeterminism, it is uncertain whether the goal will be attained. Such control is necessary for any voluntary activity, as noted, whether the voluntary activity is "will-settled" and determined or "will-setting" and not determined.

To conclude, one does not have to choose between agent (or substance) causation and event causation in accounting for free agency, libertarian or otherwise. You can—indeed, you must—affirm both. And the agent or substance causation involved is not reducible to event causation by mental states alone for the reasons explained. There is thus no "disappearing agent" problem as well.

23. Regress Objections: Responsibility and Character Development

Another common worry is that views of free will requiring ultimate responsibility lead to a vicious regress. To be ultimately responsible for a choice that issues from an agent's present will (character, motives and purposes), the agent must be at least in part responsible by virtue of choices or actions voluntarily performed in the past (self-forming actions) for having the will he or she now has. But to be ultimately responsible for these earlier self-forming actions by which we formed our present wills, would we not have to be responsible in turn for the characters, motives and purposes from which these earlier self-forming actions issued? And would this not require still earlier self-forming actions by which we formed these characters, motives or purposes?

We would thus be led backwards to the earliest choices of childhood when the wills from which we chose were not formed by us at all but were entirely the product of influences outside ourselves, parents, social conditioning, heredity, genetic dispositions and so on. It may thus appear that all responsibility for later choices in life would go back to the earliest choices of childhood when we seem to have far less freedom and responsibility than we have later in life, which is absurd.

The first response to make to this familiar worry is to note that ultimate responsibility for choices in later life need not have its source entirely in choices of childhood. This would be true only if we made no subsequent self-forming choices in later life. By contrast, the account of self-forming choices given in preceding sections implies that if self-forming choices are possible for agents at all, they would normally occur throughout our lives and more so as we mature and life becomes more complex. This is so because

It is the complexity of our lives, and of our wills and motivations, that gives rise to conflicts in our wills and to self-forming actions in the first place, and this complexity does not abate but normally grows as we develop beyond childhood. In making self-forming choices as we mature, we would be constantly forming and re-forming our existing characters, motives and purposes as we go along in ways that, though influenced by our prior characters, motives and purposes, are not determined by our prior characters, motives and purposes.

I argue, therefore, in partial agreement with philosophers such as Aristotle, who talk about the development of "character", that responsibility for our *wills* (characters, motives and purposes) accumulates over time (Kane 1996). Putting the matter in terms of the present theory: By making many self-forming choices through a lifetime, we gradually form and re-form our characters, motives and purposes in ways not determined by our past.

It would follow that, with regard to most of the self-forming choices we make, our responsibility has a twofold source: first, in the self-forming choices themselves we make in the present between our conflicting motives and purposes and, second, in the conflicting motives and purposes themselves from which the choices are made, many of which had *their* source in earlier self-forming actions by which we gradually formed our present wills over time.

The only exceptions, of course, would be the very earliest self-forming actions of childhood when it *is* normally true, if we go back far enough, that the motivations among which we choose all come from sources outside ourselves, parents, society, upbringing, etc. I have discussed these first self-forming actions of childhood in a number of writings (e.g., Kane 2011c) and have a distinctive view about them, which may be spelled out as follows.

In the earliest self-forming actions of childhood, our responsibility, far from being the source of all later responsibility, *is* very limited, precisely because there is as yet no backlog of self-formed character. That is why we hold children less responsible the younger they are. I further argue that

The earliest self-forming actions of childhood have a probative (or probing or learning) character to them. Young children are often testing what they can get away with and what consequences their behavior will have on them and others (among the many reasons why child-rearing is so exhausting). Their character is thus slowly built up by how they respond to the responses to these earliest probes. Character and purposes to which they commit themselves accumulate and they become more responsible for subsequent acts that flow not just from present efforts but from past formed character and purposes as well.

If a three-year-old is told not to take more than his share of cookies but tries to do so anyway the next time, resisting his conflicting motives not to disobey his parents, then the child is responsible. But he is not as responsible as when he does it a second, third or fourth time and it becomes a pattern of behavior. The wise parent will not punish him severely the first time but may do so mildly by withholding something he wants. But

The wise parent will also know that it is a mistake never to hold the child responsible at all for these earliest probes, because it is by being so held responsible in however limited ways in our earliest years that we gradually become self-forming beings with wills of our own making.

24. The Explanatory Luck Objection: Authors, Stories, Value Experiments and Liberum Arbitrium

These reflections lead to one of the most common and powerful variants of the luck objection made against this view and many other libertarian theories during the past three decades. This objection, which has been called the "Explanatory Luck Objection", is stated in the following way by Alfred Mele (1998), one of its most astute and persistent defenders:

> **The Explanatory Luck Objection:** If different free choices could emerge from the same past of an agent, there would seem to be no explanation for why one choice was made rather than another in terms of the total prior character, motives and purposes of the agent. The difference in choice—that is, the agent's choosing one thing rather than another—would therefore be just a matter of luck.

This objection in various formulations is now so widely cited and affirmed by critics of libertarian views of free will that it is often referred to as "the" luck objection in the literature. And many philosophers assume that it is decisive. I think they are mistaken. But I also think the objection has the power it has because it teaches us something important about free will.

The first obvious thing to be said in response to this luck objection is the following: In the case of self-forming choices as described here, it is not true to say, as the objection does, that "different free choices could emerge from the same past of an agent". This is not true, if it means the agent could make opposing choices—for example, to steal or not to steal—given exactly the same prior reasoning leading up to the moment of choice.

All that follows, as argued earlier, from the fact that a self-forming choice is undetermined is that it might be made at a given time or might fail to be made at that time. It does *not* follow that the opposing choice—not to steal—would be made at that same time, given exactly the same reasoning leading up to the choice to steal. And this would be true whichever choice is made in a self-forming choice situation.

Moreover, for whichever choice should be made in a self-forming choice situation, the following things would all be true:

(a) The agent would have caused or brought about that choice by succeeding in an effort to bring it about, thereby overcoming resistance in the will to doing so.

(b) The agent would have knowingly made that choice *rather than* the alternative.

(c) The agent would have had the power to bring about the choice made and would have successfully exercised that power when it was made. This power was not unlimited because the effort through which it was exercised might have failed due to the indeterminism involved. But if the effort succeeded, the agent's power to make the choice would have been successfully exercised.

(d) The choice would have been made for reasons that inclined (without necessitating) the agent to make that choice at that time rather than the alternative—reasons that the agent then and there chose to act upon.

(e) The agent would have made the choice rather than the alternative *voluntarily* (without being coerced against his or her will).

(f) The agent would have done so *intentionally* or on purpose (not merely by mistake) and would have done so by succeeding in an effort aimed at making that very choice rather than the alternative.

If saying "the agent's choosing one thing rather than another is just a matter of luck", as this explanatory luck objection does, is meant to deny any of these things (a)–(f) about such self-forming choices, then saying that the outcome was just a matter of luck seems to be the wrong conclusion to draw. And if one were to say that "just a matter of luck" is meant to be consistent with all of these things, the argument from luck would seem to lose much of its traction.

Ah, but not quite all traction—and this is where things get interesting. With powerful arguments in philosophy, it is not enough to show that their conclusions do not necessarily follow from their premises. One needs also to show why they seem to have such power and seem irrefutable. The luck objection in this popular form does not show that libertarian free choices must be "just a matter of luck" if that entails denying any of the claims (a)–(f). But it does show that there is something to the oft-repeated charge that such self-forming choices must be *arbitrary* in a certain sense.

A residual arbitrariness seems to remain in all self-forming choices (SFAs) because the agents cannot in principle have *sufficient* or *overriding* (*conclusive* or *decisive*) prior reasons for making one option and one set of reasons prevail over the other. Therein lies the truth in this explanatory luck objection: *An undetermined free choice cannot be completely explained by the entire past, including past causes or reasons*, and I think it is a truth that reveals something important about free will. I have argued elsewhere that such arbitrariness relative to prior reasons tells us that

> Every undetermined self-forming choice is the initiation of a novel pathway into the future, whose justification lies in that future and is not fully explained by the past (Kane 1996: 145–46). In making such a choice we say, in effect, "I am opting for this pathway. It is not required by my past reasons but is consistent with my past and is one branching pathway my life can now meaningfully take. Whether it is the right choice, time will tell. Meanwhile, I am willing to take responsibility for it one way or the other".

Of special interest here, as I have often noted, is that the term "arbitrary" comes from the Latin *arbitrium*, which means "judgment"—as in *liberum arbitrium voluntatis* ("free judgment of the will"—which was in fact the medieval designation for free will). Imagine a writer in the middle of a novel. The novel's heroine faces a crisis and the writer has not yet developed her character in sufficient detail to say exactly how she will act. The author makes a "judgment" about this that is not determined by the heroine's already formed past, which does not give unique direction. In this sense, the judgment (*arbitrium*) of how she will react is "arbitrary" but not entirely so. It had input from the heroine's fictional past and in turn gave input to her projected future. In a similar way,

> Agents who exercise free will are both authors of and characters in their own stories at once. By virtue of "self-forming" judgments of the will (*arbitria voluntatis*; self-forming actions or SFAs), they are "arbiters" of their own lives, "making themselves" out of a past that, if they are truly free, does not limit their future pathways to one.

If we should charge them with not having sufficient or conclusive prior reasons for choosing as they did, they might reply:

True enough. But I did have "good" reasons for choosing as I did, which I'm willing to endorse and take responsibility for. If they were not sufficient or conclusive reasons, that's because, like the heroine of the novel, I was not a fully formed person before I chose (and I still am not, for that matter). *Like the author of the novel, I am in the process of writing an unfinished story and forming an unfinished character who, in my case, is myself.*

25. Contrastive Explanations: Concluding Remarks on Huck Finn and Other Literary Figures

Closely related to this explanatory luck objection is another objection concerning "contrastive explanation" that is frequently made against theories of free will requiring indeterminism. A contrastive explanation is an explanation for why one thing occurred *rather than* another. In the case of free choices, it would be an explanation in terms of an agent's prior character, reasons or motives for why the agent made one choice rather than another.

The objection in this case is that, if a self-forming choice (e.g., between A and B) is undetermined up to the moment when it is made, there could be no adequate contrastive explanation for why it was made rather than the alternative choice, because the fact that the choice was undetermined would mean that either choice (of A or of B) might have occurred, given the totality of the agent's traits of character, motives and reasoning preceding the moment of choice. And there thus could not be an explanation for why one choice was made rather than the other at that moment in terms of the totality of the agent's character, motives and reasoning prior to choice.

The first thing to be said in response to this familiar argument is similar to the first thing said in response to the explanatory luck objection: In the case of self-forming choices as understood here, it is *not* true to say, as this objection does, that either choice (of A or of B) might have occurred, "given the totality of the agent's traits of character, motives and reasoning preceding the moment of choice". All that follows from the fact that a self-forming choice (e.g., the choice of A) is *undetermined* at a given time is that it might be made at that time or might *fail* to be made at that time. It does *not* follow that if the choice (of A) fails to be made at that time, the opposing choice—(of B)—would be made *at that same time*, given exactly the same reasoning that led to the choice of A.

But those who make this objection concerning contrastive explanation to views of free will requiring indeterminism usually have
another assumption in mind that also needs to be addressed. They
often assume that for an explanation of a free choice to be adequately contrastive in the sense they require, the following would
have to be the case: If making the choice that was made during a
deliberation rather than any alternative was the rational or reasonable thing to do, given the totality of the agent's reasons or motives,
then making an alternative choice during that same deliberation,
given the totality of the agent's reasons or motives, would *not* have
been rational or reasonable.

If making an alternative choice in the circumstances might also
have been a rational or reasonable thing to do, we would not have
an adequate contrastive explanation, in the sense these critics would
require, for why one choice was made *rather than* the other in terms
of the agent's reasons and motives.

But if this is what contrastive explanations would require, there
clearly could not be contrastive explanations in the sense these critics require of self-forming choices or SFAs. It is an essential feature
of self-forming choices that no *such* strong contrastive explanations could be given for them, because, in addition to being undetermined, self-forming choices must satisfy *plurality conditions* for
free choice; that is, the power to make them and the power to do
otherwise, either way, voluntarily, intentionally *and rationally*. And
this rules out the requirement that any other choice that might have
been made in the course of a deliberation, other than the choice
actually made, would have been unreasonable or irrational.

Moreover, this feature is not a defect of self-forming choices,
according to the account given of them, but it is a consequence of
their power, because it is precisely because agents have the power
to make such choices and the power to do otherwise, voluntarily,
intentionally and rationally either way that makes it possible for
such choices to be *will-setting* rather than *will-settled*. And the
power to make will-setting choices at some points in our lives is
what makes it possible for us to be makers or creators to some
degree of our own wills rather than to be always acting from wills
already formed.

It is also important to emphasize, however, that though agents
who make such will-setting or self-forming choices may not have
conclusive or decisive reasons for making the choice that is made
rather than any other, such agents do nonetheless have reasons for

choosing as they do that are "good enough" to render the choices they do make reasonable and rational ones, given their total reason sets when they choose. Some mathematical decision theorists speak in this connection of

> **Satisficing Reasons:** reasons that are good enough to justify a choice or action even though they are not sufficient to render any possible alternative choice or action that might have been made in the circumstances unreasonable or irrational.

Reasons for will-setting or self-forming choices are satisficing reasons in this decision-theoretic sense.

Moreover, the fact that the reasons for self-forming choices (SFAs) are satisficing in this sense is related to something important about free will that was spelled out in the previous section. It is related to the fact that *"every undetermined self-forming choice is the initiation of a novel pathway into the future, whose justification lies in that future and is not fully explained by the past"*. In making such a choice, we say, in effect, "I am opting for this pathway. It is not *required* by my past reasons but is consistent with my past and is one branching pathway my life can now meaningfully take".

This "narrative" conception of self-formation, as we might call it, is nicely captured in an important recent book by John Doris, *Talking to Ourselves: Reflections on Selfhood, Agency and Responsibility* (2015). In a section of this book in which Doris talks about my views of agency and responsibility, he notes (2015: 162) that in my defense of libertarian free will, I "develop the intriguing suggestion that ambivalence", about what one's true values are "and its resolution in action", is not contrary to responsible agency but is essential to responsible agency. It is so at least at some points in our lives when we are torn between conflicting values.

At such times, Doris says, when on my view we are engaged in self-formation, it is possible that more than one path into the future could represent our "true values" and it would be "up to us" which path we will take. We decide then and there which of our *possible* true values our actions will express. If we were never ambivalent—ambi-valent, I would say—in this way, we could not be self-creating beings, because our choices and actions would always be expressing what we *already* were, the formed will we already had.

At this point in his book, where Doris references these views of mine on conflicting values and ambivalence, he also discusses the example of Huckleberry Finn—an example that has played such a prominent role in contemporary philosophical writings on agency and ethics. On one telling of the Huck story, Doris says, "Huck held values favoring *both* the conventional course of action", that he should turn his friend and companion Jim, a black man who had escaped from slave owners, over to the authorities and, on the other hand, "the course [Huck] actually followed," of not turning Jim over. In sum, Doris says, "Huck's values *conflicted* ... he suffered a kind of *ambivalence*" (2015: 161):

That, I believe, is how Mark Twain himself tells the story. As I have put it:

> Huck is growing and developing as a self or agent. In deciding not to turn Jim in, Huck is not merely *expressing* what sort of a self he already is; he is also *deciding* what sort of a self he is going to be by deciding from among the conflicting values he has, which ones he will follow. He is thereby not merely engaged in self-*expression* , but in self-*making* , of the kind I believe *freedom of will* and not mere *freedom of action* sometimes requires. Such conflicts in the will and their resolution or lack thereof (as my wife, a writer, continually reminds me), are the stuff of most great literature and drama, Huck Finn, Madame Bovary, Hamlet, Anna Karenina, you name it.

These sections answer further common objections to libertarian free will. Section 22 addresses the so-called disappearing agent objection often made against views of libertarian free will of the kind defended here. I argue that, in the exercise of free will, agents are to be understood as "information responsive complex dynamical systems" exercising "teleological guidance control" over some of their own processes. These notions and their relations to free will are explained and used to answer disappearing agent objections. Section 23 addresses certain "regress" objections to libertarian free will, or the worry that if we are to be ultimately responsible for our present wills we must also be ultimately responsible for the earlier self-forming actions by which we formed our present wills, and so on indefinitely back to the earliest actions of childhood. I argue that we are constantly forming and re-forming our characters, motives and purposes throughout our lives and offer a distinctive account of the earliest self-forming actions of childhood. Section 24 discusses one of the most influential "luck objections" to views of free will requiring indeterminism. In answering this objection, I develop the view that "agents who exercise free will are both authors of and characters in their own stories at once". In making "self-forming" actions, they are arbiters of their own lives, "making themselves" out of a past that, if they are truly free, does not limit their future pathways to one". Finally, section 25 discusses objections related to this luck objection concerning "contrastive explanations": If choices were undetermined, it is argued, we could not explain why one choice was made *rather than* another. In answering this objection, I further develop the "narrative" conception of free will presented in section 24, relating it to characters in stories, such as Mark Twain's account of Huckleberry Finn.

Chapter 2

Free Will and Determinism
A Compatibilism

Carolina Sartorio

Contents

Introduction

Most of the things we do in our lives we do freely. Or so we tend to think. For example, right now you probably think you're reading these words freely. But what is it to act freely? What must be true about us, what we do, and the world around us in order for us to act freely? This is what philosophers wonder about when they think about the problem of free will.

In this chapter, I develop and defend a conception of what having free will amounts to. It is a "compatibilist" view, in that it takes free will to be compatible with a natural way of thinking about the causal structure of the world typically known as *determinism*. We'll give a more precise definition of this term in due course but, roughly, determinism is the idea that for everything we do there is a complete explanation in terms of prior facts and the natural laws—one in virtue of which it was physically impossible for us to have done anything else. Thus, the view of free will that I will defend here is a particular way of answering one of the oldest philosophical

DOI: 10.4324/9781003212171-3

problems: the so-called problem of free will and determinism. But, more generally, it is a view that fits well with a naturalistic conception of the world and of human agency, one that many people nowadays find plausible.

The plan for the chapter is the following. First, in section 1, I introduce the concept of free will and I explain what we're after when looking for an account of that concept. Then, in section 2, I give a sketch of such an account. In section 3, I introduce the problem that will be our main focus here, the problem of free will and determinism, and I explain what it is to give a compatibilist answer to that problem. In section 4, I illustrate the compatibilist conception of free will with the account of freedom developed in section 2, and I explain why I find compatibilism in general appealing. In sections 5 and 6, I discuss some important challenges to compatibilism, and I respond to those challenges. Finally, I end with some concluding remarks in the Conclusion.

This chapter has two main goals. One is to introduce you, the reader, to the classical problem of free will and determinism and to the compatibilist answer to that problem. But another, equally important, goal is to prompt you to think about these issues for yourself and to help you develop your own views on this matter. The problem of free will is a fascinating topic, and I hope you'll enjoy thinking about it as much as I do!

1. What Is a Theory of Free Will?

Imagine the following scenario. A good friend of yours suddenly dies from unknown causes. An autopsy is performed on his body and it surprisingly reveals the presence of a series of mechanisms or "chips" implanted in different parts of your friend's brain. The chips are of alien origin (a material that has never been seen on Earth), and they involve technologies that are far more advanced than anything known by humans. Imagine that, after studying the chips, scientists conclude that they are remotely activated devices used to manipulate human choices. Imagine that scientists establish, on this basis, that sometime before his death your friend was subject to direct manipulation by aliens: at least some of his choices were not made in the ordinary way (say, as the upshot of a process of deliberation on the basis of reasons) but they were instead the result of the aliens' messing with his brain in certain ways. When you find out about this, you recall your friend telling you about an odd dream he'd had, where he was abducted by aliens, experimented on for a few days and then let go. You'd had a good laugh together while discussing that dream...

Call this scenario the "**Alien Manipulation**" scenario. In the **Alien Manipulation** scenario, you find out that your friend was not a free agent, at least during the time when he was being manipulated: he was the aliens' "puppet" and was not in control of his own choices. For example, when he uncharacteristically broke his promise to meet you for lunch last week (imagine that this was one of the choices manipulated by the aliens), he didn't do that freely. Knowing that now, the resentment you felt at the time seems unwarranted: if he didn't choose to do it freely, if he wasn't in control, then he is not morally responsible for breaking his promise. Although breaking a promise is a bad thing, he doesn't deserve to be blamed for it, if he didn't do it *of his own free will*.

The **Alien Manipulation** scenario illustrates the fact that acting freely, or being in control, is a requirement for being morally responsible for what we do (the actions we perform, the choices we make—in general, everything that we do). When we lack this kind of control, as your friend does in the **Alien Manipulation** scenario, we are not blameworthy (or praiseworthy) for what we do.

This concept of freedom, or free will, and the concept of moral responsibility connected with it will be the main focus of this chapter. Briefly, these concepts can be defined as follows:

> **Free Will:** The kind of control required for being morally responsible for what we do.
>
> **Moral Responsibility:** A kind of moral assessment of people that can warrant blaming them or praising them for what they do.

Basically, then, you are morally responsible when you are blameworthy or praiseworthy for what you do. (Whether you are blameworthy or praiseworthy will, of course, depend on whether what you do is a bad thing or a good thing.) Many people also assume that in cases of serious harm, such as murder or assault, responsibility is what warrants punishment for the harm caused. Intuitively, being responsible in these kinds of ways requires being in control of what you do.

But what does it take for us to have this kind of control over our actions? And do we have it? The **Alien Manipulation** scenario is just an example (a purely hypothetical or imaginary example, hopefully!) where someone doesn't have that kind of control. But what we are after now is a *general* account of free will—in other words, a *theory* of free will, or an account of the conditions that have to be met, in *any* case, for someone to have free will. We know that a free agent is one that is not subject to the type of manipulation described in the **Alien Manipulation** case. But what other conditions does an agent have to meet in order to act freely? And why? These are the kinds of questions one hopes to answer when giving a theory of free will.

In the next section, I'll sketch a theory of free will. It's just that: a sketch (and it's a sketch of just one possible theory of free will, one that I find plausible), but it should be enough to give you an idea of how a theory of free will can be developed. Then we'll discuss how this view fits within the overall *problem* of free will. The problem of free will, as we'll see, arises when one reflects on the nature of the world we live in and our place in it. Different views say different things about what the world has to be like for us to have free will. So, a debate arises among different theorists about whether we can have free will if we live in certain kinds of worlds. This is a complex, fascinating debate, and we'll look at some aspects of it in the sections that follow.

2. A Sketch of a Theory of Free Will

The theory of free will that I propose starts from the following simple idea: *causes matter*. That is to say, how we make choices, what motivates us to make them, or what their causal sources are matters to whether we make those choices freely and, thus, to whether we are morally responsible for them. For example, in the **Alien Manipulation** scenario, your friend's choice to break his promise to meet you for lunch wasn't free because it was the result of direct manipulation by the aliens. In contrast, when we make choices in ordinary circumstances and apparently do so freely, the causes of our choices are very different: they involve, for example, things like a process of deliberation or acting for reasons.

Causes matter to free will in two important ways. First, the causes of our acts set us apart from other beings that are not morally responsible beings in general—notably, most other animals. If you have pets, you likely don't think of them as morally responsible beings. If, despite your repeated attempts to train your cat, he scratches your couch for the nth time or jumps to the table and eats your food at dinnertime, you may get mad at him (again), but you probably won't think of him as being genuinely *blameworthy* for what he did. In contrast, if your neighbor keys your car or takes your mail simply because he feels like it, knowing that it will upset you, you will likely blame him for what he did. The difference is that, at least according to a view that many people seem to have about non-human animals, animals like cats lack the capacity to recognize and respond to certain kinds of reasons. This includes moral considerations, such as the fact that acting in a certain way will be upsetting or harmful for someone and that this is a morally bad outcome. In contrast, (most) human beings can recognize and respond to moral reasons, and moral reasons are, quite commonly, among the causes or motivations of our acts. This capacity to be driven by moral reasons seems to be an essential part of what makes us—human beings—morally responsible things. Thus, causes matter to our free will in that acting freely, or having the kind of control required to be morally responsible, requires the capacity to be motivated to act by those kinds of causes.

Second, the causes of our acts also matter to our free will in that they can be used to distinguish, *within human behaviors themselves*, those that are free from those that are not free. This is the feature that will help us develop a theory of free will that applies to us, human beings. We drew attention to this feature already when we noted that your friend, the victim of manipulation in the **Alien Manipulation** scenario, didn't act freely because of the kinds of causes that his behavior had. But how can we offer a general theory of free will in terms of the causes of our behavior?

My suggestion (developed in detail in Sartorio 2016) is that we can do this by building on and extrapolating from the distinction between your neighbor (a morally responsible being) and your cat (a non-morally responsible being). The difference between the neighbor and the cat was supposed to be that your neighbor is the sort of being who is in general capable of recognizing and responding to considerations like moral reasons but your cat is not. On reflection, this means that the causes of human behavior are often *more complex* than the causes of feline behavior, in that they involve more reasons, or reasons of a more sophisticated kind. Similarly, I will suggest, when human beings act freely, this is reflected in a larger complexity in the causes (or the types of causes) of the behavior. In other words, I will argue for the following:

> Correlation between freedom and the complexity of causes:
>
> Non-free human behavior ↔ Less complex causes
> Free human behavior ↔ More complex causes

To see why this correlation exists, imagine that you have another neighbor, one who has acquired during his life, and through no fault of his own, a series of irresistible compulsions or uncontrollable urges. Once these urges are triggered, he is truly incapable of resisting them. Imagine that one of them is the urge, when he sees a car in front of him and he happens to be holding a key in his hand, to produce the sound of the sharp edge of the key scraping across the side of the car. Given that he is aware of his condition, he usually avoids acting in this way by taking some reasonable precautions: say, by not carrying a key with him and by walking on the side of the street where usually no cars are parked. But, as it turns out, unfortunately, you parked your car in an unusual spot because the other spots were taken and an emergency came up at the last time that required him to pick up a key, so he's now holding a key in his hand and your car happens to be parked right there in front of him. Predictably, the compulsion kicks in and he keys the car. Call this case the "Compulsive Keying" scenario and call the parallel scenario with the noncompulsive neighbor the "Noncompulsive Keying" scenario.

So now two of your neighbors have keyed your car! Although this is very unfortunate, you probably feel that there is a difference between the two acts. Namely, the compulsive neighbor didn't key your car freely and the noncompulsive neighbor did and, as a result, the compulsive neighbor is not to blame for keying your car and the noncompulsive neighbor is. But what lies behind the difference between the act of keying a car when it's done compulsively and the same kind of act when it's done freely? What does this difference amount to, exactly?

As I anticipated above, I think that the answer to these questions can be found, again, in the causes of the acts: the difference in freedom between the compulsive and free behavior can be traced back to a difference in the causal history of their behavior, in a way that reflects their responsiveness or unresponsiveness to reasons of certain kinds.

To be clear, this doesn't mean that *all* of the causes have to be different. In fact, some of the causes are likely to be the same in both cases. For example, both neighbors keyed the car out of a desire to key it. In fact, the desire may have been very strong in both cases: although it was resistible for the noncompulsive and irresistible for the compulsive, this may simply be due to their different psychological predispositions and not to the fact that the desire was inherently stronger in one case than in the other.

Still, there are important differences between the causes in each case. These differences can be identified by reflecting about questions of this kind:

Would the compulsive/noncompulsive neighbor have been drawn to keying the car:

... if they had believed that the police were watching?
... if they had believed that there were security cameras recording the activity in the area?
... if they had believed that it would give you a heart attack to find your car in that state?
... if they had believed that it would give others a heart attack to learn that your car was keyed?
(etc.)

Given the circumstances that the compulsive neighbor found himself in (there is a car in front of him and he's holding a key in his hand), he is drawn to keying your car basically no matter what, so the answer to questions of this kind in his case is (for the most part) "yes". The noncompulsive neighbor, on the other hand, is not drawn to keying your car no matter what but just in the actual circumstances. If the circumstances had been different in any of the ways described above, he probably would have resisted the desire to key your car. After all, although he is an inconsiderate neighbor, he probably didn't want to cause you a heart attack, and he probably thinks it isn't worth getting in trouble with the police over this sort of thing. So, the answer to questions of this kind in his case is (for the most part) "no".

But notice what follows from this: the full explanation of the behavior will be different in each case. For example, circumstances such as the fact that the police weren't watching, that there were no video cameras and that nobody would suffer a heart attack (or, rather, the fact that your neighbor *didn't believe* that circumstances of this kind obtain) will be part of what explains the behavior of the noncompulsive neighbor in the **Noncompulsive Keying** scenario, because he keyed your car, at least partly, *because* of these facts. The compulsive neighbor, on the other hand, wasn't sensitive to these kinds of facts (at least for the most part, we're assuming), so those circumstances don't play a similar role in explaining his behavior in the **Compulsive Keying** scenario.

In other words, the noncompulsive behavior had causes that the compulsive behavior lacked. Those causes include facts such as these:

Examples of causes of the noncompulsive behavior (but *not* of the compulsive behavior):

> Cause 1: He didn't believe that the police were watching.
> Cause 2: He didn't believe that there were security cameras in the area.
> Cause 3: He didn't believe that keying your car would give you a heart attack.
> Cause 4: He didn't believe that keying your car would give anybody else a heart attack.
> (etc.)

As a result, the causal history of the free (noncompulsive) behavior is *much more complex* than the causal history of the compulsive behavior, in that it includes causes of this kind.

This is the sense, then, in which free behaviors have more complex causes than behaviors that are not free: they have more complex causes because those causes reflect the fact that, when agents act freely, they are more *causally sensitive* to certain kinds of considerations than when they don't act freely. As a result, acting freely goes hand in hand with an increased complexity in the causes of the behavior.

Still, you might want to know more about why it is that this causal complexity is what *makes* us agents who act freely. For example, why think that this increased complexity in the causal history is what explains the fact that the noncompulsive neighbor acts freely whereas the compulsive neighbor does not?

The answer is that it is plausible to believe that free agents are, precisely, beings who are *sensitive to reasons* in this kind of way. Instead of being driven by irresistible forces that compel them to act in a certain way, they control and guide their behavior in accordance with considerations that they recognize (or would recognize) as counting in favor or against certain kinds of behaviors—in other words, *reasons* for or against acting in certain ways. And this sensitivity to reasons is what we see in the causal history of free behaviors and don't see in the causal history of compulsive behaviors, as illustrated by the two neighbors example.

Let me expand a bit on this important concept, the concept of being "sensitive to reasons". Sensitivity to reasons is a concept that involves a mix of considerations of different kinds. One type is *self-interested reasons*, a class of reasons that track the promotion of our self-interest—as in the case of causes 1 and 2 above. When we respond to reasons of this kind, this indicates that we are acting rationally, at least to some minimal extent that seems to be required to be morally responsible for anything (because sanity, or some minimal degree of rationality, is arguably required for moral responsibility—human beings who are utterly insane aren't morally responsible for their actions). But another type is *moral reasons*, or reasons that have their source in morality—what is morally right and wrong, or morally good or bad, as in the case of causes 3 and 4 above. In general, the thought is that the capacity to respond to reasons, including moral reasons, is essential to our human nature and it is what can support our free agency and moral responsibility. However, sometimes, as in the case of the compulsive behavior, our reasons-responsiveness capacities are impaired or bypassed and we can't respond to reasons in the appropriate way. When that happens, we don't act freely.

Briefly, then, sensitivity to reasons is a concept that can be defined as follows:

> **Sensitivity to Reasons:** Our capacity to be motivated to act by reasons, including both self-interested reasons (considerations that have to do with the promotion of our self-interest) and moral reasons (considerations that have to do with morality).

As we have seen, it is plausible to believe that acting freely is a matter of being sufficiently sensitive to reasons of these different kinds.

To clarify, I am not suggesting that acting freely requires responding to reasons in the sense of being *perfectly rational* or *perfectly moral*. The noncompulsive neighbor is certainly not acting as a perfectly moral being would act: he shouldn't have keyed your car! (And he is responding to some reasons that are objectionable on moral grounds—for example, the desire to piss you off.) The claim is, simply, that he is still *sufficiently* reasons-responsive to be acting freely. For example, he is responding to the considerations described above (causes 1 through 4), and this is enough to distinguish him from the compulsive neighbor, who doesn't act freely because he is not reasons-responsive to a sufficient extent.

Now, you might be wondering: *How much* reasons-responsiveness is required to act freely? Although this is a fair question to ask, we are not going to worry about it here. In fact, there might be some borderline cases where it's not clear whether people are acting freely, and this is precisely because it's not clear whether they are sufficiently reasons-responsive. Hence, there may not be a sharp dividing line. Anyway, the **Noncompulsive Keying** and **Compulsive Keying** scenarios are meant to be clear-cut cases where no such indecision arises, and this is why we focus on scenarios of that kind.

Another important clarification concerns the nature of the capacity to respond to reasons. The way I'm understanding this capacity, we can respond to reasons *without doing so consciously*. This is as it should be: We don't have to be conscious of all of the factors that play some role in explaining what we do in order for those factors to be explanatory. For example, the neighbor who keyed your car freely may not have been actively thinking about the possibility of anything like security cameras or heart attacks when he made the choice to key your car. Still, part of the explanation of why he made that choice can be that there were no witnesses or security cameras (or that he didn't believe that there were) and that he wasn't going to be doing anybody any serious harm (or that he didn't believe that he would). So, although the difference between him and the compulsive neighbor may not concern anything that they do consciously, it's still an important difference in the explanation of their behavior. In fact, it is such an important difference, in my view, that it can account for the difference in freedom between them.

The role played by unconscious causes is especially clear when we consider things that we do rather automatically but still freely. When you open the car door at your destination (say, upon arriving at the grocery store), this doesn't take much conscious thinking or deliberation. But, if you open the door freely, you are still sensitive to reasons in the relevant way, and this is reflected in the full explanation of your behavior. Part of the explanation of your behavior is, of course, that you opened the car door because you wanted to walk toward the store. But a complete explanation of your behavior will also include considerations such as the fact that the car is not parked in an unsafe area (or the fact that you don't believe that it is), the fact that there is nobody standing next to the car who may be harmed by the opening door (or the fact that you don't believe that there is), etc. And, again, this is so even if at the time you don't consciously recognize the explanatory relevance of factors of this kind.

Notice that the factors that we have been focusing on involve reasons of a very specific kind, namely, reasons to *refrain* from doing what you're doing. And these aren't just any reasons but particularly strong reasons, or what philosophers call "sufficient" reasons—basically, reasons that in your view would defeat other reasons that you may have to behave differently. For example, the presence of a person standing next to the car may be a sufficient reason for you not to open the door as soon as you arrive at the store. The presence of witnesses or security cameras may be a sufficient reason for your neighbor not to key your car when it's parked on the street. And the same goes for the belief that you will suffer a heart attack if he keys your car.

Now, in the actual circumstances, those reasons are absent: there is no person standing next to your car, and there are no witnesses or security cameras, etc. As a result, what the agents are responding to in these cases is not the reasons themselves but the *absence* of those reasons. Interestingly, this feature is what seems to make those agents "sensitive to reasons" in the relevant sense, as the examples of **Noncompulsive Keying** and **Compulsive Keying** illustrate. Moreover, as those examples also illustrate, there will typically be a large number of these absences of reasons that play an explanatory role in a free agent's behavior, and at least some of them will do so only unconsciously.

I have sketched a view of freedom in terms of the concept of reasons-sensitivity. The view can be summarized as follows:

The Reasons-Sensitivity View

Acting freely is a matter of being sufficiently sensitive to reasons, where this involves being sensitive to a range of reasons and absences of reasons of various kinds.

Again, the thought is that when we act freely we are responding to reasons in the relevant way, because our reasons-responsiveness capacities are not being bypassed in any significant manner, and this is something that is reflected in the causal history or the causal explanation of what we do. As a result, causal histories of free acts are quite complex in that they include a substantial range of reasons and absences of reasons: whereas the reasons are simply reasons to do what you are actually doing, the absences of reasons are, instead, absences of reasons to *refrain* from doing what you are actually doing (and usually there will be many of these).

For example, on this view, the noncompulsive neighbor acts freely when he keys your car because, given that he is not acting compulsively, he is sensitive to the absence of a range of reasons to refrain from keying the car (whereas the compulsive neighbor, by contrast, is not). Similarly, when you open the car door upon arriving at the grocery store, you do so freely because you are sensitive to the absence of a range of reasons to refrain from opening the door (for example, you don't believe that you're parked in an unsafe area, and you don't believe that somebody will be harmed by the opening door). In contrast, if aliens had been directly manipulating all of your choices at the time, you wouldn't have been sensitive to considerations of that kind, and this explains why you wouldn't have acted freely.

The view generalizes to other cases of free/unfree acts. (Exercise for you, the reader: think of other scenarios where an agent seems to be acting freely/not freely and work out how the view would account for those cases.)

To sum up the contents of this section: I have sketched a view of free will, the reasons-sensitivity view, which accounts for our free will in terms of the causes of our behavior. The view draws on the important connection that seems to exist between acting freely and being sensitive to reasons. I argued that, when we act freely, our sensitivity to reasons is reflected in the causal explanations of our acts, given the role played in those cases by certain reasons or absences of reasons. I illustrated with examples of free and unfree acts. As anticipated, the reasons-sensitivity view entails that free acts have quite complex causal histories or explanations. The complexity of those causal histories is what reflects our sensitivity to reasons or absences of reasons and, thus, the fact that we're acting freely.

Now, this may strike you as odd, on reflection, because isn't this the opposite of what "free" intuitively stands for? Isn't freedom supposed to be something that requires the *lack* of causal influences on our behavior? How can freedom be something that *requires* causes or more complex kinds of causes, then?

However, recall our main focus here: it is a concept of freedom that is tightly connected with moral responsibility. As explained in section 1, freedom *in this sense* is a certain type of control over our acts that is required for us to be morally responsible for what we do. And if we are going to be in control of our acts in this sense, our acts should better have causes. Compare, again, somebody who is totally insane and constantly finds herself acting for no reason whatsoever. That kind of person lacks control over her acts and thus is not morally responsible for anything. Moreover, in order for our acts to be free, they should arguably have causes of a certain *kind*: causes that somehow concern *us* or that have to do with complex processes that are "internal" to us in the relevant sense and that don't bypass our capacities for rational and moral deliberation. According to the reasons-sensitivity view, free acts are acts that have precisely those kinds of causes, because they are the result of processes that involve our recognizing and responding to reasons of various kinds.

This concludes my sketch of the reasons-sensitivity view of free will. Again, it's just a sketch, but I hope that by now you have a good idea of how it works—in particular, how it distinguishes free from unfree behaviors and what motivates the view in general. In the next section, I'll introduce the problem of free will and determinism. After that, I'll return to the reasons-sensitivity view and I'll explain what the view has to say about that problem.

3. The Free Will Problem: Compatibilism and Incompatibilism

The problem of free will arises once we realize that the causes of our acts include more than just the immediate ones (processes such as our deliberating, our recognizing and responding to reasons, etc.). For, surely, those processes themselves have prior causes that explain why they happened. And those causes, in turn, have other causes prior to those, which explain why *they* happened. And so on and so forth.

Thus, we may ask:

- Does this chain of causes go on indefinitely or, at least, does it go back to a time before we were even born? And:
- Are those causes "necessitating" causes? In other words, did the existence of those past causes *guarantee*, given the natural laws that govern our world, that we would act in the ways we do in the present?

Imagine that, as it turns out, the answer to both of these questions is "yes". Then this means that our acts have causes in the remote past, including times before we were born (say, thousands of years ago), that ensured that we would act in those ways. That is to say, given those past causes and the natural laws, the world was bound to evolve in exactly the way it did, and this includes our existence and everything that we ever do: all of our acts, our choices and our deliberations.

The idea that our acts have remote necessitating causes of this kind is typically known as the thesis of determinism, or *causal* determinism. Here is one possible formulation of such a thesis:

> (Causal) Determinism: The thesis that our acts are the necessary consequence of causes in the remote past and the natural laws.

(From now on, I'll drop the qualifier "causal" and I'll just use the expression "Determinism" with this definition in mind.) Notice that, if there are such remote causes, given that they are events that happened a long time ago, before we were even born, they are in some clear sense outside our control. Thus, given that we also don't have any control over the laws of nature, this means that, if Determinism is true, our acts are the inevitable result of factors that are beyond our control.

Note that the statement of Determinism doesn't specify any particular size that a full set of causes in the remote past would have to have. For all it says, any such set could be extremely large—it could even be the *whole* state of the world at the time. In fact, any such set of causes will likely be very large. For notice that, when you go back in time searching for the causes of a present event, the set of causes will grow exponentially every time you take a step back: for each immediate cause of the event, there will be a high number of prior contributing causes; for *each* of those, there will be another high number of prior contributing causes and so on. But, regardless of how large any such set of remote causes of our present acts is, we can confidently say this: if Determinism is true, then, given the *full* state of the world at, say, the time of the Big Bang (which is not in our control), and given the natural laws (which are also not in our control), it follows that the world had to evolve in exactly the way it did—it couldn't have evolved in any other way.

There are other forms of determinism that people sometimes talk about and that we won't be concerned with here. For example, *genetic* determinism: the idea that everything we do is a necessary consequence of (much more specifically) our genes. This is a considerably less plausible thesis, precisely given how specific it is. It is very hard to believe that our genes completely determine our actions, in and of themselves; clearly, environmental factors play some role in what we do. (Just think of identical twins who act differently!) In any case, we won't be concerned with any such alternative forms of determinism here but only with Determinism as defined above.

We also won't be concerned with the potential role of God as the creator of everything that exists. The problem that Determinism poses for our free will arises independently of what you think about this issue. Imagine that God created the world at the time of the Big Bang and everything evolved deterministically from there. Or imagine that there is no God and the world started (on its own) at the time of the Big Bang and evolved deterministically from there. Either way, the question arises: *Can* we act freely in such a deterministic world?

The problem that the possible truth of Determinism poses for our free will is the "classical" problem of free will:

> **The Problem of Free Will and Determinism:** The problem that seems to arise for our free will on the assumption that our acts have deterministic causes beyond our control.

Now, why has anyone wondered about the possibility of Determinism being true? Do we actually have any reason to think that it is?

Those who think that Determinism is probably true usually think this because they think, more generally, that basically *everything that happens* has a complete "naturalistic" explanation, or an explanation in terms of prior events and the laws of nature. (Perhaps with the exception of what happened at the very beginning of time. This might have to be left unexplained, if there is nothing that came before it! But we don't need to worry about this puzzle here. Suffice it to say that it's puzzling *precisely because* it's hard for us to believe that there are things that have no explanation, or to even make sense of this idea.)

Imagine that you see an apple falling from a tree. You'll probably think that there is an explanation of that event in terms of prior events and the laws of nature (even if you might not know what that explanation is or everything that is involved in it). Indeed, it would be odd to think of the event of the apple falling from the tree as an event that has no such explanation. It might even be odd to think of it as an event that lacks a *complete* explanation of that kind. By a "complete" explanation I mean one that entails that the apple would fall from the tree at that precise time and in precisely the way it did: given the antecedent facts of the world cited in the explanation and given the laws of nature, it follows that the apple couldn't have failed to fall at the time it did and in the exact way it did. In other words, a complete explanation is just an explanation in terms of deterministic or sufficient causes.

Now consider other natural events with more complex causes, say, a hurricane or an earthquake. As it happens, unfortunately, scientists usually have trouble predicting the exact path that a hurricane will take or the occurrence of an earthquake. But it's not like we think that those events don't have a complete natural explanation! Instead, we think that they do, but we just don't know what it is or we don't know some of the details.

These examples illustrate how natural it is to assume the existence of deterministic explanations, at least for events of this kind. Again, this is so even when we don't know what those explanations are. In those cases where we don't, we just assume that *there is* an explanation that escapes us.

So now imagine that you believe that human acts, including *mental* acts like the choices that we make, are just like those other events: they are events that take place in the natural world and, as a result, they are subject to the same fundamental laws of nature. Imagine that you believe, for example, that the event of somebody's making a choice basically amounts to a certain kind of activity taking place in that person's brain—patterns of neurons firing in a certain way or something of that sort. If events of this kind are subject to the same natural laws as other events, then, if we think that other events have full explanations in terms of prior causes, we should probably think the same about human choices (even if, again, those causes may be too complex for us to understand and to formulate reliable predictions on the basis of them). And we should probably think the same about the *causes* of human choices—and about the *causes of the causes* of human choices and so on. This way we'll end up with a deterministic chain of causes that traces back to times in the remote past.

Whether you think Determinism is true, then, will depend on what you think about the nature and the causes of human choices. So, go ahead and ask yourself:

- Do you think that human choices are natural events? And:
- Do you think that there are deterministic explanations of our choices, just like there (probably) are deterministic explanations of other events (apples falling from trees, hurricanes, earthquakes, etc.), even if we might not know exactly what those explanations are?

If your answer to both of these questions is "yes", then this means that you think Determinism is true—or, at least, it's true as it applies to the behavior of human beings like you and me.

Now, as it turns out, many people (including many scientists, philosophers and others) believe that the most fundamental or microscopic level of reality is not deterministic but *indeterministic*. This is suggested by some contemporary interpretations of quantum physics (the branch of physics that studies nature at its smallest scale). On this view, there are no complete or deterministic explanations of certain quantum events: all we have at that bottom level are probabilistic correlations, or explanations in terms of probabilistic laws. Correspondingly, the physical laws that apply to that level only assign specific probabilities to the occurrence of certain states given prior states of the world. In other words, they are indeterministic or probabilistic laws. This is the view, in sum:

> **Quantum-Level Indeterminism:** The thesis that the laws that govern our world at the bottom or fundamental (quantum)

level are not deterministic but indeterministic (merely probabilistic).

Now, imagine that this is right and the world is indeed indeterministic at the microscopic level. What follows from this about the causes of human choices?

Nothing clearly follows. The indeterminism at the microscopic level may or may not result in any significant indeterminism at the *macroscopic* level at which we (human beings) operate and make choices. Imagine, for example, that whenever you're deciding between coffee and tea for breakfast, the mental processes involved are indeterministic at the microscopic level. This means that the microscopic state that you're in when you decide in favor of, say, coffee, was not guaranteed to obtain by the prior microscopic state of the world and the natural laws (given those states and the laws, there was at least some chance that you would have ended up in some other microscopic state instead). Still, your actual choice to have coffee, which is a *macroscopic* state, could be determined by prior *macroscopic* states. For example, this is what would happen if your choosing coffee was determined by your feeling sleepy a second before (as a general rule, whenever you feel sleepy, you choose coffee), although the microscopic states that you're in when you're feeling sleepy don't determine a *single* next microscopic state that you'll be in.

In other words, this would be the case if *all* of the microscopic states that you could have ended up in are ones where you choose coffee over tea, as in the situation represented by the following diagram:

MACRO:	Feeling sleepy	→	Choosing coffee over tea
MICRO:	Microscopic state 1	→	Microscopic state 2
			(Microscopic state 3)
			(Microscopic state 4)

Here, microscopic states 1 and 2 are the states you were actually in when you felt sleepy and when you chose coffee over tea, respectively, and microscopic states 3 and 4 are merely possible states that you could have also ended up in, but they are states where you would still have chosen coffee.

As you can see, if this is what happens, then it doesn't really matter that Determinism is false at the microscopic level, given that it still holds at the macroscopic level. In other words, in that case Determinism would still be true *for all practical purposes*, when we are thinking about the causes of human behavior.

Another thing that could happen is this: the indeterminism at the microscopic level does result in some indeterminism at the macroscopic level but it is too insignificant to make any difference to our free will. Imagine, for example, that, although your choosing coffee was determined by your feeling sleepy, nothing determined *which particular coffee mug* you'd choose to drink the coffee from (imagine that you always have more than one available at home and they're all roughly similar): this is a truly undetermined event and one that has its roots in some indeterminacies at the microscopic level. In this case there is some indetermination at the macroscopic level, at the level of choices, but it doesn't seem to be one that makes any significant difference to what you choose to do. Again, *for all practical purposes*, your choices seem to be determined.

On the other hand, imagine that the world is indeterministic in a way that is reflected at the macroscopic level and in a way that significantly impacts our choices. Imagine, for example, that yesterday evening you decided to go to the movies instead of helping your friend study for an exam, which you had promised to do. Imagine that your choice to break your promise to your friend was not determined by the antecedent state of the world. This means that the *very same* state of the world, including the exact same process of deliberation that preceded your choice, could have been followed by your making the choice to keep your promise instead of breaking it. If that had been the case, then your choice to break the promise, which is a morally significant choice, would have been genuinely undetermined.

So, the possibilities reduce to two main ones: either Determinism is true, *or true for all practical purposes*, or it is not. For simplicity, from now on I'll drop the qualification "for all practical purposes" and I'll speak in terms of just Determinism being true and Determinism being false.

Which possibility is true of our world? Well, we don't know for sure (and we may never do). Still, it's important to think about how Determinism *would* affect our free will, if it *were* true. Some believe that the truth of Determinism would in fact undermine our free will (this is their reaction to the classical problem of free will introduced above: the problem of free will and Determinism). These people are called "incompatibilists" because they think that Determinism is *incompatible with* free will:

> **Incompatibilism:** The thesis that Determinism is incompatible with free will.

Others (called "compatibilists") believe that the truth of Determinism would not undermine our free will. In other words, they believe that Determinism is *compatible with* free will:

> **Compatibilism:** The thesis that Determinism is compatible with free will.

Notice that Compatibilism doesn't say that Determinism *is* true but only that it wouldn't undermine our free will if it *were* true. Thus, according to Compatibilism, even if we may not know whether or not Determinism holds, we needn't worry about it being true because it is not a threat to our free will. As a result, Compatibilism represents a more optimistic stance on free will, compared to Incompatibilism, in that it understands free will as compatible with a way of conceiving the causal structure of the world that may be (for all we know) an accurate description of the way things actually are.

To sum up the contents of this section: I have now introduced the classical free will problem (the problem of free will and Determinism), as well as the two main reactions to that problem, Incompatibilism and Compatibilism. In the next section I return to the view of free will presented in section 2, the Reasons-Sensitivity view, and I discuss how it fits within this framework.

4. The Motivation for Compatibilism

I am a *compatibilist* about the classical free will problem—that is to say, I think that the truth of Determinism is compatible with acting freely. The account that I sketched in section 2 above, the

Reasons-Sensitivity view, is a compatibilist account of free will. This was the view, in a nutshell:

> **The Reasons-Sensitivity View:** Acting freely is a matter of being sufficiently sensitive to reasons, where this involves being sensitive to a range of reasons and absences of reasons of various kinds.

And these were a few highlights of the view:

- Acting freely is cashed out in terms of our acts having the right kinds of causes.
- The right kinds of causes are causes that reflect the agent's "sensitivity to reasons".
- Being "sensitive to reasons" is a matter of causally responding to a relevant range of reasons/absences of reasons.

In section 2 I also noted that a consequence of the Reasons-Sensitivity view is that free acts have *more complex* causes than acts that are not free. I illustrated with the examples of **Noncompulsive Keying** (the neighbor who freely keys your car) and **Compulsive Keying** (the neighbor who keys your car compulsively and thus not freely): the noncompulsive neighbor is causally responding to a wide range of absences of reasons to refrain from keying the car (the absence of police, the absence of security cameras, the absence of the threat of a serious harm to anybody, etc.), whereas the compulsive neighbor is not. So, what this view requires for acting freely comes down to this: causal histories with just enough complexity to reflect that kind of reasons-sensitivity.

The Reasons-Sensitivity view is a *compatibilist* view of free will because, for all we've said, those causal histories could be completely deterministic. For example, the full causal history of the noncompulsive neighbor's behavior could be one that includes events in the remote past that determined that he would act in the way he did in the present—as well as the fact that, in so acting, he would be responding to certain reasons and absences of reasons.

To be clear: the view doesn't *require* deterministic causal histories. For all the view says, there could be some connections in the causal histories of our acts that are not deterministic but indeterministic. But the view also doesn't *rule out* the possibility of deterministic causal histories. Therefore, according to the Reasons-Sensitivity view, acting freely is compatible with the truth of Determinism.

In later sections, I'll discuss some specific challenges to Compatibilism raised by incompatibilists and I'll explain how a compatibilist could respond to those challenges. But, for now, let's just ask: How *initially plausible* is Compatibilism? How could one possibly *motivate* that view, to begin with?

Here, again, different compatibilists might say different things. What follows is my own way of looking at this issue (but I suspect that many other compatibilists have a similar approach).

The way I see it, the most natural way to arrive at a compatibilist view of free will is in stages. The first stage is the following:

Stage 1

At this first stage, we don't even worry about the remote causes of our acts. We simply start by thinking about the contrast between different kinds of scenarios or about how behaviors that appear not to be free differ from those that appear to be free. For example, we think about the compulsive behavior versus the noncompulsive behavior or scenarios of that kind. The thought is that by reflecting on the differences between these kinds of behaviors, we can get a preliminary idea of what acting freely might consist in, more generally. In section 2, I explained how this way of proceeding can motivate the Reasons-Sensitivity view of free will, in particular (but there are other compatibilist views that people have offered and that could potentially be motivated in a similar way).

Stage 2

Next, at the second stage, we may notice that the differences that we have found between, for example, compulsive and noncompulsive behaviors have to do with factors that are, in an important sense, *internal* to us: they are processes that run "within us" and that concern, for example, our reasons-responsiveness capacities. But, starting from those internal causal processes, one could then move, so to speak, "from the inside out" and inquire into the causes of those processes themselves: Where did those causes come from? Did something else cause them? If so, where did the causes of the causes come from? And so on. It is only then that the problem of free will and Determinism arises.

At this stage, the possibility of remote causes—in particular, deterministic ones—has been introduced. But, when presented with this possibility, it seems quite sensible to react by thinking: "Hmmm,

I guess I hadn't thought about this before. ... However, on reflection, is it really that surprising that our acts have remote causes? After all, doesn't *everything that happens* have remote causes? If so, wouldn't it be surprising if our acts *didn't* have such causes?"

This way of thinking can warm us up to Compatibilism because, as a result, instead of seeing Determinism as a threat to our free will, we may be inclined to see the existence of (possibly deterministic) remote causes as simply a consequence of a certain way of conceiving our world and our place in it: a "naturalistic" picture of the world and of human agency.

There is a third and final stage that can also be part of the motivation for Compatibilism. However, before discussing this last stage, I'd like to (very briefly) draw attention to a complication that arises at this point in the contemporary debate. It is this: Some compatibilists believe that, to a limited extent, a more external and distant set of causes of our acts *can* matter to whether we act freely. These are causes that include our "formative" years; those years when we are still developing as moral agents. Roughly, the thought is that we don't want to say that you act freely if what you do is the result of, for example, having being seriously abused as a child or having been the victim of indoctrination while growing up. These views are sometimes called "historical" views of free will, given the importance they assign to the history of one's life. They are still compatibilist views because they don't take more remote causes to matter (for example, it doesn't matter if there are causes that trace back to times before you were born, and it doesn't matter if those causes are deterministic). On the other hand, there are compatibilist views that don't pay attention to any such historical facts but that focus exclusively on the more recent causal histories. Here, to keep things as simple as possible, I'll just bypass this issue by focusing only on the more remote causes of our acts, those that obtained before we were born. I'll also imagine that the agents we're discussing meet any historical conditions that a compatibilist may plausibly set on free will: they were not seriously abused as children, they were not indoctrinated, etc. This way, we'll be focusing on cases where all compatibilists would likely agree about the freedom of the agents involved.

So, consider, for example, the act by the noncompulsive neighbor in **Noncompulsive Keying** and focus on the causes of that act that occurred before he was born (say, right before the time of his birth). As discussed in section 3, the full set of causes at that time will likely be extremely large, because we arrive at that set by thinking about, first, the immediate causes of the act; then, the causes of *each* of those immediate causes; then, the causes of *each* of the causes of each of the immediate causes, etc.

Now, the question arises: Do those pre-birth causes, in turn, have causes? If so, what kinds of causes do they have? There are three main possibilities:

(a) They don't have any causes at all.
(b) They have causes but those causes *don't determine* your neighbor's choice to key your car.
(c) They have causes and those causes *determine* your neighbor's choice to key your car.

If you are like me, (a) will strike you as incredibly implausible: things don't happen for no reason whatsoever, at least not in our world. So that leaves (b) and (c) as the only two reasonable possibilities.

As discussed in section 3, we don't know (and may never know) for sure whether our world is deterministic or indeterministic; as a result, we don't know (and may never know) for sure whether (b) or (c) is true. Still, reflecting about the difference between (b) and (c) may lead to one final thought in favor of Compatibilism. This is our third and final stage.

Stage 3

Notice that the difference between (b) and (c) concerns the explanatory power of the remote causes: if (b) is true, then those remote causes don't constitute a deterministic explanation of your neighbor's choice in **Noncompulsive Keying**, because they don't guarantee (given the laws) that the world would evolve in a way that includes his making that choice. If (b) is true, the world could have evolved in more than one way, given those causes; in particular, it could have evolved in a way that resulted in the neighbor choosing to key the car (as in the actual case), or it could have evolved in a way that resulted in the neighbor choosing not to key the car. But then, it is natural to want to ask: *Why* did things happen in the way they did? Why did your neighbor end up choosing to key the car instead of choosing not to key it?

Recall that when, in section 3, we discussed the possibility of indeterminism being true of our world, we talked about how indeterminism introduces an element of randomness or chance. If a certain quantum event is truly undetermined, then there is no "full" explanation of why it happened. At most, there is an explanation in terms of probabilities: given the prior state of the world, there was some probability that the world would evolve in that way but also some probability that it wouldn't. There is no deeper explanation than this. We can think of this in terms of "possible worlds" or different ways that our world could have been: we could have ended up in a world like the actual (one where the quantum event happens) or in a world different from the actual (one where the quantum event doesn't happen). Both kinds of worlds were consistent with the prior state of our world.

So, now imagine that this is what happens, too, in the case of your neighbor choosing to key your car. If that event was similarly undetermined by the remote causes, then at most there is a probabilistic explanation of what happened (there was some probability that he would key the car, given the state of the world in the remote past, and some probability that he wouldn't key it) but nothing more than that. In terms of possible worlds: although, as a matter of fact, he ended up in a world where he keyed your car, he could have easily ended up in a world where he didn't key it. Both kinds of worlds were consistent with the full state of our world in the remote past. If so, here, too, there seems to be an important element of randomness or chance involved.

As a result, this may naturally lead you to think that, in circumstances like this, your neighbor had no control over whether he ended up in one world or in the other, because *he* didn't "settle" which way things were going to go. Things just happened the way they did, and there is no deeper explanation. And, if this is right, then this suggests that the falsehood of Determinism (or the truth of *Indeterminism*) wouldn't help our freedom, because it wouldn't make us any *more* free, or any more in control of our acts, than if our acts had been causally determined. All that would change is that there would be some "openness" in how the world could evolve from one time to another. But given that it wouldn't be *up to us* to decide which way it does evolve, intuitively this is not something that could give us any more control over what happened.

In conclusion, although we may not know whether (b) or (c) above is true (we may not know whether our acts are determined or undetermined by remote causes), perhaps we may know this: the truth of (b) wouldn't make us be *more in control* than the truth of (c). In other words, the truth of Determinism wouldn't deprive us of any significant form of control over our acts, one that we could only have if Determinism were false. So, this may lead us to think, too, that Determinism is not a threat to our free will and may move us even closer to Compatibilism.

To sum up the results of this section: I have explained how one may naturally arrive at a compatibilist view of free will. I described one such possible route that includes three stages. In the first stage, we start by thinking about free will in terms of contrasts between cases of free and unfree action. Those cases differ with respect to their more immediate causes, so at this first stage that is where our focus is. Then, at the second stage, we start to wonder about the existence of much more remote causes of our acts and, in particular, deterministic causes of that kind. However, we then come to realize that the existence of such causes actually matches our tendency to assume that everything that happens has an explanation (even a "full" explanation) in terms of prior events and the natural laws. At that point, instead of regarding the possibility of (potentially deterministic) remote causes as an obvious threat to our free will, we may simply see it as a consequence of a naturalistic conception of the world, one that understands human agency and the capacities for moral responsibility in line with other complex but natural phenomena. Finally, at the third stage, we may corroborate this impression by reflecting on what Indeterminism (or the failure of Determinism) would bring to the table. We come to appreciate that Indeterminism wouldn't boost our free will, compared with Determinism, because all it would do is inject an element of randomness or pure chance that cannot enhance our control. That completes the motivation for Compatibilism.

To be clear: none of this shows that Compatibilism is *actually* true. But it can explain why some people (like me, and maybe you too) may be drawn to this kind of view.

In the following sections, we'll look at some major incompatibilist challenges. These are philosophical *arguments* against Compatibilism. That is, they are attempts to show, on the basis of independently plausible reasons and regardless of one's initial inclinations on this matter, that one should be an incompatibilist about free will. I think that these challenges can be successfully met, though, and so, as a result, I remain a compatibilist about free will. After discussing each of the arguments, I'll explain how I think the compatibilist could or should respond to them, so that you can judge for yourself.

Because I'll be mostly concerned with defending Compatibilism from those incompatibilist challenges, I will have to set aside other arguments and views that people have proposed and that come apart from the compatibilist view of free will in more radical ways. In particular, I have in mind highly "skeptical" views of free will. These are views according to which we *cannot* have free will, basically *regardless* of what the world is like, because having free will requires meeting conditions that it's impossible for us to meet. Those who embrace these kinds of views believe that we can't have free will in a deterministic world, as typical incompatibilists think, but they also believe that we can't have free will in an *indeterministic* world. (Hence, we can't have free will, period.) Although these are interesting challenges to the commonsense idea that we have free will, I will have to set them aside here because my main focus in this chapter is the classical free will problem—that is, the problem posed by Determinism.

5. Incompatibilist Arguments: Part I

An argument for Incompatibilism is an argument that attempts to show that if Determinism is true, we can't have free will. One of the main arguments for Incompatibilism, commonly known as the *Consequence Argument* (developed in van Inwagen 1983), goes as follows.

If Determinism is true, then everything that happens, including everything we do, is the *necessary consequence* of the remote past and the natural laws. This includes, for example, the act by your noncompulsive neighbor in the **Noncompulsive Keying** scenario (introduced in section 2). When your neighbor keyed your car, his act was the necessary consequence of the state of the world in the remote past and the natural laws. The past and the laws guaranteed that he would key your car. But, also, in many respects your neighbor is an ordinary human being. Because he doesn't have time travel powers, he has no control over the past (let alone the remote past): the past is what it is and there is nothing he could have ever done to make it be any different. And, because he doesn't have God-like powers, he has no control over the natural laws that govern our world: the laws are what they are and there is nothing he could have ever done to make them be any different. So, in effect, if Determinism is true, your neighbor's behavior is the necessary consequence of factors (the past and the laws) over which he has no control whatsoever. As a result, you might think that this seriously undermines his freedom, because if he has no control over those factors, and if they determine what he does, you might think this shows that he also has no control over his own behavior: *his own behavior, too*, is what it is and there is nothing he could have ever done to make it be any different.

Note that, if this argument works, it easily generalizes to other cases where people seemingly act freely, because the scenario involving your neighbor is a quite standard case where somebody apparently acts freely and is morally responsible for what he does. But it will be easier to use a particular example to illustrate, so we'll stick with the **Noncompulsive Neighbor** example.

It will also be helpful to cash out this argument, as philosophers typically do, in terms of premises and conclusion. The **premises** of an argument are the claims that the argument relies on, and the **conclusion** is the claim that the argument aims to establish on the basis of those premises. In this case, the conclusion of the argument is the claim that, if Determinism is true, your neighbor doesn't act freely—that is to say, the incompatibilist thesis.

Also, to simplify the formulation of the argument, we'll introduce an expression, being *powerless over something*, as shorthand for: there is nothing the agent could have done to make that thing be any different from what it is. With this expression in hand, the argument can be reconstructed in the following way:

The Consequence Argument for Incompatibilism

(Premise 1) If Determinism is true, your neighbor's behavior is a necessary consequence of the remote past and the natural laws.

(Premise 2) Your neighbor is powerless over the remote past and the laws.

(Premise 3) If your neighbor is powerless over the remote past and the laws, and if his behavior is a necessary consequence of the remote past and the laws, then he is also powerless over his own behavior.

(**Premise 4**) If your neighbor is powerless over his own behavior, then he doesn't act freely when he keys your car.

Therefore,

(**Conclusion**) If Determinism is true, your neighbor doesn't act freely when he keys your car.

Let's briefly review the motivation behind each of the premises:

Premise 1: This premise is just an application of the definition of Determinism to the specific case in point: the case of your noncompulsive neighbor.

Premise 2: This premise captures the fact that your neighbor is an ordinary human being with regular capacities, which don't include the capacity to control what the remote past or the laws are.

Premise 3: This premise captures the idea that powerlessness transmits from one fact to another fact when the latter fact is a necessary consequence of the former fact. (It is easy to come up with examples that corroborate this principle. For example: I am powerless over the fact that today is, say, Monday. But a necessary consequence of today's being Monday is that tomorrow will be Tuesday. And I am also clearly powerless over that fact.)

Premise 4: This premise captures the idea that we can't act freely if we are powerless over our own behavior—that is to say, if we couldn't have acted in any other way.

Is the Consequence Argument for Incompatibilism successful? For an argument to be successful, it must meet two requirements:

First, the argument must be *(logically) valid*. This means that, *if* the premises of the argument were all true, *then* the conclusion would also have to be true. Valid arguments are logically structured in a way that guarantees that this is the case. When this happens, we say that the conclusion "logically follows" from the premises:

Validity: An argument is logically valid when the conclusion logically follows from the premises: *if* the premises were true, *then* the conclusion would also have to be true.

Second, the premises must be true. This means that *all* of the premises must be true. When an argument meets both of these requirements, we say that it is *sound*:

> **Soundness:** An argument is sound when it is logically valid *and* its premises are all true.

Notice that when an argument is sound (and not just valid), its conclusion is true, because if it has true premises and if the conclusion logically follows from the premises (given that it is valid), the conclusion also has to be true.

Ultimately, of course, this is what we want from an argument: we want an argument that successfully establishes the truth of its conclusion. So, for an argument to be successful, it must be sound.

Now, is the Consequence Argument sound? To determine the answer to this question, we must see whether it meets the two requirements we've mentioned: it must be logically valid and its premises must be true.

The argument clearly meets the first requirement. Again, for an argument to be logically valid, it has to be the case that, *if* the premises were all true, the conclusion would also have to be true. Thus, to see that the argument meets this requirement, start by assuming that Determinism is true. If Determinism is true, it follows from Premise 1 that your neighbor's behavior is a necessary consequence of the remote past and the natural laws. But it follows from *this*, in conjunction with Premises 2 and 3, that he is also powerless over his own behavior. In turn, it follows from *this*, in conjunction with Premise 4, that he doesn't act freely when he keys your car. In sum, the assumption of Determinism leads to the claim that your neighbor doesn't act freely, under the supposition that all of the premises of the argument are true. As a result, the conclusion of the argument ("If Determinism is true, your neighbor doesn't act freely") follows logically from the premises. This shows that the argument is logically valid.

But does the argument meet the second requirement? Are all of its premises in fact true? Here things are much less clear. Compatibilists have replied to this style of argument in different ways, by launching attacks on the premises. Here we will focus on two different types of reply: first, attacks on Premise 2 and, second, attacks on Premise 4.

First Compatibilist Reply: Rejecting Premise 2

Here is, again, Premise 2:

> (**Premise 2**) Your neighbor is powerless over the remote past
> and the laws.

The thought of rejecting this premise might strike you as crazy: How could your neighbor possibly have any power over the remote past or the laws of nature? We don't have the capacity to travel back in time, and we also don't have the capacity to do miracles. How, then, could one deny that we, as ordinary human beings, are powerless over the remote past and the laws?

But a compatibilist might say, in response, that rejecting Premise 2 doesn't require attributing to ourselves magical or extraordinary capacities of any kind. In particular, it doesn't require the capacity to time travel or the capacity to do miracles.

Let me explain. At this point, too, it will be helpful to proceed in steps:

Step 1

First of all, it is clear that, if the Consequence Argument is going to establish Incompatibilism, it cannot start by simply assuming that Compatibilism is *false*. So, it cannot start by simply assuming that your neighbor cannot act freely if our world is deterministic or that he is powerless over his own acts.

Step 2

So now think about what would have to be the case if Compatibilism were, in fact, *true* and, in particular, if your neighbor were not really powerless over his determined behavior. This would mean that he was able to refrain from acting in the way that he was determined to act. Recall that we are understanding his being "powerless" as shorthand for: there is nothing that he could have done to make his behavior be any different from what it is. As a result, his *not* being powerless over his own behavior basically means that he *could* have acted differently (he could have failed to key your car).

At this point, you are surely wondering how a compatibilist could pull this off. You might ask: how *could* he have acted any differently, if his behavior was fully determined? But, whereas incompatibilists would argue that nobody could have acted differently in a deterministic world, the compatibilists we are considering would argue that this doesn't capture the concept of ability that is relevant to free will. So, at this point, the debate between incompatibilists and those compatibilists would center around the nature of the relevant ability.

Here we'll sidestep most of this debate (because it isn't important for our purposes here). But, very briefly, the compatibilist's thought here is simply this: Imagine that we live in a deterministic world and a child starts to drown in the sea at a crowded beach. Imagine that among the witnesses there are some good swimmers and some bad swimmers and that none of them try to save the child, so the child eventually dies. Surely, there is a sense in which it is true to say that the good swimmers could have saved the child (unlike the bad swimmers), even if it was determined that none of them would. If so, this suggests that Determinism is compatible with *some* ability to do things differently—an ability that the good swimmers in this case have. Very roughly, this is the sense of "could have done otherwise" that compatibilists would argue is compatible with Determinism and that might be relevant to free will.

In any case, the main point so far is that incompatibilists cannot simply assume that Determinism rules out the ability to do otherwise, and thus free will, if this is what they're trying to prove. So, it's an open question at this stage whether agents who live in causally determined worlds have the ability to do otherwise, in the sense relevant to free will: for all we know at this point, your neighbor *might* have had the relevant ability.

Step 3

The next step is to ask yourself: What *else* would have to have been true of the world if your neighbor had *exercised* that alleged ability to do otherwise—the one that we're assuming he may have still had? That is to say, what else would have to have been true of the world if he *had* acted differently (in other words, if he had failed to key your car)?

Now, this is important because, given that we are assuming that the world is deterministic, this means that something in either the past or the laws would have to have been different in that case. Under the assumption of Determinism, if the past and the laws had been exactly the same, your neighbor would have to have acted in exactly the same way he did—that is to say, he would have to have keyed your car. (This is, after all, what Determinism says: that the present is a necessary consequence of the past and the laws.)

Step 4

Putting this all together, what we have is this: If Compatibilism is true and your neighbor was not powerless over his determined behavior, then he could have acted differently from the way he was determined to act. Plus, if he had acted differently, then either the past or the laws would have to have been different, too. So, if Compatibilism is true, and if your neighbor was not powerless over his determined behavior, then he in fact had the ability to do something that is such that, had he done it, *either the past or the laws would have been different*. In a certain sense, then, it seems that your neighbor had the ability to affect the past or the laws!

Again, at first this might seem incredible, but it will probably seem less incredible once you realize what exactly is being claimed. Emphatically, the claim is *not* that your neighbor could have performed a miracle or traveled back in time to affect the past. Rather, the claim is only that your neighbor had a certain ability to act differently that happens to result in another interesting kind of ability: a certain ability to affect the past or the laws. But this is not an ability to do miracles, or to time travel or to do anything of that sort.

It might help to think of this in terms of a distinction between "strong" and "weak" abilities to affect the past or the laws (a distinction taken from Lewis 1981):

> **Strong Ability:** Someone who has a strong ability to affect the past or the laws is someone who could have *caused* the past or the laws to be different from what they are.
> **Weak Ability:** Someone who has a weak ability to affect the past or the laws is someone who had the ability to do something differently in their lives and, had they exercised that ability, then either the past or the laws would have to have been different for them to do so.

What the compatibilist is saying here, in effect, is that, although it is wildly implausible to attribute to your neighbor (or to any other ordinary human) the *strong* ability to affect the past or the laws, it is much less implausible to attribute to him the *weak* ability. In fact, the compatibilist might argue that if Compatibilism is true and your neighbor is not powerless over his own determined behavior, then he automatically has that weak ability, simply *as a result of* having the ability to act differently in a deterministic world. One ability leads to the other in a quite straightforward way:

Ability to act differently in a deterministic world → Weak ability to affect past/laws.

You might remain unconvinced. You might think that it's not at all clear that your neighbor even had the *weak* ability to affect the past or the laws, simply because it's not at all clear that he had the ability to act differently in a deterministic world *to start with*. As we have seen, it would only follow that your neighbor has the weak ability to affect the past or the laws *if* he really had the ability to act differently in a deterministic world. But you may think that he cannot have the ability to act differently if his behavior was fully determined.

Fair enough. But, if this is your reaction, then this just means that you don't find the idea that we can act differently in a deterministic world (an idea that some compatibilists want to embrace) initially plausible. However, note that what we are discussing now is not whether the idea is initially plausible on its own but, instead, possible *arguments to believe that it's false* (or, in other words, independently plausible reasons on the basis of which to conclude that it fails). And, as noted above, such arguments cannot start by simply assuming that the compatibilist idea is false, because they're supposed to *prove* that it's false.

This is worth emphasizing: all the compatibilist is claiming at this point is that this particular argument against Compatibilism—the Consequence Argument—fails. The compatibilist is arguing that it fails because, in a way, one of its premises (Premise 2) already *assumes* that Compatibilism is false, or that your neighbor is powerless over his own behavior in a deterministic world. It already assumes this, the thought is, because if the compatibilist were right and one *could* somehow retain the ability to do otherwise in a deterministic world, then that would thereby give us a reason to reject Premise 2, because it would follow that one also has a certain ability to affect the past or the laws (again, this follows Lewis 1981). And an argument cannot be successful if it already assumes what it's trying to prove.

Thus, even if you're not convinced that Compatibilism (or this particular form of Compatibilism) is true, you could still agree with the compatibilist that the Consequence Argument isn't successful, in that it doesn't show what it's trying to prove.

Second Compatibilist Reply: Rejecting Premise 4

But there is at least another way to defend Compatibilism from the challenge posed by the Consequence Argument, one that doesn't insist on the idea that we can retain the ability to act differently in a deterministic world. It is to reject another premise in the argument, namely, Premise 4:

> (Premise 4) If your neighbor is powerless over his own behavior, then he doesn't act freely when he keys your car.

Recall that here "powerless" means that he couldn't have acted differently (he couldn't have failed to key your car). So, Premise 4 in effect says that, if your neighbor couldn't have failed to key your car, then he didn't act freely.

The second way of resisting the Consequence Argument consists in arguing that this premise is false, because we *can* act freely despite lacking the ability to do otherwise. In other words, acting freely *doesn't require* having the ability to do otherwise. If so, even if Determinism really did deprive us of the ability to do otherwise, Compatibilism could still be true, given that acting freely doesn't require any such ability.

How could one argue for this? Consider the following scenario. Imagine, again, that yesterday your neighbor keyed your car. He didn't do it out of compulsion (like your compulsive neighbor) but simply because he hates your guts and he knows that it will upset you to find your car in that state. As it turns out, unbeknownst to him, the previous night some evil aliens had sneaked into his house while he was sleeping and had implanted a highly sophisticated mechanism in his brain that allowed them *both* to monitor his thoughts to the very last detail *and* to manipulate his choices. Typically, the evil aliens use these mechanisms on humans to manipulate them to make evil choices (in particular, choices to key other people's cars) that they wouldn't have made on their own. However, in the case of your neighbor, they didn't have to intervene at all because, to their surprise and delight, your neighbor made the choice that they wanted him to make completely on his own. (And they could tell that he would, a few seconds before he did, because they were closely monitoring his thoughts by means of the mechanism.) That is to say, in this case the aliens remain completely idle; they don't intervene in the formation of his choice. Call this case "**Idle Aliens**". This type of scenario is typically called a "Frankfurt-style" case, because it has the structure of scenarios described by Frankfurt in his 1969 paper.

Notice that two claims seem to be true of **Idle Aliens**. First:

(Claim 1) Your neighbor acted freely in making the evil choice.

This claim seems to be true because your neighbor made his evil choice completely on his own and in a way that doesn't appear to undermine his freedom. He didn't do it compulsively, for example. And he also didn't do it as a result of having been manipulated by the aliens. Although the aliens were present and they were ready to intervene if they found out that he wasn't going to make the evil choice on his own, they didn't need to intervene, because as it turned out he did make it on his own. As a result, the presence of the evil aliens doesn't seem to excuse his behavior in any way. He acted freely and is just as responsible for what he did as if the aliens hadn't been there.

Next, the following claim also seems to be true of this case:

(Claim 2) Your neighbor couldn't have failed to make the evil choice.

This claim seems true of **Idle Aliens**, too, because, by assumption, the aliens wouldn't have let your neighbor fail to make the evil choice. They were there to ensure that he would make the evil choice and they are really good at their job—in fact, they never fail. Had they found out that your neighbor wasn't going to make the evil choice on his own, they would have immediately intervened by forcing him to do so and he would have ended up making the choice (the very same evil choice) as a result.

In other words: On the one hand, Claim 2 seems true because the aliens were *present* (and they had certain intentions and capabilities by virtue of which your neighbor couldn't do otherwise). On the other hand, Claim 1 seems true because, although the aliens were present, they *stayed idle* (and, as a result, their presence doesn't excuse your neighbor's behavior).

By the way, notice that this is a key difference between this scenario and the **Alien Manipulation** scenario we discussed in section 1. There we were assuming that the aliens had *in fact* manipulated your friend's choices and, as a result, he didn't act freely. By contrast, in **Idle Aliens**, we are assuming that the aliens never had to intervene because your neighbor made the evil choice completely on his own. This is why your neighbor seems responsible for what he does in **Idle Aliens**, whereas he is not responsible in **Alien Manipulation**.

So, Claim 1 and Claim 2 both appear to be true. And when you put them together you get this: Your neighbor freely made his choice to key your car, but he couldn't have failed to make that choice. In other words, he freely did something that was unavoidable for him. So, this suggests that it *is* possible, after all, to act freely *despite* lacking the ability to do otherwise. In other words, this suggests that Premise 4 in the Consequence Argument is false.

At this point, you might want to ask: If acting freely doesn't require having the ability to do otherwise, then why was it so tempting to think that it does? Why did it seem so natural to assume that if a choice was unavoidable for us, we couldn't have acted freely? The fact that it's so natural to assume this suggests that we think of the ability to do otherwise as simply essential to our free will!

But the compatibilist has a reply to this, too. It goes as follows. When we think about scenarios where our choices are unavoidable, it is very natural to think about scenarios where we don't act freely. But this is only because of the *kind* of scenario we're thinking about. For example, consider your compulsive neighbor in **Compulsive Keying**. Unlike your noncompulsive neighbor, he acted compulsively when he decided to key your car: his choice was unavoidable; he couldn't have done otherwise. But notice that his compulsion is also what *drove* him to decide to key your car: he made that choice as a result of having been compelled to make it. In other words, the very same factors that rendered his choice unavoidable were also the factors that caused his choice.

By contrast, consider a scenario like **Idle Aliens**: in that case, the factors that rendered your neighbor's choice unavoidable—the aliens—were *not* the factors that drove him to act. (The factors that drove him to act were his own reasons and deliberation; he never even found out about the aliens!) And notice that, in this type of case, where the factors that render the choice inevitable were not the ones that explained why he acted, the agent appears to act freely and be responsible for what he does, *despite* lacking the ability to do otherwise.

So, this suggests that what determines whether we act freely is *not*, after all, whether we could have done otherwise. Rather, it's the *actual causes* of our behavior or whatever explains why we acted. If we acted on the basis of our own reasons, deliberation, etc. (and not on the basis of compulsion, etc.), then we acted freely, and this is so *even if* we lacked the ability to do otherwise.

But notice that this is something that we can only see by focusing on quite atypical and artificial cases like **Idle Aliens**. (Luckily for us, these are not realistic cases—or, at least, we don't have any reason to think that they are.) Again, it's hard to think of cases where the factors that render our choices unavoidable are not also the factors that explain why we act. Irresistible compulsions, on the other hand, are a real thing. Unfortunately, so are other factors that can compel us or force us to make certain choices that we wouldn't otherwise want to make (think of people acting under duress or under the influence of coercive threats, for example). As a result, when we think about scenarios involving unavoidable choices, we naturally think of scenarios where agents also don't act freely, because their acts have causes that are freedom undermining.

In conclusion, this suggests that the basic presumption that free will requires the ability to do otherwise may have been misguided. Acting freely doesn't really require the ability to do otherwise. The reason it seemed so tempting to think that it does is just that the most obvious scenarios involving unavoidable choices also tend to be scenarios where we don't act freely and thus we tend to associate lacking the ability to do otherwise with not acting freely. But, even in those cases, what explains why we don't act freely is not the fact that our choices were unavoidable but the fact that they were caused in a certain kind of way.

As a result, this provides compatibilists with a different way to challenge the Consequence Argument—one that consists, again, in rejecting Premise 4 in the argument. But, at the same time, it motivates a different way of cashing out the concept of *free will* that is at the basis of the discussion. Recall that (as explained in section 1) we are working under the following understanding of free will:

> **Free Will:** The kind of control required for being morally responsible for what we do.

But what *is* the kind of control required for being morally responsible for what we do? One might think that it requires having the ability to do otherwise, as those who believe in Premise 4 in the Consequence Argument assume. Or you might (perhaps on the basis of the previous discussion) think that it does not and that all it requires is for our behavior to have certain kinds of causes.

So, there are these two different conceptions of what having free will amounts to:

> **Leeway Freedom:** The idea that acting freely requires some "leeway" in action, in the sense of having the ability to do otherwise.
>
> **Source Freedom:** The idea that acting freely only requires having the right kinds of "sources" or actual causes (and not, in particular, the ability to do otherwise).

As we have just seen, there are some powerful reasons to think that **Source Freedom** does a better job than **Leeway Freedom** at capturing what is really essential to our free will. And, if so, the compatibilist can use this to resist the Consequence Argument for Incompatibilism, by rejecting Premise 4 in the argument.

Personally, I believe that **Source Freedom** is the right view of free will. Perhaps it's not obvious *at first sight* that this is what acting freely consists of. But, for the reasons offered, I think this is the best view, on reflection.

Notice that when I presented a sketch of my theory of free will in section 2, I developed it as a view in terms of just actual causes. This was the view, once again:

> **The Reasons-Sensitivity View:** Acting freely is a matter of being sufficiently sensitive to reasons, where this involves being sensitive to a range of reasons and absences of reasons of various kinds.

Here the concept of reasons-sensitivity was spelled out in terms of actual causes: we act freely to the extent that we are *causally sensitive* to reasons in the right kind of way. In other words, we act freely to the extent that our acts have certain kinds of causes. As a result, the Reasons-Sensitivity view says nothing about the ability to do otherwise being required for having free will. Thus, it fits the general conception that understands freedom in terms of actual causes, and actual causes only, which is captured by **Source Freedom**.

As we have seen, this results in an important advantage for compatibilists. If we don't rely on a view of freedom based on the ability to do otherwise, we can easily rebut the Consequence Argument for Incompatibilism by rejecting Premise 4 in that argument. Again, this is because if freedom doesn't require the ability to do otherwise, then it follows that Determinism *needn't be* a challenge to our free will, even if it robs us of such an ability.

To sum up the contents of this section: In this section, I developed and explained one major incompatibilist challenge: the *Consequence Argument* for Incompatibilism. I discussed two different ways in which compatibilists can resist that challenge. One consists of rejecting Premise 2 of that argument and in claiming that there is a sense in which we may not be powerless over the remote past and the laws. The other (my preferred response) consists of rejecting Premise 4 of the argument and in embracing a conception of freedom ("source" freedom) that doesn't require the ability to do otherwise. I conclude that the Consequence Argument fails to establish Incompatibilism.

6. Incompatibilist Arguments: Part II

The second type of incompatibilist challenge that we'll discuss is a challenge that affects Compatibilism *even if* one thinks of free will in terms of **Source Freedom**. That is, it's a challenge that cannot be avoided by giving up the commitment to **Leeway Freedom**, because it doesn't rely on the thought that Determinism threatens our free will by virtue of undermining the ability to do otherwise.

The challenge is the following. We'll start by considering another purely imaginary scenario, one that will require to stretch your imagination even further—but not too far, if you've read science fiction works such as Douglas Adams' (1979) fascinating book, *The Hitchhiker's Guide to the Galaxy*. (The scenario we'll introduce is not exactly the same as the one described there, but it's similar in some important respects.) As we will see, thinking of this imaginary scenario can trigger intuitions about freedom and responsibility that make trouble for Compatibilism. Thus, this will provide the basis for an argument for Incompatibilism (see Mele [2006] for an argument closely related to the one presented in this section).

So, here it goes: Imagine that there is a highly intelligent alien race with amazing God-like powers: they can create whole universes, and they can do this with complete foresight of what will happen in those worlds after their creation. Imagine that we learn that our whole world was created by those aliens and that they designed the Earth and the rest of our universe with full knowledge of what we would do at every point in our lives. This is because their immense knowledge and computational powers allowed them to foresee how the world would evolve from the beginning of time, given the state of the world at that initial time of creation, in accordance with natural laws that are fully deterministic.

Imagine, moreover, that such aliens are also quite evil and so they created our world not just foreseeing but also *intending* for human beings to perform evil acts and rejoicing at that fact. In particular, imagine that they created our world with full knowledge that a certain human being—your noncompulsive neighbor described in the **Noncompulsive Keying** scenario—would choose to key your car on a particular day and anticipating that to happen. The rest of the story is exactly the same as before: we are to imagine, for example, that when your neighbor keyed your car he didn't act compulsively, that he was responding to various reasons and so on and so forth.

Call this new imaginary scenario "**Alien Design**". Now ask yourself how you feel about your neighbor's responsibility in **Alien Design**: Does your neighbor seem considerably less responsible, or perhaps not responsible at all, for keying your car in this kind of case? If this is how it seems to you, you're not alone: it seems that way to me, too. It's a very natural reaction to have about this case. Somehow, imagining that the evil aliens designed our world knowing full well that your neighbor would act that way at that point in his life, and in fact intending that to happen, seems to undermine his freedom and responsibility.

But recall that, given how we have described the case, when your neighbor keyed your car, he did it voluntarily, he didn't act compulsively and he was sensitive to reasons in the way described in section 2 (for example, he is responding to the absence of security cameras, to the absence of police in the area, etc.). As a result, a compatibilist account of free will would have trouble explaining why he seems to be less responsible. This goes for the account that I have proposed in section 2, the Reasons-Sensitivity View of free will, but also for most other compatibilist accounts. After all, as we have seen, what's behind Compatibilism is the idea that the remote causes of our acts don't matter to our free will, even if they fully determine what we do at every point in our lives. And, if this is the case, then it shouldn't matter to your neighbor's free will if his behavior was the necessary result of, in particular, an act of intentional design by aliens that took place many years ago. But, again, this is not how we feel about the **Alien Design** scenario: somehow, we feel it *does* matter!

Here, too, it will help to reconstruct the argument in the form of premises and conclusion. Once we do this, we see that its structure is quite simple. This is basically it:

The Design Argument for Incompatibilism

(**Premise 1**) Your neighbor is not responsible for his acts in **Alien Design**.

(**Premise 2**) If your neighbor is not responsible for his acts in **Alien Design**, then Compatibilism is false.

Therefore,

(**Conclusion**) Compatibilism is false (in other words, Incompatibilism is true).

Again, the motivation for the premises is briefly the following:

Premise 1: This premise is just an expression of an intuition that I predict many people would have about the **Alien Design** case. It seems to arise from the fact that your neighbor's behavior in this case is the result of an act of *intentional design* by the evil aliens: the aliens knew he would act that way and designed the world wanting him to act that way. Somehow this seems to undermine your neighbor's responsibility.

Premise 2: This premise is based on the idea that Compatibilism is committed to the irrelevance of the existence of remote deterministic causes of our behavior to our having free will. It shouldn't matter if those causes involve evil intentional agents or just natural processes: if Compatibilism is true, we should be able to act freely regardless of the precise nature of those remote deterministic causes.

Is the Design Argument for Incompatibilism successful? Again, for it to be successful it would have to be sound, and this means that it must be logically valid and have true premises. The argument is clearly valid, because the conclusion logically follows from the premises. That is to say, on the assumption that the premises are both true, the conclusion couldn't fail to be true. But are the premises *true*?

Given that there are two premises, there are two main ways in which the argument could be rejected: by rejecting Premise 1 or by rejecting Premise 2. I'll discuss both of these options.

First Compatibilist Reply: Rejecting Premise 2

I'll start with the second premise. Here it is again:

> (Premise 2) If your neighbor is not responsible for his acts in **Alien Design**, then Compatibilism is false.

How could this premise be rejected?

Rejecting Premise 2 amounts to claiming that whether we could have free will and be responsible in a deterministic world depends on the exact nature of the remote deterministic causes. If these were just "natural" causes, as in a standard deterministic scenario, then we would have free will and we would be responsible. However, if they involved intentional design or malice of some kind, as in the **Alien Design** scenario, then we wouldn't have free will and we wouldn't be responsible. If we could defend this view, we could accept Premise 1 and reject Premise 2 on the grounds of that conception of free will. Notice that this would still be a form of Compatibilism, because it entails that we can have free will and be responsible in *standard* deterministic scenarios, where the remote causes are purely natural processes.

But there is a problem with this response. The problem is that this addition complicates the compatibilist picture in a way that might make it seem unmotivated. At bottom, the compatibilist conception of free will can be seen as embracing the idea that when thinking about what grounds our free will, *we shouldn't worry about remote causes at all.*

This is something we touched on in section 4, when we were discussing the motivation for Compatibilism. I pointed out then that part of that motivation consisted in starting from an intuitive difference between behaviors that seem to be free (such as many ordinary human behaviors) and behaviors that seem not to be free (such as compulsive behaviors) and then noting that the existence of remote causal explanations of the behaviors, including potentially deterministic ones, doesn't undermine those differences. In fact, the existence of remote causes can come to be seen as something that is not surprising news in any way but only as a consequence of a naturalistic conception of the world and our place in it. We tend to think that events don't just happen for no reason, at least not in the kind of world we live in, but have explanations in terms of prior causes. And those prior causes have explanations in terms of even more distant causes and so on until the time of the Big Bang.

But then it also seems natural to assume that there will come a point, when we reach the very remote causes, where it shouldn't matter at all what those causes are like. If so, questions such as "What caused the Big Bang?" (Was it God? Evil aliens? Some physical feature of our universe? Nothing at all?) are simply irrelevant to our free will and responsibility. And, if that is the case, the compatibilist cannot reply to the Design Argument by rejecting Premise 2.

Fortunately for the compatibilist, there is another option, rejecting Premise 1 of the argument, which I think is more promising. I'll discuss that option next.

Second Compatibilist Reply: Rejecting Premise 1

Here is Premise 1 again:

> (Premise 1) Your neighbor is not responsible for his acts in **Alien Design**.

When I introduced the argument, I noted that Premise 1 seems to be strongly supported by intuition: somehow, your neighbor seems to be much less responsible, or perhaps not at all responsible, in this case. But is this a *reliable* intuition? Can we trust it?

Compatibilists could attack Premise 1 by arguing that the intuition about this case is not reliable. In particular, they could note that it's quite unstable, in that it quickly changes or loses its force as soon as we consider slight variants on the case.

Consider, for example, this variant: This time imagine that the aliens are not evil and that the reason they designed the world the way they did is that they wanted some good things to happen in the world, and this inevitably meant creating human beings who would act wrongly on some occasions.

> By the way, notice that this is, in essence, what some religious people think about God: that God created us knowing that we wouldn't always do the right thing. But, of course, they also think that God's intentions in so doing were not bad but good and that God had his reasons for doing this. For example, the reason could be that God wanted us to retain our freedom and regarded our acting wrongly on some occasions as the result of our exercising our freedom in the wrong ways.

So, think about how you feel about a "good aliens" case like this, where the aliens who created our world had good intentions, not bad intentions. Is your intuition that your neighbor didn't act freely in this case as strong as in the original "evil aliens" case? For what it's worth, mine is not: I am much more hesitant and less inclined to feel that way when I think about this case than when I think about the other one.

Or (following the Douglas Adams story just a bit more closely) imagine that the aliens were instead driven by philosophical curiosity: they created our world to play the role of a powerful computer, which they needed as part of their quest for finding the meaning of life, the universe and everything. Is your intuition that your neighbor didn't act freely in this "philosophical aliens" case as strong as in the original "evil aliens" case? Again, mine is not; I'm much more hesitant in this case.

But now ask yourself: Could it matter to your neighbor's freedom and responsibility if the world was designed by aliens with *bad* intentions or with *good* (or, at least, not bad) intentions?

Personally, I don't see how that could plausibly matter. The intentions that the aliens hypothetically had when they created the world should have no effect on your neighbor's free will. Why would it matter what was going through the aliens' minds while they were designing the world? It seems that, if anything, all that would matter to our freedom and responsibility is what the aliens actually *did*: what kind of world they created and what kinds of features we (human beings) have in that world. But what intentions motivated their creation, or which intentions they had while creating it, seems to be irrelevant to the freedom of the agents that exist in that world, if it had no effect in the product of their creation. And, if so, this suggests that there must be something messing with our intuitions about these cases if we can't help but see an intuitive difference between the different cases when, on reflection, we judge that there really is none.

Now, what could be messing with our intuitions about these cases? I suspect it's the fact that in the original case with the evil aliens, **Alien Design**, the aliens *themselves* seem to be to blame for what your neighbor does. After all, they created the world intending for your neighbor to act wrongly and rejoicing at that fact. Given that the aliens are a much clearer target of blame, we tend to see your neighbor himself as much less responsible, or perhaps even as not responsible at all. In contrast, in the variants with the good (or not bad) intentions, the aliens themselves don't seem to be equally blameworthy and your neighbor is left as the only obvious culprit.

Notice that what I'm suggesting is not that this is how things really are but only that this is what explains how we might be tempted to *see* things. That is, what I'm suggesting is that how responsible your neighbor *seems* to us to be depends on whether there are others who are more clearly to blame. But this doesn't change the fact that, as things stand, your neighbor can be equally to blame in both cases.

To motivate this some more, consider the following scenario. A group of three boys are spending the afternoon together at a park. One of the boys, Jimmy, sadly tells the others that he doesn't have any treats to eat (his family is very poor and can't afford to buy some for him). The other two boys, Jack and Max, pretend they didn't hear him and fail to offer Jimmy one of theirs. Obviously, we want to blame both Jack and Max for acting very selfishly on this occasion. But now imagine that later we find out that though they were both carrying chocolate boxes, one of the boys (Jack) had 5 chocolate pieces left, whereas the other boy (Max) had 100 pieces left. So, Max is now a much more obvious target of blame. And doesn't Jack seem to be a bit less responsible in this case as a result?

Imagine that you have this reaction. Now, arguably, this doesn't change Jack's *actual* responsibility in any way. Assume that, at the time, Jack didn't know that Max had many more chocolate pieces left than him. So, he should have offered one chocolate piece to Jimmy, and he acted very selfishly when he didn't. The fact that (unbeknownst to him) Max was acting in a way that was even *more* blameworthy doesn't get Jack off the hook and doesn't make him any less blameworthy. He just *appears* to be less blameworthy in this case, simply because we have a much clearer target of blame (Max).

Thus, one could argue that our intuitions about somebody's moral responsibility can be quite unreliable, at least in these kinds of cases. And this, in turn, can be used to support the rejection of Premise 1 in the Design Argument for Incompatibilism. The response consists, again, in suggesting that Premise 1 fails because your neighbor is, in fact, responsible for keying your car in the **Alien Design** scenario. He just *appears* not to be responsible, or to be less responsible than in other cases, because in that scenario the evil aliens are a much more obvious target of blame.

I conclude that the compatibilist can plausibly resist the challenge posed by the Design Argument, and thus, that the argument doesn't succeed in establishing Incompatibilism.

To sum up the contents of this section: In this section, I developed and explained another major incompatibilist challenge: the *Design Argument* for Incompatibilism. I discussed two different ways in which compatibilists could try and resist that challenge: one is rejecting Premise 1 of the argument and the other is rejecting Premise 2. I argued that, whereas one of the responses faces some serious problems, the other one is much more promising. On that basis, I concluded that the Design Argument fails to establish Incompatibilism.

Conclusions

In the last two sections of this chapter I examined two influential arguments for Incompatibilism, the Consequence Argument and the Design Argument. I argued that compatibilists have plausible responses to both of those arguments. As a result, I concluded that those arguments fail. But where does this leave us?

Well, it depends on how you feel about Compatibilism to begin with. In particular, if, like me, you think that Compatibilism is an independently plausible view of free will, then you should take the failure of the incompatibilist arguments we have reviewed as further reason to be a compatibilist. Earlier in this chapter, I explained what I take to be the main motivation for being a compatibilist, and I gave a sketch of a compatibilist view that I find particularly plausible—roughly, a view that takes our freedom to depend on our being suitably sensitive to reasons. I won't rehash the whole case for Compatibilism here, but I'll summarize what I see as the main takeaways.

First, despite possible appearances to the contrary, acting freely is not a matter of being "unburdened" or "unencumbered" in the sense of *lacking causes* when we act. Quite the contrary, acting freely is acting *from* causes (of the right kind). This is because acting freely amounts to having the kind of control over our acts that can make us morally responsible for what we do. And we cannot be in control of (and be morally responsible for) what we do if we act for no reason or if our acts don't have any causes.

Moreover, the kinds of causes that our acts have when we act freely are in fact quite *complex* and, in particular, much more complex than when we don't act freely (as when our acts are the result of freedom-undermining factors such as compulsions, addictions, phobias, etc.). That complexity reflects the fact that when we act freely, we are sensitive to the presence and absence of reasons of various kinds, including reasons that are moral in type. This same complexity in the causes of our acts also sets us apart from beings who are not morally responsible because they are not sensitive to reasons in the same kind of way, such as most other animals.

So, far from being uncaused, free acts are acts that have rich and substantial causes. In other words, the causes of our acts can *make* us free, rather than unfree, because they can explain why we act freely when we do.

Now, according to most compatibilists, the causes that make us free do not include the very remote ones. The causes that are relevant to our free will have to do with factors like our deliberations, the reasons that motivate us to act and maybe some events that helped shape our lives and our values in certain ways, but they don't go all the way back to times before we were even born. In fact, *it doesn't really matter*, according to most compatibilists, what kinds of remote causes our acts have. In particular, for all we know there could be remote deterministic causes of everything we do—and, more generally, of everything that happens in our universe. It could be, for example, that back at the time of the Big Bang it was already determined that the world would evolve in precisely the way it did, given the full state of the world at that time and, thus, that we would act in exactly the way we did. But according to these compatibilist views, this would have no effect on our free will, because we could still respond to reasons in such determined worlds and our acts could still have the complex kinds of causal histories that acting freely requires.

Of course, at this point some might still want to complain that if our acts were causally determined in the way we are imagining, then we couldn't have responded to any other reasons than the ones we actually responded to and our acts couldn't have had any other causes than the ones they actually had. How could we have acted freely, then?

But notice that this complaint is, in essence, another instance or application of the Consequence Argument for Incompatibilism or of the idea that underlies it: the thought that Determinism robs us of free will because it robs us of *the ability to do otherwise.* And, as we have seen, there are some plausible ways in which compatibilists can respond to that argument. Recall that one of them (the reply that I take to be the most promising) consists in claiming that freedom doesn't really require any such ability to do otherwise; instead, it only requires acting from the right kinds of causes. So, even if Determinism did rob us of the relevant ability to do otherwise, this wouldn't undermine our free will, according to this form of Compatibilism that I endorse.

At bottom, embracing Compatibilism amounts to coming to terms with the idea that we are part of the natural world and so are our actions; as a result, our acts have prior causes just like other natural events do. And those causes, in turn, have other causes even more into the past, and so on, until you reach a time in the remote past before any human beings existed. Compatibilism understands human agency and the capacities for freedom and moral responsibility in line with other complex but purely natural phenomena. As a result, the existence of those very remote causes of our acts (which could, at least potentially, be deterministic) is nothing more than a consequence of this naturalistic conception of the world. And it's not really a big surprise, at least not on reflection, given that it matches our tendency to assume that everything that happens has an explanation—even a "full" explanation—in terms of prior events and the natural laws.

Finally, even if it turned out that the world we live in is in some important ways indeterministic and not everything that happens has a full (deterministic) explanation, the compatibilist would point out that such indeterminism wouldn't boost our free will in any way or make us any *more* free, because at most what it would do is inject an element of randomness or chance that cannot enhance our control. Arguably, we could still be free in an indeterministic world of a certain kind. But indeterminism is not what would *make* us free in that case. What would make us free is, again, the fact that we are capable of responding to reasons in the relevant way and the fact that our acts can still have the relevant kinds of causes.

If you find this defense of Compatibilism persuasive, then it's likely to pay off because, as it turns out, Compatibilism (and, in particular, the compatibilist view that I have advanced here) has some main advantages over other views on the free will problem. Let me end by listing some of its virtues.

First, as I have already pointed out but is worth emphasizing once more, Compatibilism is a good match for a general conception about the world we live in, and our place in it, that many people nowadays find attractive. This is a *naturalistic* conception of the world. According to this naturalistic conception, events have explanations in terms of prior causes and the natural laws—explanations that could, at least potentially, be deterministic. And, although we (human beings) are "special" or different from other beings in some important ways, this is not because we have magical, supernatural or God-like powers of any kind. Instead, it's just because we have more complex or sophisticated powers of reasoning, emoting and understanding than other natural beings. And, among those sophisticated (but still purely natural) powers are the powers to act freely and to be morally responsible for what we do.

Second, unlike highly skeptical or revisionary views of free will, Compatibilism also follows commonsense in its vindication of human free will. It upholds and lends support to the intuitive sense that we have the power to act freely and that we often get to exercise it in our ordinary lives. Plus, compatibilist views tend to draw the line between free and unfree behaviors in roughly the way commonsense does—for example, they entail that the behavior by your noncompulsive neighbor in **Noncompulsive Keying** is free and the behavior by your compulsive neighbor in **Compulsive Keying** is not free. They do this while still allowing for the possibility that we could be wrong about specific cases. For example, if it turned out that aliens had been directly manipulating your friend's choices by the use of chips that they had secretly implanted in his brain, as in the **Alien Manipulation** scenario described in section 1, then it would follow that your friend didn't act freely after all. But all of this is, again, in accordance with commonsense. We would intuitively agree that if your friend really had been subject to manipulation in this way, then he wouldn't have acted freely at all.

So, Compatibilism has at least these two main virtues: it is a good fit for a naturalistic picture of the world and of human agency and it also respects commonsense. Finally, Compatibilism has a third important virtue. It is the following: As we have seen, the world could be (in broad strokes) deterministic or indeterministic. For all we know (and perhaps will ever know), it could be one way or the other. The third virtue of Compatibilism is that it can fit a naturalistic picture of the world and respect commonsense, *regardless of which is the deep truth about the world.* As we have seen, most compatibilist views would say that it's simply irrelevant whether determinism is true or not. For example, on the view that I favor, to the extent that we can be responsive to reasons in the right kind of way, we can act freely, and this is so regardless of whether our acts are causally determined by remote states in the past or not.

Again, this is not to say that freedom doesn't depend on what the world is actually like or on how we make our choices. It *does* depend on that. Rather, it's only to say that it doesn't depend on whether determinism or indeterminism is the truth about the deep causal structure of the world. That's just irrelevant to our freedom, according to most compatibilist views (and according to the compatibilist view that I favor). The final main virtue of Compatibilism is, then, that it helps "protect" our freedom in ways that other views of free will cannot.

———

For their comments on my contribution to this debate, thanks to Juan Comesaña, Tomás Comesaña, and Michael McKenna. For all their help and support along the way, thanks to Andy Beck and to the series editors, Ty Goldschmidt and Dustin Crummett. Finally, many thanks to Bob Kane for the lively discussion.

First Round of Replies

Chapter 3

Reply to Carolina Sartorio's Opening Statement

Robert Kane

Contents

Introduction: On Acting Freely: Some Significant Agreements

In the first half of Carolina's opening statement in this debate, she lays out her compatibilist view of free will and responsibility in some detail. In the second half, she offers criticisms of some common arguments in favor of opposing incompatibilist views. I think her criticisms of incompatibilist views in the second half fall short and will show why I think so in this response. But I first want to briefly address the first half of her statement about acting freely,

DOI: 10.4324/9781003212171-5

because I agree with much that she says there about free action. I just don't believe that it captures all we need to say to give a full and adequate account of free will and hence also of moral responsibility, and I want to explain why.

I agree with her, for example, that to act freely, one's acting cannot be the result of compulsion. It cannot be triggered by uncontrollable compulsions or urges one cannot resist, as in her scenario of the compulsive neighbor who cannot resist keying your car ("Compulsive Keying"). Nor would your action be free if someone coerced you into doing what you do (e.g., by holding a gun to your head) or if you were controlled or manipulated in more subtle ways by other agents (as in her "Alien Manipulation" scenario). Nor would you be free in many other cases different than these but where you are also not in control of your own behavior.

Moreover, I agree with much that she says positively about what is required to act freely and, in particular, about the importance of "reasons-sensitivity" to acting freely. For example, she says that "free agents are ... beings who are sensitive to reasons. ... Instead of being driven by irresistible forces that compel them to act in a certain way, they control and guide their behavior in accordance with considerations that they recognize as counting in favor or against certain kinds of behaviors. ... And this sensitivity to reasons is what we see in the causal history of free behaviors." In her opening statement here, and even more thoroughly in her carefully argued and original book, *Causation and Free Will* (Sartorio 2016), she spells out this "reasons-sensitivity view," as she calls it, of acting freely in detail. And there is much in this reasons-sensitivity view about acting freely, as she describes it, with which I agree.

But I do not believe that such an account of free action *alone* gives us a full and adequate account of free will and hence of moral responsibility, though it gives us an important part of such an account. Why not all?

Because, as argued in my opening statement, *free will is not just about free action*, though it involves free action. It is about *self-formation*, about *the formation of our "wills"* or how we got to be the kinds of persons we are, with the characters, motives and purposes we now have. Were we ultimately responsible to some degree for having the *wills* (characters, motives and purposes) that lead us to act as we do, or can the sources of our wills be completely traced back to something over which we had no control, such as Fate, or the decrees of God, heredity and environment, social conditioning or hidden controllers and so on? That is the key kind of question that has given rise to the traditional problem of "free *will*" wherever it has arisen in human history.

To have free will in this sense, as also argued in my opening statement, it must be that at least *some times in our lives* we face forking paths into the future, either of which may be taken by us, given the past and the laws governing the universe. At such times, it is "up to us" which of these paths is taken, in the sense that either path may be taken and *whichever* path *is* taken would be taken by us *in accordance with our wills* (voluntarily, intentionally and rationally). Actions satisfying these conditions are special because in performing them we do not merely *express* the will we already have but we also *form* or *shape* the will we may then express in action in future. I thus call them "self-forming" (or "will-setting") actions.

1. Acting Freely and Free Will: Some Significant Differences

Importantly, such self- or will-forming actions must also satisfy the conditions for acting freely generally that Carolina requires. But the agents must satisfy further conditions as well. For example, like other free actions, self-forming actions could not be coerced or otherwise controlled or manipulated by other agents. The agents would in addition have to be "sensitive to reasons", as she says, and not "driven by irresistible forces that compel them to act in a certain way". The agents would also have to "control and guide their behavior in accordance with considerations that they recognize as counting in favor or against certain kinds of behaviors".

But, in addition, for self-forming actions the reasons to which agents are sensitive would be complex and conflicting and the agents must choose which conflicting reasons to set their wills upon by making efforts to overcome resistance in their wills coming from the reasons to do otherwise.

One might thus say that agents who are capable of such self-formation—and hence free will—have reached a higher evolutionary stage of self-consciousness in which they are not only sensitive to reasons but sensitive to conflicting sets of reasons.

They have a richer and more complex inner life and they must choose which of the conflicting sets of reasons to set their wills upon as they go forward. Different choices may be made at such times, voluntarily, intentionally and rationally. Whichever choice is made would thus be sensitive to reasons the agent has and chooses to act upon at the time. But the reasons the agent chooses to act on would be different depending on which choice is made and the competing reasons to do otherwise would have to be overcome by effort whichever choice is made.

Will John choose to steal from the poor box because he desperately needs the money or will he choose not to do so for his moral reasons that tell him it would be wrong to steal money that is used to help others? Will the recent law graduate accept the offer of the smaller firm because it is nearer her home, friends and family or will she accept the offer of the larger firm in the big city because she desires the prestige it would bring?

Now a key point here regarding the age-old problem of free will and determinism is that such self-forming and will-setting choices would not be possible, if whichever choice was made at such times was *determined*. For then, only one of the choices the one actually made, would have been causally possible. We might have *believed* that either choice was open to us and it was possible for us to make either choice "at will". But, in reality, if the choice was determined, this would not be so. It may have been possible to make the choice that was made, voluntarily, intentionally and rationally. But if the choice made was determined, it would not have been possible to have made any alternative choice.

Not all of our *free* actions have to be self-forming in this manner. In many cases we may act from a will already formed and may do so *freely* in a sense that nothing prevents us from doing what we will to do at such times. We may be able at such times to do *what* we will without being coerced or controlled, or acting from compulsions, having reasons for acting as we do and being sensitive to those reasons. We may even at such times be determined to will as we do and yet be free to act *as* we will without any constraints or persons preventing us.

But if what we did at such times was determined, it would have been causally impossible for us to have willingly done anything else. So, though many of our free actions might be like this, if *all* of our free actions in the course of our lives were like this—if none were self-forming, that is—we would never be free to *form* our wills *in one way or another* rather than to act in accordance with the wills we already had. We might then have *freedom of action* but not *freedom of will.*

In the Introduction of this response to Carolina's opening statement I argue that there is much that I agree with in the "reasons-sensitivity" account of free action that she presents in the first half of her opening statement. In section 1, I then explain why, despite these agreements, I believe such an account of free action does not alone gives us a full and adequate account of free will and moral responsibility, though it may give us a part of such an account; and I explain what else is needed to give a full and adequate account of free will and moral responsibility.

2. Critique of Incompatibilist Views (Part I): The Consequence Argument and Being Powerless over the Past and Laws

With this background, let us turn to the second half of Carolina's opening statement where she criticizes some well-known arguments for believing that free will must be incompatible with a thoroughgoing determinism. The first argument she considers for the incompatibilism of free will and determinism is the Consequence Argument, so named by its leading defender, Peter van Inwagen (1983). She formulates the argument as follows:

(**Premise 1**) If Determinism is true, your neighbor's behavior is a necessary consequence of the remote past and the natural laws.

(**Premise 2**) Your neighbor is powerless over the remote past and the laws.

(**Premise 3**) If your neighbor is powerless over the remote past and the laws, and if his behavior is a necessary consequence of the remote past and the laws, then he is also powerless over his own behavior.

(**Premise 4**) If your neighbor is powerless over his own behavior, then he doesn't act freely when he keys your car.

(**Conclusion**) If Determinism is true, your neighbor doesn't act freely when he keys your car.

She then considers two replies that compatibilists might make (and have made) to this Consequence Argument for incompatibilism. Compatibilists might reject Premise 2 of the argument or reject Premise 4. Consider Premise 2 first.

"The thought of rejecting this premise may strike you as crazy", Carolina says. "How could your neighbor possibly have any power over the remote past or the laws of nature? We don't have the capacity to travel back in time, and we also don't have the capacity to do miracles. How, then, could one deny that we, as ordinary human beings, are powerless over the remote past and the laws?" She asks us to recall that being "**powerless**" in Premise 2 is shorthand for: "*there is nothing [your neighbor] could have done to make his behavior be any different from what it is.* As a result, his *not* being powerless over his own behavior", she says, "basically means that *he could have acted differently* (he could have failed to key your car)".

She then adds: "At this point, you are surely wondering how a compatibilist could pull this off. You might ask: how *could* [your neighbor] have acted any differently, if his behavior was fully determined?"

My own reaction at this point is to say: "Good question! How *could* he have acted differently if his behavior was fully determined?" If you also wonder about this, I'm completely with you. Philosophy begins in wonder. But then it shouldn't end there. So let's see how she attempts to answer the question.

Her answer begins by asking us to focus on the meaning of "could have acted differently", which, she says, expresses a certain kind of *ability*: "Whereas incompatibilists would argue that nobody could have acted differently in a deterministic world," she says, "the compatibilists we are considering would argue that this doesn't capture the concept of ability that is relevant to free will". She then distinguishes between two kinds of abilities:

Strong Ability: Someone who has a strong ability to affect the past or the laws is someone who could have *caused* the past or the laws to be different from what they are.

Weak Ability: Someone who has a weak ability to affect the past or the laws is someone who had the ability to do something differently in their lives and, had they exercised that ability, then either the past or the laws would have to have been different for them to do so.

Compatibilists, she then argues, can concede that though "it is wildly implausible to attribute to your neighbor (or to any other ordinary human) the *strong* ability to affect the past or the laws, it is much less implausible to attribute to him the *weak* ability". In fact, she adds, "The compatibilist might argue that if Compatibilism is true and your neighbor is not powerless over his own determined behavior, then he automatically has that weak ability, simply *as a result of* having the ability to act differently in a deterministic world".

In response, one might grant, for the sake of argument, that the "strong ability" to make the past or laws different than they are, as she defines it, is not an ability that ordinary humans could have. Still, this alternative notion of "weak ability" to affect the laws or the past—which she offers as an alternative and says compatibilists *can* affirm—is, it seems to me, *way too weak* to give us the freedom of will we need. Think about it a minute. This weak ability to make the past or the laws different than they are is not an ability we could ever *exercise* in the actual world in which we live and must act. This is so because, by the very definition of this weak ability, if someone ever exercised such a weak ability to do something differently in their lives, then "either the past or the laws would have to have been different" in some way than they actually are. And from this it follows directly that

> **Such a Weak Ability** could *not* be exercised in a world in which the past and the laws were *not* different in some way than they actually are. So, by definition, *it is not an ability that could ever be exercised in the world as it actually is* in which we must live and act.

Carolina says that "compatibilists could say that agents could have such a weak ability to do otherwise even in a determined world." Indeed, compatibilists *could* say this. But what they would thus be offering us is a notion of an ability that Immanuel Kant rightly called a "wretched subterfuge" and William James a "quagmire of evasion" in place of what is really needed for free will. What is really needed for free will at least at some times in our lives is the ability to do otherwise that it is possible for us to *exercise in the real world in which we live and act*, with the past as it really is and the laws as they really are. And such an ability cannot be had if determinism is true of that real world. What compatibilists would be giving us instead is an ability that could only be exercised in merely hypothetical or possible worlds that never actually existed.

In this section, I respond to the first of three arguments Carolina puts forward in her opening statement against views of free will that are incompatible with determinism. In order to explain how agents could have acted any differently than they actually did if their behavior was fully determined, she distinguishes two kinds of "abilities" to do otherwise. If determinism is true, she argues, agents could not have the "strong ability" to do otherwise because they could not change the past or the laws. But agents might still have a certain "weak ability" to do otherwise if determinism were true: an ability such that if they had exercised that ability, then either the past or the laws would have to have been different for them to do so. In response I argued that, because such a weak ability could *not* be exercised in a world in which the past and the laws were not different than they actually are, it would not be an ability that could ever be exercised in the world as it actually is in which we must live and act.

3.   Critique of Incompatibilist Views (Part II): Being Powerless and Acting Freely

The second way Carolina considers that compatibilists might respond to this Consequence Argument for the incompatibilism of free will and determinism is by rejecting Premise 4 of the argument:

> (**Premise 4**) If your neighbor is powerless over his own behavior, then he doesn't act freely when he keys your car.

We are again asked to recall that being "powerless" means your neighbor couldn't have acted differently when he keyed your car. So, she says, **Premise 4 amounts in effect to saying:** "If your neighbor couldn't have failed to key your car, then he didn't act freely when he did so."

Her response to this Premise 4 is then to argue that "acting freely *doesn't require* having the ability to do otherwise." So "even if Determinism really did deprive us of the ability to do otherwise," she says, "Compatibilism could still be true, given that acting freely doesn't require any such ability." To argue for this, she introduces a science fictional scenario she calls

> **Idle Aliens:** In this scenario, we imagine that the night before your neighbor keyed your car "some evil aliens had sneaked into his house while he was sleeping and had implanted a highly sophisticated mechanism in his brain that allowed the aliens *both* to monitor his thoughts to the very last detail *and* to manipulate his choices".

These evil aliens use these mechanisms on humans to manipulate them into making evil choices the humans would not have made on their own. But if the implanted mechanism monitoring the thoughts of the humans tells the aliens a few seconds before the humans act that the humans are going to perform *on their own* the evil acts the aliens want, the aliens and their mechanism do not have to intervene and do not intervene.

This, we are to imagine, is what happens in your neighbor's case. He made his evil choice to key your car completely on his own, in the sense that he did it for his own reasons, without being coerced or acting compulsively and the aliens' mechanism did not have to intervene and did not in fact intervene. As a result, she says, "The presence of the evil aliens doesn't seem to excuse [your neighbor's] behavior in any way. He acted freely and is just as responsible for what he did as if the aliens hadn't been there". Yet he *couldn't have done otherwise than make this evil choice* to key your car, because if the mechanism implanted by the aliens monitoring his thoughts had indicated seconds before that he was *not* going to make the evil choice they wanted on his own, this mechanism would have intervened and made him make that evil choice anyway.

So it seems that in this case where your neighbor made the evil choice to key your car on his own and the aliens and their mechanism did not intervene, your neighbor would have acted freely and would be responsible for what he did, even though he couldn't have done otherwise. Premise 4 of the Consequence Argument would be false: It would not be generally true that "if your neighbor couldn't have failed to key your car, then he didn't act freely when he did so." In this scenario, he acted freely and responsibly on his own, yet he could not have done otherwise, because the aliens and their mechanism would not have let him do otherwise.

4. Idle Aliens, Frankfurt-Style Examples and the Ability to Do Otherwise

You may have recognized by now that this Idle Aliens scenario is a version of a strategy for arguing against the incompatibility of free will and determinism that, as I noted in my opening statement, has become especially popular in contemporary philosophy among compatibilists. This strategy does not involve arguing (as classical compatibilists tried to do) that the ability to do otherwise is really compatible with determinism. Rather, this new strategy is to argue more radically that "even if Determinism really did deprive us of the ability to do otherwise, Compatibilism could still be true, given that acting freely" in a sense required for moral responsibility "doesn't require any such ability" to do otherwise.

This strategy, which was discussed in my opening statement, usually takes the form of appealing to what have come to be called "Frankfurt-style examples" in contemporary debates about free will and moral responsibility, named for Harry Frankfurt (1969), who formulated the first of these influential examples. Idle Aliens is a version of this general strategy of appealing to Frankfurt-style examples to show that acting freely in a sense required for moral responsibility does not require any such ability to do otherwise at all.

To see the similarity, recall Frankfurt's original example discussed in my opening statement. Frankfurt asked us to imagine that a controller, Black, has direct control over the brain of another man, Jones, and wants to allow Jones to do only what he, Black, wants Jones to do. Black prefers, however, to allow Jones to act on his own whenever possible and so will only intervene if Jones is about to do something that he, Black, does not want. Frankfurt then asks us to consider situations in which Jones is about to do what the controller Black wants, so that Black does not have to intervene and does not intervene.

In such situations, Frankfurt argues, Jones could be acting freely and could be responsible for what he does, because he would have acted *on his own*, from his own motives and for his own reasons, and nothing and no one (including Black) would have interfered with or prevented him from doing what he chose to do. Yet in such situations, Jones, Frankfurt argues, could not have done otherwise, because if he had given any indication of doing otherwise, Black would have prevented him from doing so. Frankfurt thus concludes that *acting freely and responsibly doesn't require having the ability to do otherwise.*

It is not difficult to see that this is how the **Idle Aliens** scenario unfolds as well. The aliens have direct control over the brains of all humans, as Black does over Jones. And, like Black, the aliens prefer to allow those they control to act on their own whenever possible and will only intervene if those they control are about to do something that the aliens do not want.

We are then asked to consider situations in which a human (such as your neighbor) under the control of these aliens is about to do what the aliens want (an evil act of keying your car), so that the aliens do not have to intervene and do not intervene. In such situations, it's then argued, this agent (your neighbor) could be acting freely and could be responsible for what he does, because he would have acted on his own, from his own motives and for his own reasons, and nothing and no one (including the aliens) interfered with or prevented him from doing what he chose to do. Yet your neighbor could not have done otherwise, because if he had given any indication of doing otherwise the aliens and their mechanism would have intervened to prevent him from doing so.

From this scenario, Carolina concludes, as does Frankfurt from his example, that "acting freely *doesn't require* having the ability to do otherwise." So Premise 4 of the Consequence Argument, she says, would be false. We *can* act freely and responsibly even when we could not have done otherwise. Thus, she concludes, "Even if Determinism really did deprive us of the ability to do otherwise, Compatibilism could still be true, given that acting freely doesn't require any such ability" to do otherwise.

5. Will-Setting, Responsibility and the Ability to Do Otherwise

Now the first thing to be said in response to this argument for compatibilism by appeal to **Idle Aliens** is the same thing that was said in my opening statement about other arguments for compatibilism that appeal to Frankfurt-style examples generally: Namely, *we don't need to appeal to such unusual and exotic examples to show* *that agents can sometimes and often do act freely and responsibly, even when they could not have done otherwise.* We have already seen from the example of Luther and other examples, which could be multiplied, that agents can be free and responsible for actions that flow from their wills at the time they acted and such that they could *not* have done otherwise *at that time.*

In everyday life, we often perform actions freely from a will already formed and such that we had no good reasons at the time to do otherwise. One can be responsible, as we saw, for such "will-settled" actions, as Luther was for his saying, "Here I stand, I can do no other", even if such actions were determined by one's existing will at the time so that one could *not* have done otherwise than perform them when they were performed.

But it was also argued in my opening statement that not *all* of our actions in our lifetimes could be determined or already will-settled in this way when we act, *if we are ever to be ultimately responsible for our wills being set the way they are when we act.* For this to be the case, we would have to have the ability *at some times in our lives* to make not merely "will-settled" but also "will-setting" or "self-forming" choices or actions that were not already determined by our existing wills when we performed them.

Though **Idle Aliens** and other such Frankfurt-style examples thus show that we can sometimes—even often—perform actions freely and responsibly, though we could not have done otherwise *at the time we performed them*, such examples fail to show the falsity of a more complex principle that I called in my opening statement:

> **Will-Setting Condition:** Agents are ultimately responsible for having the wills (characters, motives and purposes) they express in action only if at some times in their lives they willingly (voluntarily and intentionally) perform certain ("will-setting" or "self-forming") actions (SFAs) such that the agents had not only the power to willingly perform them but also the power to have willingly done otherwise.

It can be shown that if *all* of an agent's actions were under the control of these aliens, there could be no such self-forming choices or actions and hence no will-setting of the kind required for agents to be ultimately responsible for having the quality of wills they do have. This is the case because if the aliens were to have such control over all of the actions of humans, the one thing they could never allow is the following: The aliens could never allow the agents an opportunity to bring to completion "will-setting" or "self-forming" actions that were undetermined, because the aliens could not know whether or not the will-setting or self-forming actions would be performed until the moment they were either performed or failed to be performed.

The aliens would thus always have to intervene, either beforehand or at the time of the action, in some way to prevent such will-setting actions from occurring so that *they* themselves—*the aliens and not humans*—could *ensure* that humans always do what the aliens want them to do and never do what the aliens do not want them to do.

As a consequence, those who argue from examples such as **Idle Aliens** and other such Frankfurt-style examples that the ability to do otherwise is not needed *at all* for free will and moral responsibility are guilty of what logicians call a fallacy of composition: From the fact that *some*—even *many*—choices and actions in the lifetimes of agents can be such that the agents can perform them freely and responsibly even though the agents did not have the power to have done otherwise at the time they were performed it does not follow that *all* actions in the lifetimes of agents could be like this.

It does not follow that all actions could be like this *if* agents are ever to be responsible for their wills being set the way they are when they act. For this to be the case, agents would have to have the power, at some times in their lives, to engage in ("will-forming" or "self-forming") choices or actions that were such that the agents not only had the power to willingly perform them but also the power to have willingly done otherwise.

To illustrate these will-forming or self-forming actions and their relation to free will, recall the example of Huckleberry Finn discussed in my opening statement. As John Doris (2015) was quoted there, Huck held conflicting values favoring both the conventional course of action, that he should turn his friend and companion Jim, a black man who had escaped from slave owners, over to the authorities and the course Huck actually took, of not turning Jim over. This, I added, is how Mark Twain himself tells the story. Huck is growing and developing as a self or agent.

> In deciding not to turn Jim in, Huck is not merely expressing what sort of a self he already is; he is also deciding what sort of a self he is going to be by deciding from among the

conflicting values he has which ones he will follow. He is thereby engaged not merely in self-expression but in self-making, or self-formation, of the kind that freedom of will and not mere freedom of action sometimes requires.

And as we have seen here, such choices would not be possible if we were always under the control of other beings such as Frankfurt-style controllers like those imagined here in the scenario of **Idle Aliens**.

Carolina's argument in these sections is that acting freely and responsibly "doesn't require having the ability to do otherwise" at all. So "even if determinism really did deprive us of the ability to do otherwise," she says, "Compatibilism could still be true", given that "acting freely and responsibly doesn't require any such ability". In section 3, I discuss the argument she makes for this in terms of a science fictional scenario involving Idle Aliens. In section 4, I show that this argument in terms of Idle Aliens is a version of modern arguments for the claim that moral responsibility does not require the power to do otherwise based on so-called Frankfurt-style examples. And in section 5, I argue that all such arguments involving Frankfurt-style examples, including this argument about Idle Aliens—though they may show that we can *sometimes* perform actions freely and responsibly, even when we could not have done otherwise—fail to show that we could be ultimately responsible for our wills being the way they are if we could *never* in our lifetimes have acted otherwise than we actually did.

6. Critique of Incompatibilist Views (Part III): Design Arguments

The second class of arguments for incompatibilist views of free will that Carolina examines are what she calls Design Arguments. Her discussion of these arguments begins by asking us to consider yet another imaginary scenario, this one inspired by Douglas Adams'

(1979) book *The Hitchhiker's Guide to the Galaxy*. She calls this scenario

> **Alien Design:** We are to "imagine a highly intelligent alien race with amazing God-like powers. They can create whole universes and can do this with complete foresight of what will happen in those worlds after their creation. Imagine that we learn that our whole world was created by those aliens and that they designed the Earth and the rest of our universe with full knowledge of what we would do at every point in our lives. This is because their immense knowledge and computational powers allowed them to foresee how the world would evolve from the beginning of time, ... in accordance with natural laws that are fully deterministic. Imagine, moreover, that such aliens are also quite evil, and so they created our world not just foreseeing but also *intending* for human beings to perform evil acts and rejoicing at that fact. In particular, imagine that they created our world with full knowledge that ... your neighbor ... would choose to key your car on a particular day."

She then asks how we feel about this case and continues as follows: "Does your neighbor seem considerably less responsible, or perhaps not responsible at all, for keying your car in this kind of case? If this is how it seems to you, you're not alone: it seems that way to me, too. It's a very natural reaction to have about this case. Somehow, imagining that the evil aliens designed our world knowing full well that your neighbor would act that way at some point in his life, and in fact intending that to happen, seems to undermine his freedom and responsibility".

"But recall that," she continues, "when your neighbor keyed your car, he did it voluntarily, he didn't act compulsively and he was sensitive to reasons". "As a result", she says, "a compatibilist account of free will would have trouble explaining why he seems to be less responsible. This goes for the account that I have proposed ... the Reasons-Sensitivity View of free will, but also for most other compatibilist accounts".

Here, as elsewhere in her work, Carolina is both honest and perceptive about why libertarians and other incompatibilists about free will might have doubts about the truth of compatibilism. As a libertarian and incompatibilist about free will, I certainly share the immediate reactions to this **Alien Design** scenario that she expresses here (immediate reactions she says she also shares and perhaps you may share as well). It *does* seem to matter in important ways to the responsibility and free will of your neighbor and all other persons in this imagined world that it was created by these aliens in such a way that all events, including all human choices and actions, were completely *determined* from the moment the world was created.

But philosophy cannot rest on immediate reactions alone. So once again we must consider her response to these sorts of incompatibilist worries about compatibilism. She begins by reconstructing the argument she believes lies behind design arguments of this sort, which she calls

The Design Argument for Incompatibilism

(**Premise 1**) Your neighbor is not responsible for his acts in **Alien Design**.

(**Premise 2**) If your neighbor is not responsible for his acts in **Alien Design**, then Compatibilism is false.

(**Conclusion**) Compatibilism is false (or, in other words, incompatibilism is true).

Her critique of this argument focuses on Premise 1: Why, she asks, do we so readily believe your neighbor and others would *not* be responsible for their acts in such a determined world created by these evil aliens?" She then floats the suggestion that "we tend to believe this because the aliens' intentions are evil and so the aliens *themselves* seem to be to blame for what your neighbor does. Given that the aliens are a much clearer target for blame, we tend to see your neighbor himself as much less responsible, or even perhaps not responsible at all.

To test such intuitions, she then asks us to consider alternative scenarios. "Consider, for example," she says, "that the aliens are not evil and they designed the world they did because they wanted some good things to happen in the world and this inevitably meant creating human beings who would act wrongly on some occasions." She asks us to think about this "good aliens" scenario, as she calls it, where the aliens who created our world have good intentions, not bad intentions.

She then asks: "Is your intuition that your neighbor didn't act freely in this case as strong as in the original 'evil aliens' case?"; and she answers: "For what it's worth, my intuitions are not" as strong. "I am much more hesitant and less inclined" to think your neighbor did not act freely and responsibly in this good aliens scenario than in the bad aliens scenario.

Why is she less inclined to think that humans do not act freely and responsibly in the good aliens case than in the evil aliens case? She says it is because in the evil aliens case we feel that the ultimate *blame* belongs to the aliens who created a world in which your neighbor and other humans were determined to perform evil acts, whereas in the good aliens case, because their intentions are good, we cannot *blame them* for the actions of humans (some of which may have been bad) in the world the aliens created.

Now I find both her reaction here and the reasons given for it unconvincing. Keep in mind that in *both* scenarios, good aliens or bad, "our whole world was created by those aliens and they designed the Earth and the rest of our universe with full knowledge of what we would do at every point in our lives". Moreover, in both universes everything that happened from the moment of creation, including every human action, good *or* bad, was completely determined.

As a result, those who lived in the world created by the evil aliens might be said to be *less lucky* or less fortunate than those humans who lived in the world created by the good aliens. But would they be less *free* in their behavior? I think not. Consider that humans in both worlds were determined to do everything they did, *good or bad*, and were not free in either world to have avoided doing anything they did *in either world*. Our freedom and responsibility are not just a matter of being *blameworthy* for the bad things we might do but also of being *praiseworthy* for the good things we might do.

On the view of free will I've been defending, we want free will because we want to be ultimately responsible for being the kinds of persons we are and hence for the actions we perform.

We want such Ultimate Responsibility so that what we accomplish in life redounds to us and not to some all-powerful aliens who made us the way we are and determined everything we do for their own purposes. And this is true not merely when we might be blamed for what we do but also when we might

> be praised for our accomplishments and the good things we might accomplish. We want to be deserving of our good or great achievements as ultimately caused by our own efforts and not ultimately caused by some alien beings. And we want to be ultimately deserving of approval and gratitude and being deserving of being loved and appreciated by those we care about and by others for the good things we may do. We want these things to be the results of our ultimately free and responsible doings and not the results of the actions of some manipulative aliens who have made us the way we are and determined everything we would do.

It is true that if we wish to be ultimately responsible and hence praiseworthy for the good things we do and for the admirable things we may accomplish by our efforts, we must also risk being ultimately responsible and blameworthy for the bad things we may do. We must also have had the power at some times to have willingly done blameworthy as well as praiseworthy things. But if we are to be ultimately responsible for doing *either* good *or* bad, we could not be *determined* to do one or the other, whenever we act, as would be the case in these deterministic worlds created either by evil aliens *or* good aliens.

Moreover, being able to do good *or* evil, to act well *or* poorly, is the price we pay for having free will, the price to be paid for it to be ultimately "up to us" whether we are blameworthy or praiseworthy, deserving of resentment and dislike when we do badly or of gratitude, love, appreciation and admiration when we do well. The good aliens allowed both good and evil. But in determining everything we do, they were the ultimate causes of everything we do, good and evil, and we were merely their instruments. We don't want to be pawns in someone else's chess game, however sophisticated the game may be.

All of this is even more true of the third alien scenario Carolina considers, which follows more closely Adams' (1979) story in *The Hitchhiker's Guide to the Galaxy*. Here we are asked to "imagine that the aliens were instead driven by philosophical curiosity: they created the world to play the role of a powerful computer, which they needed as part of their quest for finding the meaning of life, the universe and everything". They also allowed humans to do good or evil out of curiosity. But in also creating a world in which every-thing humans did was determined, the aliens in this third "philo-sophical aliens" scenario, as in the other two scenarios, would have been the ultimate causes of everything we did, good or evil, and we humans would have been merely their instruments.

Of course, in any of these three scenarios it might be imagined that the worlds created by the aliens allowed for some *indetermin-ism* in human affairs that would make it possible that the humans involved might in some cases do good *or* do evil as a result of their own choices that were not determined. Then the aliens would not have taken over all of the ultimate responsibility. They would have left some of the ultimate responsibility to human beings themselves. But such a scenario that would require some human choices and actions to be undetermined would not be one that *compatibilists* such as Carolina could accept as *required* for free will. Compatibil-ists believe we can have all the free will and responsibility "worth wanting" even if determinism is true and hence without requiring indeterminism.

7. Free Will, Design Arguments and Religious Questions

In the course of her discussion of these alien design arguments, Carolina rightly mentions some similarities between the second of her three scenarios, the "good aliens" scenario, and what some reli-gious people think about God and God's creation of our world. Like the good aliens in her second scenario, she says, God's inten-tions were good and, like these good aliens, God created us know-ing that we wouldn't always do the right thing.

There are indeed some similarities here between this good aliens scenario and traditional discussions of free will in religious con-texts. Yet there are also some significant differences between these aliens and God as usually conceived in most theistic traditions. The good aliens of her scenario "wanted some good things to happen in this world, and this inevitably meant creating human beings who would act wrongly on some occasions." And because creat-ing humans who would do wrongly on some occasions was "inevi-table" in the world these aliens created, the aliens were "powerless" to avoid it. So these aliens went ahead and created their world in which every action of every creature was *determined*, though some were determined to do good and some were determined to do evil.

But this is not how most religious believers usually think about God. In most theistic views, God is not only *all-good* but also *all-powerful* (*omnipotent*). Unlike the good aliens of her second scenario, therefore, an omnipotent God could not have been *powerless* to avoid creating a world in which some beings would do evil on some occasions.

This consequence of God's omnipotence has in fact been the source of central questions in the long history of theological speculation about God: *Why* would God, who is all-powerful *and* all-good, have created a world in which some beings do evil? What might have been God's reasons for allowing this? In his classic poem *Paradise Lost*, John Milton describes the angels debating these very questions. They wondered how some of them could have sinned "of their own free wills" and why they, and not God, were ultimately responsible for their sins, because God had made them the way they were and had complete foreknowledge at the creation of the world of what they would do. While debating these questions, even the angels, according to Milton's poem, were "in Endless Mazes lost".

The most common response to these deep questions in the long history of theological thought is the following: God wanted to leave it "up to" humans themselves whether they would choose God's way or some evil way, whether they would choose to love God or to abandon God "of their own free wills". Love is greater when it is freely given. And for this to be the case, God could not have created a world like the world of these "good" aliens of her second scenario, in which all the actions of humans, whether good *or* evil, were *determined* by the creator or creators from the moment of creation. If that were the case, the ultimate responsibility for good *and* evil acts would lie with the creator or creators of the world. And though this might be alright in the case of these aliens, it would not be alright for God, who is supposed to be, in the theistic traditions, not only all-powerful but also *all-good*.

This way of absolving God from being ultimately responsible for the evil done by humans is in fact often called in the theological traditions

The "Free Will Defense" for why an all-powerful and all-good God might have allowed evil in the world. According to this common defense, God did it because the love of creatures is greater when it is freely given. And if it were to be freely given, God could not determine that creatures would choose to love and follow God's way. So the price to be paid for this greater good of freely chosen love and following God's way was that some creatures might also choose and do evil. God would therefore allow the possibility of evil for this greater good.

Such a "free will defense" does not entirely solve the "problem of evil" in religious thought by itself, as many critics of theistic religions have argued. For example, it does not solve the problem of so-called natural evils in the world, such as earthquakes, floods, droughts, genetic and other diseases and other disasters that cause untold pain and suffering to innocent persons, including children, and do not seem to be caused by humans. It is interesting, however, that when such disasters strike (as in the case of the pandemic of 2020, going on as I write) many people have a tendency to want to find *some* other *humans* to blame. *Other* people, of course, are usually picked out to blame, not those who are like *us*; not those who share many features that we value or who believe what we believe. To complicate matters further, in some cases where natural disasters cause untold evil in the world, such as with climate change, many choices and actions of humans *are* to a considerable degree to blame.

Still, though this free will defense might not be the whole story in theistic defenses of God concerning the problem of evil, many religious thinkers believe that the free will defense would have to be a necessary part of such a defense. And I think they are correct in believing this much. An *all-powerful* God might be able to create a thoroughly determined world in which all of the actions of creatures, whether good or evil, would be determined from the moment of creation, but an *all-good* God would not do so.

It is worth adding that there have also been some religious believers who accept the fact that if God is all-powerful and all-knowing, then in creating the world, God, like these aliens, would inevitably know from the beginning everything that was going to occur in it, including all actions of humans, good or evil. In a religious context, such a view is a form of determinism often referred to as *predestinationism*. God predestines all things in the world, including both the good actions and the evil actions of humans, simply by creating a world in which everything is determined from the moment of this creation and foreknowing how it will all unfold from the moment of creating, and humans cannot do other than they are predestined to do in this world.

This is a difficult doctrine to accept, especially when it is coupled, as it often is in these religious views, with the belief that God rewards those who do good with heaven and punishes those who do evil with eternal torments in hell. This is frequently held to be a consequence, despite the fact that, on these predestinationist views, it is God who, from the moment of creation, by virtue of creating such a universe, foreordained that some persons would do good and some would do evil. Such a predestinationist view is not a religious view I could accept. I leave it to you to decide for yourselves whether you could accept it.

In section 6, we have looked at Carolina's criticism of a second class of arguments for the incompatibility of free will and determinism, which she calls "Design Arguments". In such arguments we are asked to imagine some highly intelligent and powerful aliens who created the world we live in and *determined* everything in it, including every human action. She then argues that whether agents, such as your neighbor, seem to be responsible in such design scenarios depends on whether the aliens who designed them had evil intentions or good intentions. If their intentions were evil, she argues, we could blame the aliens and not the humans for the humans' evil acts. But if the intentions of the aliens were good, we could *not* blame the aliens for the evil acts of humans and therefore could blame the humans. I argue against such claims by asking us to consider that humans in both worlds were determined to do everything they did, *good or bad*, by the alien designers and humans were not free in either world to have avoided doing anything they did *in either world*. I then argue that our freedom and responsibility is not just a matter of being *blameworthy* for the bad things we might do but also of being *praiseworthy* for the good things we might do. In section 7, such arguments about alien designers are then related to theological arguments about whether and to what extent humans are free and responsible for their actions if God has created them to be the way they are with full knowledge of everything they would do. Would God be responsible for evil-doing or the humans? Section 7 discusses this and other religious questions regarding human free will and responsibility.

Conclusion: Freedom, Determinism, Indeterminism, Causation and Control

(1) In her final section, Carolina concludes that "*it doesn't really matter*, according to most compatibilists, what kinds of remote causes our acts have. In particular, for all we know there could be remote deterministic causes of everything we do—and, more generally, of everything that happens in our universe. It could be, for example, that back at the time of the Big Bang it was already determined that the world would evolve in precisely the way it did, given the full state of the world at the time and, thus, that we would act in exactly the way we did. But according to these compatibilist views", she argues, "we could still respond to reasons in such determined worlds and our acts could still have the complex kinds of causal histories that acting freely requires".

"Of course, at this point", she adds, "some might still want to complain that if our acts were causally determined in the way we are imagining, then we couldn't have responded to any other reasons than the ones we actually responded to and our acts couldn't have had any other causes than the ones they actually had. How could we have acted freely then?"

These are also good questions. In attempting to answer them, she then asks us to "notice that this complaint is yet another instance ... of the ... idea that underlies" the Consequence Argument and other arguments for incompatibilism, namely, "the thought that Determinism robs us of free will because it robs us of the *ability to do otherwise*". She then reminds us, however, that, as she has argued earlier, "there are some plausible ways in which compatibilists can respond to that argument".

The reply compatibilists might make that she "take[s] to be the most promising consists in claiming that freedom doesn't really require any such ability to do otherwise; instead, it only requires acting from the right kinds of causes. So even if Determinism did rob us of the relevant freedom to do otherwise, this wouldn't undermine our free will, according to this form of compatibilism that I endorse".

In response, I have argued here and in my opening statement that it *does* matter to our freedom of will and responsibility that we have the ability to do otherwise—not for every free action we might perform but at least *at some times in our life* when we engage in *self-formation*, when we engage in making ourselves into the kinds of persons we are with the wills we do have. She is right to say that we can make some—even many—free and responsible acts in the course of our lives for which we could not have done otherwise at the time we performed them. But to engage in ultimate *self-formation* and not merely *self-expression*, all of the choices or actions in our lifetimes could not be like this.

To engage in self-formation, agents would have to have the ability, at some times in their lives, to act in such a manner that they not only had the ability to willingly perform the actions but also the ability to have willingly done otherwise, and this could not be the case if these actions were determined. I have argued that the various arguments she deploys appealing to alien scenarios of various kinds fail to show that this is not the case.

(2) In her concluding section, she also says that "if it turned out that the world we live in is in some important ways indeterministic … such indeterminism wouldn't boost our free will in any way or make us any *more* free, because at most what it would do is inject an element of randomness or chance that cannot enhance our control".

I have also argued that this is not the case. Indeterminism makes possible a kind of freedom (freedom of will) and a kind of responsibility (ultimate responsibility) that are valuable and worth wanting and that we could not have in a thoroughly determined world. Indeterminism does this by making it possible at times in our lives for us to perform certain actions (self-forming or will-setting actions) such that it is possible that we are able to perform them *in accordance with our wills* (voluntarily, intentionally and rationally) and also possible that we are able *to do otherwise*, also *in accordance with our wills*.

Indeterminism thereby makes possible a kind of *plural voluntary control* over some of the crucial choices and actions in our lives, the power or ability to make them and the power or ability to do otherwise, voluntarily, intentionally and rationally, *either way* they should be made. Such *plural* voluntary control would not be possible if all of our choices and actions were determined.

(3) Finally, she says in her conclusion that "acting freely is *not* a matter of being 'unburdened' or 'unencumbered' in the sense of *lacking causes* when we act. Quite the contrary, acting freely is acting *from* causes (of the right kind). This is because acting freely amounts to having the kind of control over our acts that can make us morally responsible for what we do. And we cannot be in control of (and morally responsible for) what we do if we act for no reason or if our acts don't have any causes".

I agree wholeheartedly with all of these claims and have made this clear in my opening statement and this response. In the view I have defended it is also true that "acting freely *is* acting *from* causes of the right kind" and that "we cannot be in control of (and morally responsible for) what we do if we act for no reason or if our acts don't have any causes." But while accepting these claims, I have strongly rejected arguments supported by many compatibilists and others that if some choices or actions were *undetermined*, they must therefore be *uncaused*. To the contrary, I have argued that

> Indeterminism is a technical term that merely rules out deterministic causation, not causation altogether. Indeterminism is consistent with probabilistic forms of causation, where outcomes are caused but not inevitably. It is thus a mistake, I noted—one of the most common mistakes in the long history of debates about free will—to assume that "undetermined" must mean or imply "uncaused".

Indeterminism, I further argued, does diminish control of certain kinds over what we are making efforts to do. But I added that in cases of self-forming choices or actions, such as that of the young law graduate, the indeterminism that is admittedly diminishing her control over the choice she may be trying to make (to join one law firm or another) is coming from her own will. It is coming from the motives she has for making the opposing choice (to join the competing firm).

In each case, the indeterminism is functioning as a hindrance or obstacle to her realizing one of her purposes—a hindrance or obstacle in the form of resistance within her will that has to be overcome by effort. If there were no such hindrance—if there were no resistance in her will—she might indeed in a sense have "complete control" over one of her options. There would be no competing motives standing in the way of her choosing it and therefore no interfering indeterminism. But then she also would not be free to *rationally* and *voluntarily* choose the other purpose (to choose otherwise), because she would have no good competing reasons to do so.

In such a manner, I argued that by being a hindrance to the realization of some of our purposes, *indeterminism opens up the genuine possibility of pursuing other purposes*—of choosing or doing otherwise *in accordance with, rather than against, our wills*. By diminishing to some degree a certain kind of one-way control (which I called *teleological guidance control*) over certain of our choices, indeterminism makes possible a more-than-one-way control (*plural voluntary control*) over those choices, or the ability to make them or to do otherwise, in accordance with our wills, *either way they are made*. To be genuinely self-forming agents (creators of ourselves)—to have free will—there must at times in life be obstacles and hindrances in our wills of this sort that we must overcome. Free will, as I said, is a gift, but it is also a struggle—and an achievement.

Carolina concludes by saying that "far from being uncaused, free acts are acts that have rich and substantial causes. In other words, the causes of our acts *make* us free, rather than unfree, because they can explain why we act freely when we do".

Again, I agree. But I would add that if the causes of our acts were always *deterministic* causes, that would not make us more free but less free in an important sense. It would mean that we would never have the power to choose different forking paths into the future and to do so in accordance with our wills, whichever path we might choose. We would then have a measure of freedom of action but not a deeper freedom of will.

In the Conclusion, I question several further claims Carolina makes in her opening statement. The first claim is that "*it doesn't really matter, according to most compatibilists, what kinds of remote causes our acts have*". I argue that it *would* matter to our freedom and responsibility if there were remote fully determining causes of *everything* we do. Second, she says that "if it turned out that the world we live in is in some important ways indeterministic … that … wouldn't boost our free will in any way". It would merely inject randomness or chance that cannot enhance our control. I argue in response that this is not the case. Indeterminism makes possible a kind of freedom (freedom of will) and a kind of responsibility (ultimate responsibility) that are valuable and that we would not have in a thoroughly determined world. Third, she says that free actions are not uncaused but have to have the right kinds of causes. I agree with this but argue that the right kinds of causes could not always be deterministic causes if we are to have freedom of will.

Chapter 4

Reply to Bob Kane's Opening Statement

Carolina Sartorio

Contents

Introduction

In his opening statement, Bob proposes a theory of free will that has the following features:

- Determinism is incompatible with free will and thus with moral responsibility.
- Free will is possible under certain (indeterministic) conditions.
- Those conditions involve the opportunity to perform, at some key points in our lives, *will-setting* or *self-forming acts* (SFAs).
- SFAs are acts by means of which we resolve a deep conflict in our will, in cases where we are torn between competing visions of who we want to become.
- In those cases, the conflict is resolved when one set of such motivations wins out over the others: an SFA is the result of the winning motivations *indeterministically causing* the choice.
- SFAs are free because in those cases (i) we are the *ultimate sources* of our acts and (ii) we had *alternative possibilities* of action (we could have done otherwise).

For example, a young man who is a freshman in college and is figuring things out as he starts a new chapter of his life may face

DOI: 10.4324/9781003212171-6

difficult choices: he may be torn between different career paths, between considerations such as prioritizing his present desires and his long-term goals, between the desire to fit in with his group of friends and the value to stand up for what he believes in, etc. To the extent that the outcome of those choices is truly *undetermined* (that is to say, it's not determined by factors such as his genes, his environment or the whole state of the world in the past and the laws of nature), Bob believes that in making these choices—the SFAs—the young man is exercising his freedom as he charts his own path into the future, by setting his will in a certain direction.

Even for those of us whose will is already set at the time when we act (like Martin Luther when he claimed, "Here I stand; I can do no other"), Bob believes that we can only act freely to the extent that there was some earlier time when our will was conflicted, the outcome of that conflicted will was, again, undetermined and we set our will in a certain direction by means of an SFA. It is only then, Bob thinks, that *we* (and not some factors external to us and beyond our control) are the ultimate sources of what we do. Thus, Luther can still be responsible for what he did at the time, even if at that time his will was completely set, if he is responsible for his will having been set in that way as a result of some prior struggle or conflict in his will. If, on the other hand, there is nothing he could have ever done differently in his entire lifetime to make himself different than he was, then he is not responsible.

Bob's view combines different elements in an ingenious way, which results in an attractive picture of free will. In particular, the requirement of *indeterminism* yields a certain kind of "openness" that allows him to say that free agents are agents who could have done otherwise, in some important sense. And this is something that, as we have seen, accords with a natural way of thinking about our freedom. (This is the *leeway* conception of freedom discussed in section 5 of my opening statement.) But, at the same time, given that in an SFA each of the alternatives is highly appealing to us, it is also true that we will have made our choice voluntarily, rationally or supported by reasons, regardless of what we end up deciding to do. This is important because it allows Bob to address the problem that *indeterminism* seemed to pose to our free will: basically, the charge that all indeterminism does is introduce chance or luck instead of more control. (This is a problem I discussed in section 4 of my opening statement.) Bob notes that if in an SFA we would have chosen voluntarily and rationally regardless of what we had chosen to do, then what we choose still remains, in some important sense, within our control. And this is the case *despite* the indeterminism. This is an attractive result of Bob's view, one that puts it at a significant advantage over other "libertarian" views of free will (views according to which indeterminism is required for free will). Bob and I agree about some things and disagree about others. We agree about the fact that we can have free will under certain favorable conditions and about the fact that those conditions don't require the exercise of any mysterious, supernatural or God-like powers. These are both important points of agreement. However, we disagree about what free will *does* in fact require. In particular, Bob thinks that it requires a form of *ultimate responsibility* grounded in *indeterministic causation*, whereas I think that it doesn't, and Bob thinks that it requires a *conflicted will*, whereas I think, again, that it doesn't.

In what follows, I examine these points of disagreement between us. In some cases, I develop them in more detail in order to bring out more clearly what I see as the root of the disagreement. In other cases, I offer reasons in support of a compatibilist view of free will like the one I developed in my opening statement or reasons to resist an incompatibilist view like the one Bob developed in his opening statement.

The debate between compatibilists and incompatibilists is, like most other major philosophical debates, at the same time easy to grasp but difficult to settle. Both sides are supported by forceful arguments and potent intuitions. As a result, I cannot hope to offer here a definite proof of compatibilism or a knockdown objection to incompatibilism. All I can hope for is that at the end of the day you'll come to see compatibilism in a plausible light and to appreciate the extent of its virtues and the appeal of the reasoning behind it.

1. Incompatibilist Arguments and Incompatibilist Intuitions

Bob is an incompatibilist because he believes in the following two claims:

- Free will and moral responsibility require that we be the *ultimate sources* of our acts.
- If Determinism is true, then the ultimate sources of our acts are not us but factors external to us and beyond our control.

In turn, Bob believes in this latter claim because he believes in the following two other claims:

- Being the ultimate sources of our acts requires bearing some responsibility for any sufficient cause (reason or motive) of those acts. (This is Bob's "**UR**" or *Ultimate Responsibility* principle.)
- If Determinism is true, then there are sufficient causes of our acts that are completely beyond our control—and thus for which we are not at all responsible.

That is to say, Bob is an incompatibilist because he believes that Determinism cannot give us what free will requires—which is ultimate sourcehood, or the capacity to be responsible for any sufficient causes of what we do.

Now, imagine that one tried to turn this basic reasoning into a full-blown *argument* for Incompatibilism. (To be clear: I don't mean to suggest that this is an argument that Bob is in fact offering; I'm just interested in exploring what the argument would have to look like if one tried to turn the above observations into one.) The argument would have to look basically like this:

The Ultimate Sourcehood Argument for Incompatibilism

(**Premise 1**) If Determinism is true, then there are sufficient causes of our acts that are completely beyond our control—and thus for which we are not at all responsible.

(**Premise 2**) Having free will and being morally responsible for what we do require that we be the ultimate sources of what we do, in the sense of bearing at least some moral responsibility for any sufficient causes of what we do.

Therefore,

(**Conclusion**) If Determinism is true, we cannot have free will or be morally responsible for what we do.

Notice that Premise 1 in this argument is an immediate consequence of the thesis of Determinism itself. This is the definition of Determinism that I gave in section 3 of my opening statement:

(**Causal**) **Determinism:** The thesis that our acts are the necessary consequence of causes in the remote past and the natural laws.

We are clearly not responsible for events in the remote past or for the natural laws. So, it immediately follows from this definition of Determinism that if Determinism is true, our acts have sufficient causes that we are not responsible for.

But then if Premise 1 in the argument is an obvious consequence of the thesis of Determinism, this means that the whole weight of the argument lies on Premise 2. And this, in turn, suggests that this is not a real *argument* for Incompatibilism at all, because what the "argument" is saying is basically this:

> Notice that Determinism would mean that the world is a certain kind of way. But, surely, free will requires the world *not* to be like that. Hence, Incompatibilism is true.

Clearly, this doesn't provide any new *reason* to believe in Incompatibilism but is simply a restatement or an expression of the incompatibilist thesis itself.

I suspect that Bob would agree with all of this. In particular, I suspect that he would say that the **UR** principle is basically that: an expression of the incompatibilist thesis or of the incompatibilist "gut intuition". But, if so, note how different this is from the arguments for Incompatibilism that we discussed in the last sections of my opening statement (we discussed two: the Consequence Argument and the Design Argument). Those were real attempts to *argue for* the incompatibilist thesis on the basis of prior assumptions or reasons. **UR** doesn't give us that.

So, now imagine that all we really have in **UR** is the expression of an incompatibilist intuition. How *strong* or *powerful* is that intuition?

This is likely to vary from person to person (especially from convinced incompatibilist to convinced compatibilist!). This is why, in what follows, I will limit myself to explaining how a compatibilist would approach this and, in particular, how a compatibilist might try and account for some of the cases used by Bob to *evoke* such incompatibilist intuitions. The hope is that this way we'll at least be able to see in clearer light what the nature of the disagreement is between Bob and me or between incompatibilists and compatibilists in general. Being clear about the terms of a debate is key before one can make up one's mind about it. So, if you haven't yet made up your mind about the compatibilism–incompatibilism debate, then this should help you do so—or, at least, it should put you in a better position to do so.

In his opening statement, Bob uses some powerful examples to evoke the relevant incompatibilist intuitions. One of them is the case of a young man who assaulted and raped a teenage girl in Bob's own neighborhood. Bob's initial reaction, he reports, was anger and resentment toward the young man, but that reaction changed when he attended the trial and learned about the young man's history of parental neglect and sexual abuse. As a result, he found himself transferring some of that blame to those who had abused the young man. Any residual blame for him, Bob reports he then thought, would be appropriate only to the extent that those influences didn't fully *determine* his behavior. If those circumstances were completely determining of his behavior, then he deserved no blame at all for it; otherwise he did.

This thought is captured in the following passage by Bob:

> My question became: Was his behavior *all* a matter of bad parenting, neglect and abuse and like factors, or did he have any crucial role to play in choosing it? [...] We know that parenting and society, genetic makeup and upbringing have a profound influence on what we become and what we are. But were these influences entirely *determining,* or did they "leave anything over" for the young man to be responsible for?
>
> (Bob's opening statement, section 9)

Here Bob is suggesting that reflecting on the case of the young man can help bring out the kind of incompatibilist intuitions that motivate his view of free will (the thought that if what we do is *fully determined* by factors outside our control, then we can't be responsible).

However, notice that in the passage cited above Bob isn't focusing on causal determinism, or determination by events in the remote past and the natural laws. Instead, he is focusing on a much narrower kind of determination: determination by *the formative circumstances in one's childhood.* As a result, a compatibilist about *causal* determinism and free will (like me) could agree with Bob that the young man is not responsible for his criminal behavior, if it turns out that his formative circumstances indeed determined his criminal behavior. It may be, for example, that the way he was abused as a child turned him into an agent who cannot respond to reasons in the right kind of way (he may be unable to recognize the moral reasons to refrain from engaging in sexually abusive behavior, or he may be unable to respond to them). If this were the case, then a compatibilist view of free will that understands free will in terms of sensitivity to reasons (like the view I defended in my opening statement) would entail that the young man is *not* in fact responsible for his behavior in that kind of case. And, if so, this is not a case that lends support to Incompatibilism over Compatibilism, when these are understood as theses concerning the broader form of Determinism: causal Determinism.

Now, an incompatibilist like Bob would want to say that if it turned out that the young man's behavior was not determined by his formative circumstances but was instead determined by events in the remote past and the natural laws, then the young man would *still* lack the relevant kind of freedom, because it would still be true, in that case, that his behavior was the *inevitable result of external factors beyond his control*. And, if so, it's equally unfair to hold him responsible, because this means that he is still not the ultimate source of his behavior but, rather, that some factors that are external to him are.

But notice what has happened here. We have now circled back to the bare incompatibilist intuition—that "gut intuition" we referred to before—according to which if our behavior is the deterministic result of factors that are beyond our control, then we cannot be responsible for it. But, to me, this doesn't have the same intuitive plausibility as the claim we started out with, when Bob first introduced the example: the claim that determination by the young man's *formative circumstances* would undermine his free will.

Consider the following two excuses:

> **Excuse 1**: "Don't blame me: I am not responsible for what I did. My environment and formative circumstances made me do it!"
>
> **Excuse 2**: "Don't blame me: I am not responsible for what I did. The whole state of the universe in the remote past (together with the natural laws) made me do it!"

Do these excuses sound equally good to you? To me, they don't: the first one sounds much more like an excuse—a *good* excuse—than the second. The two excuses seem to have a very different "ring" to them.

Imagine that you agree with me about this. Why could there be such a difference? Let me suggest: because it's not at all obvious that the full state of the world in the remote past is a real *excuse* for what you're doing. Perhaps it's an *explanation* of what you're doing. But it's an explanation of what you're doing in the same way that it's an explanation of *everything else that happens*! (Recall: if the world is deterministic, then anything that actually happens has an explanation in terms of a complete description of the state of the world in the remote past and the laws; this is just what Determinism is.) In contrast, not everything—in fact, very little—can be fully explained by appeal to the formative circumstances that shaped a person's life. This is why, I suggest, determination by one's formative circumstances strikes us as a much better excuse: because on those rare occasions where it obtains, we see it as something that abnormally constrains the development of individuals in ways that limit, or even undermine, their freedom.

At any rate, these are my (admittedly, compatibilist) intuitions. What this helps bring out is that, at bottom, the debate results from a *clash of basic intuitions*. Incompatibilists see causal determination by the remote past and the laws as on a par with (or just as freedom-undermining as) other narrower forms of determination. Compatibilists, in contrast, don't: whereas they see one as a genuine excuse, they see the other as a mere explanation—an explanation that applies much more broadly to all other natural phenomena.

How do *you* see it? What is the right way to think about this issue, in your view?

> To sum up: in this section, I explained how part of the disagreement between Bob and me arises from a clash of intuitions. In particular, the UR principle, which is central to Bob's view, is not something that can be used to *argue* for Incompatibilism, because it's an expression of the basic incompatibilist intuition itself. I explained how compatibilists like me would disagree with that basic intuition and how we would want to distinguish between certain forms of determination that undermine freedom and responsibility and others that don't.

2. Does Free Will Have to Be a Struggle?

"Free will is a gift, but it also involves struggle", Bob writes (opening statement, section 21). This is, again, because he thinks that our freedom can only be ultimately grounded in SFAs, which involve a deep conflict in our wills. But does free will really *have* to be a struggle? In this section, I'll take issue with this interesting claim of Bob's.

Imagine that an omnipotent, omniscient and benevolent God created the world as we know it. (You don't have to believe in God to follow along; if you don't believe in God, just consider this as a mere hypothetical.) Surely, when God did that, He did it freely. If anything, it seems that the acts of an omnipotent being are the ultimate or purest expression of freedom, because they are the expression of powers that are fully unlimited. But, presumably, God didn't have to be conflicted to create our world freely! His act of creation needn't stem from any conflict of will whatsoever.

In the figure of an omnipotent God, then, we find freedom (or the purest expression of freedom) coexisting with the lack of a conflicted will (or even with a fully resolute will). If God's freedom could work like that, then why think that human freedom must fundamentally *not* be like that? Why think that, for us to act freely, our behavior must always trace back to some inner conflict in our wills, whereas it doesn't have to be like this for God?

I suspect that Bob would say, in reply, that God's freedom is necessarily different in kind from our freedom. This is because if God exists, He is the start of the causal chain that is the sequence of events that take place in our universe, instead of a mere link in that chain, as we humans are. As a result, even under the assumption that God's will was set from the very beginning, He remains the ultimate source of his acts. In contrast, the only way in which *we* could be the ultimate sources of what we do, given that our behavior does have antecedent causes outside our control, requires a combination of Indeterminism and a conflicted will. It requires *Indeterminism*, because it's only then that those antecedent causes won't determine what we do. And it requires *a conflicted will*, because it's only then that it remains "up to us" which of those paths we take. In Bob's own words, this is because acting from a conflicted will results in our having "plural voluntary control" over what we do: it gives us the chance to choose among alternative courses of action where, regardless of what we end up doing, we act voluntarily, intentionally and rationally (Bob's opening statement, section 5).

Still, the view that human freedom requires a conflicted will seems odd to me, for two reasons. The first reason is that this results in a quite complex picture of ultimate sourcehood, one according to which there are two fundamentally different ways in which beings could potentially be the ultimate sources of their acts: God's way and the human way. The human way requires Indeterminism and a conflicted will, whereas God's way presumably requires neither. This is not a definitive argument against Bob's view, because it could turn out that the right picture of ultimate sourcehood is, in fact, as complex as this. But, in general, we tend to think that simpler views are preferable (unless given good reason to think otherwise). As a result, this at least puts some pressure on Bob's view, because it suggests that if a simpler view were available, it would in principle be preferable to Bob's.

The second reason to be suspicious of the idea that human freedom requires a conflicted will is this: Although we can't imagine human beings that are as powerful as an omnipotent God, we can easily imagine human beings who, like a benevolent God, are driven to do the right thing for the right kinds of reasons. We can even imagine human beings who are not at all conflicted when they perform those acts for those reasons and who were *never* conflicted in this kind of way, because they are *naturally* driven to perform those acts for the right kinds of motivations. Can't these human beings act freely when they behave in those ways, despite the fact that they don't act from a conflicted will?

Consider, for instance, the following example:

> **Mary:** Mary is a very nice woman who from an early age is naturally predisposed to help others. Every time Mary runs into someone who clearly needs help, she helps them. And this has always come naturally to her, so she does it happily, without struggle or inner conflict of will. Moreover, this is not a compulsion but something Mary does simply because she is naturally responsive to the needs of others.

Doesn't it seem odd to think that Mary can't act freely when she helps others because she is much more "saint-like" than the rest of us? But this is the consequence that Bob's view has: Bob's view implies that if Mary's generous acts cannot be traced back to an earlier inner conflict of her will, if Mary was never deeply torn about this in any way, then she can't act freely. And if she can't act freely, she deserves no praise for what she does.

To press this point further, compare the case of Mary with this other case:

> **Conflicted Mary:** Conflicted Mary is another woman who finds herself in similar circumstances to Mary's and who, like Mary, decides to help a stranger who is in need of help. However, unlike Mary, Conflicted Mary was deeply torn before she decided to act in this way, because she realized that helping the stranger would mean giving up some super-fun plan she had made for the rest of the day, and she really struggled with her decision as a result.

According to Bob's view, Conflicted Mary could be acting freely when she helped the stranger, because she acted from a conflicted will. She could, as a result, deserve praise for what she did. But Mary couldn't, because she didn't act from a conflicted will (and her behavior doesn't trace back to an earlier inner conflict of her will). So the fact that Mary never felt the temptation to act for selfish reasons but was always naturally drawn to help others prevents her from deserving any praise for her generous acts.

Doesn't this strike you as an odd result? Doesn't it seem like, if anything, it should be the other way around (that is, that Mary deserves *more credit* than Conflicted Mary)? If so, you'll agree with me that this is another counterintuitive consequence that Bob's view has, given Bob's commitment to the principle that human freedom requires a conflicted will.

> To sum up: in this section, I gave reasons to resist Bob's claim that human freedom requires a conflicted will. I argued that this claim results in a surprisingly complex view of freedom, one that would have to draw a sharp distinction between the kind of freedom that a being like God could have and the kind of freedom that we could have. I also argued that the view has some odd results about human freedom itself, and I illustrated with the cases of Mary and Conflicted Mary.

3. SFAs, Indeterminism and Alternative Possibilities

As I noted in the Introduction, an attractive feature of Bob's view as a libertarian view of free will is that it combines the following two claims:

- On the one hand, *indeterminism is required for our free will*, because it provides the "openness" we need to be the ultimate sources of our acts. This is because unless Determinism is false, the ultimate sources of our acts are (not us but) determining factors beyond our control, such as the whole state of the world in the remote past.

- On the other hand, *indeterminism is not a problem for our free will* if it plays the role Bob is imagining it does in the SFAs that ground our freedom. This is because the choice we make in an SFA is not the result of mere luck or chance but of an effort of will guided by inclining reasons. As a result, in an SFA we are in control of what we do: we act voluntarily, purposefully and rationally (instead of involuntarily, accidentally or irrationally). And this is so *despite* the indeterminism.

Recall that this second claim is key to Bob's project, because it aims to address the threat that *indeterminism* seemed to pose to our free will: basically, the charge that all indeterminism does is introduce chance or luck and thus it cannot give us more control than we would have if Determinism were true (which is a general problem for libertarian views of free will).

In this section, I'll examine in more detail this second claim by Bob. Is Bob right in thinking that if the conditions he imagines are met, we retain the relevant kind of control over what we do? Or is Bob's view subject to a version of the same objection that arises for other libertarian views of free will?

In order to answer these questions, we need to look more closely into the details of Bob's view. To illustrate, I'll be using one of the main examples that Bob uses in his opening statement as an example of an SFA (a case originally due to van Inwagen 1983: 127–28):

> **John:** John chooses to steal money from the church poor box after being deeply conflicted about it. John's inner conflict arises from the fact that he has powerful self-interested motivations to steal (he is in desperate need of money) and powerful

moral motivations not to steal (he recognizes that others who could use that money are just as poor or even poorer than he is). In this case, the self-interested reasons win over the moral ones and John steals the money from the poor box, thus setting his will in that direction, by making himself into the kind of person who steals in those kinds of circumstances. But his choice to steal was not determined by the events in the past: the same events in the past, including his antecedent deliberation, could have failed to result in his choice to steal. In other words, the series of events that resulted in his choice to steal was an *indeterministic* causal process.

More precisely, this is what Bob suggests about this case: John is in control of his choice to steal and he is responsible for that choice, because his choice is the result of a certain effort of his will. This is the effort to make the choice to steal and to overcome the temptation to do otherwise (the temptation that is represented by the conflicting moral motivations). At least at that specific moment in time when John made the choice to steal, he was *trying* to make that choice, guided by the inclining self-interested reasons, and he was *trying* to overcome the resistance posed by the moral reasons. Not only this but he *succeeded* in that effort. As a result, he is in control of his choice and he is responsible for it. Thus, central to Bob's argument is the thought that what puts him in control of what he does is the fact that John *exercised his willpower* at the time, because he managed to overcome the temptation to do otherwise and thus succeeded in making the choice that he was trying to make at the time.

Notice that Bob's suggestion is *not* that at the relevant moment in time John was trying to do both things at once—the immoral and the moral thing. Bob thinks that this wouldn't give us what we want. Arguably, this is because if he had been trying to do both things at once, this would turn him into a blatantly irrational being (someone who is simultaneously trying to achieve two things that he knows to be incompatible with each other), and then John wouldn't be the model of rationality and control that Bob envisages for an agent engaged in an SFA.

Instead, Bob's model of an SFA involves an effort of will to do *only one* of those things *at any particular moment in time* (an effort that could succeed or fail, given the indeterminism). Thus, Bob writes:

[I]mportantly, ... it is not being claimed that these efforts or exercises of willpower aimed at different choices would be occurring at the same time during deliberation. Nor would they be occurring throughout the entire deliberation. Rather, different efforts or exertions of willpower may be initiated at different times depending on the course of the agent's reasoning.

[...]

In other words, a distinction needs to be made between John's *not choosing to steal* at a time and his choosing *not to steal* at that time. What is assumed, if John fails in his effort to choose to steal from the poor box at a time, due to the indeterminism involved, is not that he would have made the contrary choice not to steal at that same time, but rather that no choice at all would have been made at that time. The deliberation would continue until a potential reassessment of the motivating reasons that inclined to one choice or the other led to another later effort to make the choice to steal or a potential reassessment led to a later effort to make the choice not to steal. Or the deliberation might terminate without any decision being made.

(Opening statement, section 16; emphases
in the original)

And this is what Bob says on the point about rationality:

[A] common objection is that it is irrational to make efforts to do incompatible things. I agree that it would be irrational if the efforts to make incompatible choices (say, to steal or not to steal) were being made at the same time, given exactly the same reasoning up to that time. But this is not what is being assumed here in the case of self-forming choices. Rather, one or another of these efforts or exercises of willpower may be initiated at different times, depending on the trajectory of the agent's reasoning up to that time. In particular, one such effort may be initiated when, in the course of deliberation, the agent's considered reasons at that point incline (without necessitating) the agent to make one of the choices rather than another. It is not irrational to make an effort to make a choice in such situations in terms of one's presently inclining reasons, though it would be irrational to also make an effort to make an opposing choice at *this same* time, given these same inclining reasons.

(Opening statement, section 19)

The thought, then, is that John is responsible for his choice to steal because he was, at that particular moment in time, trying to make that choice (and not the opposite choice). For that would mean that he succeeded in making a choice that he was trying to make at the time (and a choice that was rational at the time). Now, given the indeterminism, his effort of will was not guaranteed to succeed but could have instead failed. Still, this doesn't mean that it could have failed because he could have made the opposite choice at that time, given the exact same deliberation: it only means that the indeterministic process could have failed to go to completion precisely because it was an indeterministic process, and this is the mark of indeterministic processes.

I will now argue that this proposal gives rise to a series of questions and also to a potentially serious objection to the view. Let's start with the questions.

The questions concern the right way of understanding an SFA, in Bob's view. One would have thought that an SFA is just a "torn decision": a decision made in the context of a conflicted will or one that we manage to make when we are pulled by reasons inclining us in different directions at once. But in the passages quoted above Bob seems to be suggesting a more robust picture of an SFA. In this view, an SFA is a decision made not just in a context where we are deeply conflicted but in a more specific context where the following two conditions also obtain:

(i) We are trying to make a particular decision (say, the decision to do A).

(ii) We succeed in that effort.

And it's not fully clear when we should think that conflicted agents meet these conditions and, in particular, condition (i). When are conflicted agents—say, agents who are conflicted between reasons for doing A and reasons for doing B—*trying to make the decision to do A*, rather than the decision to do B?

Perhaps Bob would say that this is when the reasons to do A just happen to be (at the time) more salient to the agents in question than the reasons to do B. Or perhaps he would say that this is when those agents feel (at the time) more tempted by the reasons to do A than by the reasons to do B. But if the answer is something along these lines, then another question arises: What about cases where the opposing sets of reasons are simultaneously equally salient and equally tempting to the conflicted agents? One might have thought that these are the paradigm cases of torn decisions, because these are the scenarios where we are *really* torn about what to do. Isn't it possible to imagine such cases? And can't we act freely in them? These are the kinds of questions that one would need to answer to get a better grip on Bob's proposal, before we can evaluate it in full.

So far, I have raised a series of questions for Bob that at least hint at a potential puzzle for the view. I'll now raise a more explicit objection to the view, one stemming from the same kinds of considerations.

As Bob explains in the Introduction to his opening statement, his view of free will is an attempt to capture the ordinary picture of free will according to which free will requires alternative possibilities of action. This is, again, the "leeway" model of freedom that I discussed in section 5 of my opening statement, and it's the kind of freedom that Bob thinks one exercises in the context of an SFA. Briefly, these are the requirements of the leeway model of freedom:

(1) Free will requires the existence of multiple open paths into the future (at least sometimes).

(2) Free will requires that it be (at least sometimes) *up to us*, and to no one and nothing else, which of those paths we take.

The objection that I'd like to raise is that it's not clear, after all, that Bob's concept of an SFA satisfies this model of freedom because it's not clear that it satisfies condition (2).

Briefly put, the objection is this: As we have seen, in Bob's view, the reason it is open to us to do otherwise in the context of an SFA is that the relevant effort of will could have *failed to succeed*. Importantly, this is not because he thinks that we could have decided to do otherwise at the time but simply because the process started by the relevant effort of will was indeterministic, and this means that it was not guaranteed to succeed. But, the objection goes, the mere fact that our efforts of will could have failed to succeed in this way doesn't seem to be enough to meet condition (2) above.

To illustrate, consider once again the case of John. According to Bob, when John freely made the choice to steal, he acted freely because he was trying to make that choice and he succeeded in that effort. However, he had alternative possibilities of action (he could have done otherwise) because that effort of will could have failed to succeed. And, again, this is not because Bob thinks that he could have made the opposite choice right there and then but simply because the relevant indeterministic process (the process involving his effort of will) could have failed to go to completion. But the mere fact that such an indeterministic process could have failed to go to completion doesn't give John any control over what he does. After all, it wasn't *up to him* whether that indeterministic process succeeded or failed.

Another way to press the objection is this. If SFAs work in the way Bob imagines they do, at the time when John was trying to make the decision to steal, there is really nothing else that he could have *done*, right there and then. Although he could have failed to succeed in the effort to decide to steal, he couldn't have, more robustly, *resisted* the effort himself. A mere failure to succeed is not an expression of agency; it's just the failure of an expression of agency. Thus, failing is not really something that John could have *done*, as an agent, but merely something that could have happened to him. As a result, this is not something that gives him any real leeway of action.

I think this is a serious problem for Bob's view. On the one hand, there is important pressure for Bob to say that the agents in SFAs cannot be trying to do two incompatible things at once (choosing to do A and choosing to do B) but only one of them at any given moment in time. If they were trying to do two incompatible things at once, that would turn them into irrational beings and not into the kinds of beings that act rationally and are in control of what they do. On the other hand, however, if agents in SFAs were only trying to do one thing at a time, then the only way in which they could have done otherwise at any particular time would be by failing to succeed in the relevant efforts of will at that time. But this would undermine the idea that it was really *up to them* which path they took, right there and then. Thus, this would undermine the idea that they had real alternative possibilities of action.

In other words, this is a serious problem because it brings to light an internal tension in Bob's view, one that arises from a clash between some basic commitments of the view. At the same time, it suggests that Bob's view is subject to a version of the same kind of objection that arises for other libertarian views of free will. The basic objection to those views was, once again, that indeterminism cannot boost our control, because all it does is introduce luck or chance, not added control. I have argued that although at first Bob's view seems to be better situated than other libertarian views to address this objection, in the end it falls prey to it anyway, given the identification of alternative possibilities with the possible failure of our efforts of will.

To sum up: in this final section, I examined in more detail Bob's central concept of a self-forming act (SFA). I identified some questions that arise concerning that concept, as well as an important objection that arises for the view, given Bob's understanding of that concept. The objection is that the view fails to deliver as a leeway conception of freedom, because the alternative possibilities it posits are not really in our control.

Second Round of Replies

Chapter 5

Reply to Carolina Sartorio's Reply to My Opening Statement

Robert Kane

Contents

In her response to my opening statement, Carolina presents three objections to the incompatibilist view of free will defended there. I consider each objection in turn.

1. Determinism, Formative Circumstances and the Young Man at Trial

Carolina first considers my example of the young man on trial for assaulting and raping a teenage girl in our neighborhood. As she describes it, my initial reaction (as well as that of my wife and other neighbors of the girl in the courtroom) "was anger and resentment against the young man". But when we learned more about his "sad history of parental neglect and sexual abuse", my wife and I, along with others in the courtroom, found ourselves "transferring some of the blame to those who had abused the young man". Yet, like the others, we were not yet ready to transfer all of the blame away from the young man. As Carolina quotes my statement, our questions became:

> Was his behavior *all* a matter of bad parenting, neglect and abuse and like factors, or did he have any crucial role to play in choosing it? ... We know that parenting and society, genetic

DOI: 10.4324/9781003212171-8

make-up and upbringing have a profound influence on what we become and what we are. But were these influences entirely *determining*, or did they "leave anything over" for the young man to be responsible for?

(Section 9)

She then adds that I use this example, along with other examples, to help bring out the incompatibilist intuitions that motivate my view of free will. To put these intuitions more precisely, if all of the choices and actions in our lifetimes were fully determined, we could never have chosen or done anything differently in our lives to make ourselves any different than we are. This is what we wanted to know about the young man: Could he ever have chosen or done anything differently in the course of his life to have resisted the terrible influences upon him and made himself any different than he was?

This seems like a reasonable question to ask—of the young man or others—in assessing their responsibility for being the way they are. Yet if determinism were true, no one, given their past and the laws, could *ever* have done otherwise at *any* time in their lives to make themselves different than they are.

Compatibilists, who believe that all of the free will and responsibility worth wanting, and that we can have, is compatible with determinism must deal with this consequence. They must hold that all of the free will and responsibility worth wanting and that we can have must be consistent with the fact that no one, given the past and the laws, could ever have acted otherwise in their lives to make themselves different than they are. To accept this consequence seems to me to undercut our ordinary practices of assessing persons' responsibility for being the kinds of persons they are and acting as they do, whether it be the young man or any of the rest of us.

In response, Carolina says that in the passage about the young man just cited, I am *not* "focusing on causal determinism, or determination by events in the remote past and the natural laws". Instead, she says, I am focusing on a much narrower kind of determination: determination by the formative circumstances in one's earlier years. And this, she says, makes a difference.

To explain why, she introduces two kinds of excuses that might be given to excuse oneself from responsibility:

> **Excuse 1:** "I am not responsible for what I did. My environment and formative circumstances made me do it!"

Excuse 2: "I am not responsible for what I did. The whole state of the universe in the remote past (together with natural laws) made me do it!"

She says that Excuse 1 *is* a "good excuse" and she agrees that it *would* allow us, if true, to excuse the young man from responsibility, at least to some degree, as I in fact argue. But Excuse 2, which follows from determinism, she says, is not an equally good excuse and, even if true, in her view, it would not excuse the young man from responsibility. The reason she gives for this difference between the two excuses is the following:

It's not at all obvious that the full state of the universe in the remote past is a real *excuse* for what you're doing. Perhaps it's an *explanation* of what you're doing. But it's an explanation of what you're doing in the same way it's an explanation of *everything else that happens*! (Recall: if the world is deterministic, then anything that actually happens has an explanation in terms of a complete description of the state of the world in the remote past and the laws. This is just what Determinism is.)

There are several problems with this answer that I'll consider in turn. First, when she says that the full state of the universe in the remote past is an explanation of what you're doing "in the same way it's an explanation of *everything else that happens*" in the universe, she fails to note the following significant difference. For the majority of other things in the universe—planets, stars, galaxies, trees, amoebae, insects, dogs, tigers and many other things—we don't have to ask about whether or not they themselves are to any degree *morally responsible* for being the way they are. We don't have to be concerned, as regards the moral responsibility of planets, galaxies, trees, etc., about whether they could have ever acted differently to make themselves different than they are.

By contrast, for human beings like us who are capable of moral and legal responsibility, it *does* matter whether or not they were determined to act exactly as they did throughout their lives or whether they were ever capable of acting differently "of their own free wills" to make themselves in any way different than they are. That's what we wanted to know about the young man. Even if one supposed that animals under the young man's care—his dogs or pet tiger, for example—had killed the young woman, what we'd want to know was whether *he* was in any way responsible for allowing them to do so and whether *he* could have done anything differently to prevent them from doing so.

A second concern about her argument is this: We need to be clear that determinism doesn't *merely* imply that the state of the universe in the *remote* past and the laws determine everything we would do. If determinism were true, it would also be the case that *all* of the causes that had *any* influence on what sorts of persons we become would determine exactly how we turn out—not *only* the state of the universe in the remote past and the laws but also *including* our formative circumstances, our genes, our fetal development, our upbringing, the social and behavioral influences on us and many other causes throughout our lives, *taken together,* would determine how we turn out. If the remote past determines us at all, it would do so *through* these intermediate causes. It would not "skip over" them in some magical way but would determine us by way of determining all of these intermediate causes that had a direct causal influence on our development from the moment we came into existence.

To highlight this point, consider a third excuse in addition to the two excuses she gives.

> **Excuse 3:** If determinism were true, *all* of the causes that had *any* influence on what sort of person the young man became, *not only* the whole state of the universe in the remote past and the laws but *also* his formative circumstances, his genes, his fetal development, his upbringing and the social and behavioral influences throughout his life, would have determined that he would do what he did. If determinism were true, *all* of these causal influences on his behavior, taken together, would have made it *causally impossible* for him to have chosen or acted differently at any time in his life to make himself in any way different than he is.

What we wanted to know about the young man was whether he could have ever resisted *any* of these causal influences on him throughout his life to make himself any different than he turned out to be. And if determinism were true, this would always have been causally impossible.

Of course, we know from earlier discussion that Carolina, as a compatibilist, believes that there *is* a certain *ability to do otherwise* that agents *can* have, *even if all* of their actions were determined by all of the causes that influenced them presupposed in this Excuse 3. Perhaps, then, she might want to argue at this point that if agents had this special ability to do otherwise, despite all of these causal influences upon them, Excuse 3 would also not be a valid excuse. She calls the ability to do otherwise in question, which compatibilists *can* accept, a *"weak ability"* to do otherwise and says it is *all* the ability to do otherwise that is needed to account for free will and responsibility *even in a thoroughly determined world.*

> To have this weak ability to do otherwise is to have an "ability to do something differently in your life, such that, had you exercised that ability, then either the past or the laws would have to have been different in some way than they actually are for you to do so".

The problem, however, as argued in my earlier response, is that such a "weak ability" to do otherwise is way *too weak* to give us the freedom of will we need for true moral responsibility. For this weak ability to do otherwise is not an ability that could ever be *exercised* in the *actual* world in which we live and must act. This is so because if someone ever exercised such a weak ability to do something differently in their lives, then, by its definition, "either the past or the laws would have to have been different" in some way than they actually are. And from this it follows that such a weak ability could *never* be *exercised* in a world in which the past and the laws were *not* different in some way than they actually are. In other words, it's an ability that *could never be exercised in the world as it actually is* in which we must live and act.

Yet Carolina says this weak ability is "all the ability we need" to do otherwise for free will and moral responsibility if compatibilism is true. If this is correct, I think it is a huge strike against compatibilism, because it would amount to saying that *all the ability to do otherwise needed to account for free will and responsibility*, if compatibilism is true, is *an ability to do otherwise that could never be exercised in the actual world in which we must live and act.* That's why I agreed earlier with Kant and James, who called this weak ability to do otherwise a "wretched subterfuge" and a "quagmire of evasion" for what is really needed for free will. But you will have to decide for yourselves whether or not you agree.

In this section, by reflecting on my example of the young man on trial for assaulting and raping a young woman, Carolina concedes that it is a valid excuse to say that "the young man's environment and formative circumstances made him do it". But she goes on to argue that it is not a valid excuse to say " the whole state of universe in the remote past and the laws of nature made him do it". In my response, I raise several objections to this distinction, including the objection that if the remote past and laws determined everything he did, they would do so by determining his environment and formative circumstances, which would then determine everything he did; and this would be a valid excuse.

2.   Free Will and Struggle

In her second objection to my view, Carolina asks: Does free will really have to involve struggle? The first reason to doubt this, she says, is to reflect on the figure of an omnipotent God, in whom we find freedom coexisting with the lack of a conflicted will. She then asks: "If God's freedom could work like that, then why think human freedom must fundamentally *not* be like that?"

The proper response to this question is one I anticipated earlier and is one she herself acknowledges, namely, "God's freedom is necessarily different in kind from our freedom". The vast difference between God's freedom and ours has been a central aspect of theological debates through the centuries, as I noted in my earlier response. God is omnipotent, all-knowing and all-good, whereas humans are none of these things. Being all-good, God cannot do evil as well as good, as we humans can. In addition, being all-knowing, God knows all the possible consequences of any actions that might be performed, as we humans do not. We must therefore deliberate about the consequences of our possible choices and cannot always be certain about which of them will turn out to be the best choice. Unlike God, we must sometimes struggle to do this; and unlike God, we cannot always fully justify the choice to be made in terms of what we already know. We will only learn in time and by acting.

Carolina herself gives yet another reason for the vast differences between God's freedom and our human freedom, when she says that I might also well argue (and indeed I would argue) that

> If God exists, [God] is the start of a causal chain that is the sequence of events that take place in our universe, instead of a mere link in that chain, as we humans are. As a result, even under the assumption that God's will was set from the very beginning, [God] remains the ultimate source of [God's] acts. In contrast, the only way in which *we* could be the ultimate sources of what we do, given that our behavior does have antecedent causes outside our control, requires a combination of indeterminism and a conflicted will. It requires *indeterminism*, because it's only then that those antecedent causes won't determine what we do. And it requires a *conflicted will*, because it's only then that it remains "up to us" which of these paths we will take. In Bob's own words [she says], this is because acting from a conflicted will results in our having "plural voluntary control" over what we do: it gives us the chance to choose among alternative courses of action where, regardless of what we end up doing, we act voluntarily, intentionally and rationally.

This nicely expresses a further reason why, if God exists, God's freedom is necessarily different than ours.

But Carolina does not let the issue rest there. She adds that, despite these differences with God's freedom, it still seems odd to her that *human* freedom requires a conflicted will. To explain why, she suggests we consider the contrast between two women:

> **Mary:** is a woman who from an early age is naturally disposed to help others. Whenever a person clearly needs help, Mary helps them and she does so freely (without compulsion) and without a struggle or inner conflict of will.

By contrast,

> **Conflicted Mary:** is a woman who, like Mary, decides to help a stranger in need. But, unlike Mary, she was torn before she decided in this way because she also desired to do something else that conflicted with helping the stranger and she had to struggle to overcome resistance in her will to make her decision as a result.

Carolina then argues that Mary can be said to act freely and responsibly when she helps the stranger even though she did so without a struggle and without having to overcome any conflict in her will. In fact, Carolina argues, we might even say that Mary had *more* freedom to help the stranger than Conflicted Mary, because, unlike Conflicted Mary, Mary did not have to struggle to overcome a conflict in her will to help the stranger. So conflict and struggle are not necessary for free action and they may even inhibit free action.

There are many things that need to be said in response to this argument. The first is this: In the view I have been defending, Mary *could* be said to act freely and responsibly when she helps the stranger, even if she did so without a struggle and having to overcome conflict in her will. A crucial feature of the view I am defending is that conflicts in the will and struggle do not have to be involved in *all* of our free and responsible actions. They need only be involved in those choices or acts by which we make ourselves into the kinds of persons we are, with the wills we have—that is, the "self-forming" actions by which we form and re-form the wills we express in action.

The first question I would therefore have about Mary is whether she *ever* in the course of her life engaged in any such self-forming actions in which she had to struggle to overcome conflicts in her will. In childhood, for example, was she ever tempted to disobey her parents and do something she really wanted to do (hang out with certain friends, play video games when she should be doing homework and many other things)? Was she ever conflicted about these and many other matters and had to struggle to resolve such conflicts in one way or another? If so, she would be engaging in self-formation from an early age, as I would argue most of us have to do.

Later, such conflicts would not abate between what she desired and felt obligated to do. If anything, in teenage, they would grow more frequent and more intense and would include how far to go in sexual matters, drinking and possibly drugs, what friends to hang out with and many more such conflicts. Moreover, at this time, questions about one's future and life choices would begin to multiply—whether or not to go to college and where, what to study, what career to pursue. Further into adulthood, conflicts would get even more complex: whether or not to marry or whom to marry, whether and when to have children, how to reconcile career and child-rearing and, if a relationship or marriage is not working, whether to end it or perhaps keep it together for the sake of the children.

All of these things and many more might require self-forming actions for their resolution in which one would have to struggle to resolve conflicts in one's will, to choose between conflicting values, each of which she cared about. And the choices Mary made one way or another at all of these stages of her life would influence the kind of person she would become and the will she would have in the future. They would be self-forming choices.

Yet Carolina suggests that facing such conflicts in the will and struggling to overcome them is not necessary at *any* times in our lives if we are to be free and responsible agents. In fact, she suggests that we would be *freer and more responsible* if we *never* had to overcome such obstacles in our will. This assumption is presumably based on the thought that you are freer to do something when there are no obstacles standing in your way of doing it—obstacles that have to be overcome by effort and struggle.

But this assumption also overlooks another important distinction that I have argued is crucial for fully understanding freedom of will. It makes a difference to our freedom of will whether the obstacles that have to be overcome by effort or struggle have an external source or are coming from our own will.

For example, if my closet door is jammed, I am less free to get into it than if it is not jammed. If it is jammed, I have to struggle to open it and must make an effort to do so that might fail, so I am less free to open it. Of course, if the obstacle is coming from a conflict in my own will, I also have to struggle and make efforts to choose.

But, interestingly, in this case, where the obstacle that has to be overcome by effort is coming from my own will, and not from an external source, the struggle to overcome it also gives me more freedom of another kind, because it makes it possible for me to make different choices in accordance with my will (voluntarily, intentionally and rationally) either way I should choose and thereby enhances my freedom of will.

If you never had conflict in your will, you'd never be free to do something and also be free to do otherwise *in accordance with your will, either way*. And this is what we need at least sometimes in our lives if we are to have freedom *of will* and not merely freedom of action.

Carolina says you don't have to struggle to overcome conflicts or temptations to act freely; this is true if we are talking about freedom to act *as* you will (freedom of action). But to have freedom of will, you must also sometimes in life be free to *will otherwise than you will to do*. And this requires sometimes having conflict in one's will that one must struggle to resolve in order to determine which pathway into the future you will take.

I suggested earlier that if Mary was a normal human being, she would likely have engaged in a good deal of such self-formation required for free will throughout her life, beginning in childhood and into her teenage years and beyond into adulthood, struggling to resolve conflicts in her will of myriad kinds. Even saints aren't made in a day. If you doubt that, I suggest you read the lives of the saints. Their stories are full of inner struggles, conflicts to be resolved, temptations to be overcome. That is how they became saints.

3. Self-forming Actions, Indeterminism and Alternative Possibilities

The third of Carolina's three objections focuses on what she calls "the central threat *indeterminism* poses to our free will", namely, that "all indeterminism does is introduce chance or luck and thus it cannot give us more control than we would have if determinism were true". She notes that this is the source of the many objections from "luck" or "chance" to libertarian views requiring indeterminism. My view, she says, addresses various problems about luck and chance but, in the end, she thinks it does not adequately address all of these problems.

To explain why, she focuses on my account of self-forming actions, using my example of John, torn between stealing from the church poor box and his moral motives for not doing so. If John is to make either choice, it was said, effort would have to be made to overcome resistance in his will coming from his reasons or motives for making the alternative choice. These resistant motives and the resulting conflict in his will would give rise to indeterminism in this effort, making it uncertain that it would succeed. If he succeeds in his effort nonetheless—for example, to choose to steal—despite this indeterminism, he will have made that choice to steal voluntarily, intentionally and rationally. But what if his effort had failed, due to the indeterminism involved? Carolina asks us to focus our attention on the *failure* of efforts in self-forming choice situations. She says

> A mere failure to succeed is not an expression of agency; it's just the failure of an expression of agency. Thus, failing is not something John could have *done*, as an agent, but merely something that could have happened to him. ... [This] suggests that Bob's view is subject to a version of the same kind of objection that arises for other libertarian views of free will. The basic objection to those views was ... that indeterminism cannot boost our control, because all it does is introduce luck or chance, not added control.

There are many things to be said in response to this objection. Consider first her conclusion: "that indeterminism cannot boost our control, because all it does is introduce luck or chance, not added control". This conclusion overlooks another feature I have emphasized about my view throughout: To adequately address the free will problem, one must take into account different notions of *agential control*, as well as different notions of freedom, different dimensions of responsibility and other distinctions.

Indeterminism does indeed diminish one kind of control agents may exercise over their voluntary activities, which was called *teleological guidance control* (TGC). But in doing so, indeterminism makes possible another kind of control, namely, *plural voluntary control* (PVC), which is especially important for freedom of will.

Agents exercise *teleological guidance control* over their cognitive activities (such as their efforts in self-forming choice situations) when they are able, through feedback loops and error correction mechanisms, to guide these cognitive activities toward certain goals in the face of perturbations. Indeterminism *diminishes* such teleological guidance control, but it *does not eliminate it altogether*. As neuroscientist Marius Usher (2006) makes clear, a complex dynamical system, such as a human agent, can exhibit teleological guidance control, tending through feedback loops and error correction to converge on a goal, *even when, due to presence of indeterminism, it is uncertain whether the goal will be attained.*

If the activity (in this case, the effort or exertion of willpower) does succeed in attaining its goal (the choice aimed at), despite this indeterminism, then the agent can be said to have brought about the choice voluntarily and intentionally by making an effort to bring it about. If the effort *fails*, however, due to the indeterminism, it does *not* follow that the choice that may eventually be made will occur merely as a matter of luck or chance, as Carolina claims in making this objection.

Consider the case of John deliberating about whether or not to steal from the poor box. If, due to the indeterminism, John fails in his effort to choose to steal from the poor box at a time, the deliberation would either continue until a reassessment of the motivating reasons that inclined him to one choice or the other led to another later effort to make the choice to steal or a potential reassessment led to a later effort to make the choice not to steal. Either of these potential further efforts might also fail. But if either of them succeeds, despite the indeterminism, John would have brought about one or another of the choices (i.e., to steal or not to steal) and would have done so voluntarily and intentionally (i.e., in accordance with his will), whichever choice should be made.

> In other words, whichever choice is made in such a self-forming choice situation will not occur merely by chance or luck. Whichever choice is made will have been brought about purposefully by the agent in accordance with the agent's will.

It may, of course, also be that no choice is made in the course of a deliberation. John, as I said, may leave the church, planning to think more about it, perhaps berating himself for his indecisiveness. But in that case also, it will *not* be the case that one choice rather that the other occurs "merely by chance or luck", as the objection claims. In that case, no choice whatsoever *occurs*. So, in a self-forming choice situation, any choice that *does occur* will not occur merely by chance or luck. It will have been brought about by the agent in an effort to make it rather than an alternative, voluntarily and intentionally.

The conclusion Carolina draws from this third objection is thus not true. It is not true "that indeterminism cannot boost our control, because all it does is introduce luck or chance, not added control". To see why this is not "all" indeterminism can do, one must consider that to fully understand free will, it is necessary to distinguish not only different kinds of freedom and dimensions of responsibility but also different kinds of *control*.

By *diminishing* (without eliminating) one kind of control—*teleological guidance control* that agents have over their efforts or exertions of willpower—indeterminism makes it possible that these efforts or exertions may fail to attain their goals. But, by doing this, indeterminism also makes possible another kind of agential control that is crucial for free will, namely, *plural voluntary control*: the power at some points in our lives to be able to choose from among different possible paths into the future our lives may take and to be able to do so *in accordance with our wills, whichever path is chosen*.

Moreover, exercising such a power seems to require indeterminism. If the choice made at such times was always determined, it would not have been causally possible to have made an alternative choice and hence not causally possible to have made an alternative choice voluntarily, intentionally and rationally. Thus, as argued in my opening statement, by being a hindrance to the realization of some of our purposes, indeterminism opens up the genuine possibility of pursuing other purposes—of choosing or doing otherwise in accordance with, rather than against, our wills.

I think therefore it is simply wrong to say, as Carolina and other critics of libertarian free will do, that indeterminism cannot enhance our freedom because "all it does" is introduce luck or chance, not added control. She is right, however, to say (as she does in her opening statement) that "an important part of the motivation for being a compatibilist" is the thought that indeterminism, even if true, could not help with free will: As she puts it, "indeterminism could not give us any more control over what we do than we would have if determinism were true". This is indeed an assumption that has motivated most compatibilist views through the centuries, including her own view. Yet I believe it is mistaken. Indeterminism makes possible a kind of control—plural voluntary control—over some of our actions that we could not have if determinism were true.

What you have to ask yourself is whether it matters to you that there will be times in life when you face forking paths into the future that your life may take, that it be "up to you" at such times which of these paths you will take, because either path may be chosen by you in accordance with your will. Does this matter to you, or are you satisfied with the thought that at all times in life, only one path into the future is really possible for you?

> In section 2, I respond to Carolina's argument that a person who never had any conflicts in her will that she had to struggle to overcome would have more freedom than a conflicted person would have. I respond that such an agent might have more occasions on which she was free to do *what* she wills, but if she *never* had to struggle to overcome such conflicts in the will, she would have less freedom and control over what it is she *wills* to do (that is, less freedom of will). Section 3 considers the third of Carolina's objections, that indeterminism cannot boost our control over our actions because all it does is introduce chance and randomness, which lessens control. In response, I argue that indeterminism does diminish (without eliminating) one kind of control agents may exercise over their voluntary activities; that is, teleological guidance control (TGC). But in doing so, indeterminism makes possible another kind of control, namely, plural voluntary control (PVC), which is especially important if we are to have freedom of will.

4. Intuitions and Aspirations

Carolina says that disagreements about free will such as ours involve a "clash of intuitions". Indeed, they do. But there is more to it than a clash of intuitions. I have argued that the deepest problems of philosophy, of which the problem of free will is certainly one, also involve a clash of what I have called in past writings "aspirations" (Kane 1993, 1996, 2010). In this regard, I have often quoted Immanuel Kant, who said that there were three great philosophical questions humans can ask:

- What can we know?
- How should we act and live?
- What should we aspire to?

For most of the deepest questions of philosophy, including his second question about ethics, we cannot definitively resolve them in terms of our answers to the first question, "What can we know?" if "know" means know with certainty. We must bring in the third question as well: "What should we aspire to?"

"Aspiration" has a special meaning in this third question having to do with the search for truth. Kant himself in this third question uses the term "hope" rather than "aspiration". His actual question is "What can I hope for?" ("*Was kann Ich hoffen?*"). Hope and aspiration are related, to be sure. But hope is something you can have while doing nothing to attain what is hoped for, whereas aspiration, as I am viewing it, involves a patient spiritual and intellectual search or quest for the true and the good, as in Socrates' saying that "the unexamined life is not worth living". It is with this meaning in mind that I have altered the formulation of Kant's third question from "hope" to "aspiration".

By this alteration, I mean to emphasize that the move beyond the first two Kantian questions to the third about aspiration is not a move away from rational inquiry to "irrational" hope. To the contrary, aspiration as understood here does not preclude rational inquiry but rather requires it. Think of scientists, who aspire to find the ultimate truths about the nature of the universe. They do not merely "hope" that their speculations and theories provide such knowledge. They continually submit their speculations to experiments and tests in order to find out to what degree their theories may or may not provide such knowledge. They engage in a patient intellectual search or quest for what is worth believing about the nature of the universe.

A similar idea holds in philosophy. But what we aspire to there is to understand not only what is worth believing about the nature of the universe but also what is worth believing *and striving for* in the nature of things, if we are to give full meaning to our lives. There is plenty of room for argument here as well. If, for example, you aspire to the kind of free will I have been defending as something that would give greater meaning to your life, you must confront arguments that such a freedom is not possible in the real world because "all indeterminism does is introduce chance or luck into the world and thus it cannot give us more control than we would have if determinism were true". And you must answer many other objections, many of which were ably defended in this debate by

Carolina, suggesting that such a freedom is not "worth wanting" or that it is not a freedom we *could* have anyway.

"Aspiration" is an apt word for this radically contingent seeking. It signifies "an outflowing or going outward of the spirit," from the Latin *aspirare*, which means "to breathe (*spirare*) forth" but also "to have a desire or longing for something" and "to seek to attain it". The image suggested is of our spirits reaching beyond the finite points of view we inhabit in order to find out what would give ultimate meaning to our lives.

So why do we want free will? In my book *The Significance of Free Will* (1996), I answered this way, which is worth repeating in conclusion:

> We want it because we want ultimate responsibility. And why do we want that? For the reasons that children and adults take delight in their accomplishments from the earliest moments of their awakening as persons, whether those accomplishments are the making of a fist [as the baby may do while sitting in an infant seat] or walking upright or composing a symphony.
>
> (100–110)

They want these accomplishments to be ultimately their own doing and not ultimately caused by some aliens or hidden forces they do not control.

When a young child is first learning to walk, you may hold her hands from behind to make sure she does not fall. But when, at a certain point, she pushes your hands away as if to say, "Unhand me, I want to do this on my own", I believe "she is expressing a primordial desire that inevitably arises in creatures who attain a certain level of self-consciousness: the desire to be 'somebody' whose contribution to the world is her own. ... Belief in free will is a higher order expression of this thirst in response to the seditious influences of the world" that we do not control. "Whether that thirst can be fulfilled and what its ultimate significance may be are matters of continuing debate. But I believe the thirst goes with the territory of self-reflectiveness and is connected to higher aspirations in human beings toward a worth for their existence that transcends transitory satisfactions. If these aspirations matter, free will matters".

In this final section, I reflect on the question of why we should want free will. Free will, I argue, is something we should aspire to possess if we want to give full meaning to our lives, and I explain why I believe this to be the case.

Chapter 6

Reply to Bob Kane's Reply to My Opening Statement

Carolina Sartorio

Contents

1. Indeterminism and Free Will

In my opening statement, I sketched a theory of free will, the "Reasons-Sensitivity view," according to which acting freely is acting from the right kinds of causes. When we act freely, I suggested, the causal histories of our acts reflect the fact that we are suitably sensitive to reasons and, thus, that our agential powers are not being bypassed or impaired by freedom-undermining forces such as manipulating aliens or irresistible compulsions. Recall that this is a *compatibilist* view of free will because, on this view, acting freely is compatible with the truth of Determinism. That is to say, the causal histories of our acts could potentially trace back to a complex set of causes in the distant past that entail that we would act in the way we did (if the laws of our world are deterministic), and this wouldn't rob us of our free will. For example, we could still have free will if everything we do were already determined by the full state of the world at the time of the Big Bang or at the time when our world was initially created (by God, or aliens or what have you).

In his response to my opening statement, Bob notes that he is in agreement with much of what I suggest concerning what is *necessary*

DOI: 10.4324/9781003212171-9

for us to have free will. In particular, he agrees that a certain kind of causal history exhibiting sensitivity to reasons may be necessary. However, he disagrees with the claim that such conditions can be *sufficient* for our having free will. This is an important point of disagreement because what we are after, in giving an account of free will, are conditions that are *both necessary and sufficient* for our having free will.

As an analogy, imagine that one is wondering about what conditions a number must meet to be divisible by 6 and that somebody suggests, as a possible answer, that the number must be divisible by 2. Although being divisible by 2 is necessary for being divisible by 6, it's not sufficient. For example, the number 10 is divisible by 2 but not by 6. Thus, the answer is incomplete; it is missing something important. (Exercise for the reader: How could this answer be improved so that it doesn't have this problem? What are necessary and sufficient conditions for a number to be divisible by 6?)

Similarly, Bob is arguing that my answer to the question about the conditions for free will is incomplete: it's missing an important ingredient. And what is that missing ingredient, according to Bob? It's the *indeterminism* required for us to have the opportunity to be self-made agents. In order for us to have free will, he thinks, we must have the chance to perform self-forming actions (SFAs) that allow us to shape our own wills, at least during some key points in our lives. And this must be done in an indeterministic setting, because this is the only way in which we (instead of determining forces outside our control) can be the ultimate sources of our wills. As a result, Bob is an *incompatibilist*: he thinks that Determinism is incompatible with free will and, thus, that our acts must be undetermined for us to have free will.

Given that this is our main point of disagreement, it will be the focus of the first part of my response. But let me note that what I say here is connected with my reply to Bob's own opening statement (in particular, with my comments in section 3), so you can check out those comments as a complement to this, if it helps you understand the debate better.

Take the main example I used in my opening statement: the case of **Noncompulsive Keying.** This was a disgruntled neighbor who keyed my car out of spite and not as a result of an irresistible compulsion or any other freedom-undermining mechanism of that kind. According to the view that I proposed, my neighbor acted freely because he was sufficiently sensitive to reasons when he acted in that way (this was in contrast with the compulsive neighbor described in **Compulsive Keying**, who didn't act freely when he keyed my car). However, Bob would suggest that in order for my neighbor to have acted freely, another important condition must be met. Namely, there must have been some point in his life when he "made himself" into the kind of person who commits that type of act, by performing the relevant SFA in an indeterministic setting.

In what follows I'll argue that Bob is wrong in thinking that the opportunity to perform such an SFA can play this role in grounding my neighbor's freedom. It cannot do that, I'll argue, because it cannot give him any more control over what he does, or over how he shapes his will, than if he hadn't had such an opportunity. As a result, indeterminism (or the kind of indeterminism at play in the context of an SFA) cannot contribute positively to his freedom. Maybe it wouldn't *stand in the way of* his freedom (a point to which I'll return momentarily), but it also wouldn't promote his freedom in any significant way.

Picture that moment in time when my neighbor is about to perform the SFA in question. He's struggling between conflicting motivations—let's say the selfish motivations to attend to his own needs (and to disregard the needs and interests of others) and the moral motivations to be a good citizen (somebody dedicated to helping others in his community, to be a good neighbor, etc.). At the end of the day, the selfish motivations win over the moral motivations, and my neighbor has shaped his own character in a way that would lead him to perform inconsiderate, unneighborly acts in the future.

In Bob's view, we should understand this in terms of my neighbor's *own efforts of will* succeeding in what they were attempting to achieve then (becoming an inconsiderate person). In addition, it is key, in his view, that the outcome of that process not be determined by anything outside of his control (such as the whole state of the world in the past together with the laws), because that would make those determining factors the ultimate source of my neighbor's will, which would preclude his freedom. Hence, he thinks it's important that his effort of will could have failed to succeed or that there be a certain kind of "openness" represented by the existence of two possible outcomes of his deliberation process:

(a) His effort of will succeeds.
(b) His effort of will fails.

In sum, in Bob's view, in order for my neighbor to have free will, he must have contributed to shaping his own will at some earlier point in life by performing the relevant SFA. Plus, that SFA must have been the result of an indeterministic process involving his own effort of will, which was not guaranteed to succeed but could have failed.

My objection is, then, this: the mere fact that such an indeterministic process could have failed to go to completion (in other words, the mere fact that there was an option (b) alongside option (a)) doesn't give my neighbor any more control over what he decides to do. After all, it wasn't *up to him* whether that indeterministic process succeeded or failed. Although, under these circumstances, the process could have failed, *he* wouldn't have been the one to make it fail. Rather, it would have failed simply because it was an indeterministic process, and indeterministic processes are (by their own nature, or by definition) processes that are not guaranteed to succeed.

In other words, my objection is that the "openness" provided by the existence of option (b) is just that: *mere openness*, not a kind of openness that remains within my neighbor's control. And, if it's mere openness, it's not something that could give my neighbor more freedom or control than he would have had without it (that is, if only option (a) was a real possibility, which would have been the case if the outcome of his deliberation had been predetermined). In general, the existence of an alternative to the actual course of events is not something that can enhance our control over what we do unless the alternative is also within our control. But option (b) was not under my neighbor's control. So, the existence of (b) as an alternative to (a) is not something that can boost my neighbor's control in any way.

To clarify my response: I agree with Bob that my neighbor *can* act freely when he performs the SFA in the way that Bob imagines. According to the Reasons-Sensitivity view that I sketched in my opening statement, my neighbor can act freely in this context to the extent that when he makes that decision, he acts from the right kinds of causes in a way that reveals that he's suitably sensitive to reasons. In fact, I also agree with Bob's claim (see, e.g., the Introduction of his reply) that our freedom as human agents is expressed not just in what we do with our bodies but, more fundamentally, in what we do "in our minds"—that is to say, in our *acts of will*, or in the choices or decisions that we make. On my view, free choices are, again, choices that are sensitive to reasons in the right kind of way. And some of those reasons-sensitive choices could in principle be made in an indeterministic setting, where the relevant efforts of will are not guaranteed to succeed. In other words, I believe that indeterminism needn't *take away* our freedom, because it needn't take away the reasons-sensitivity in which our freedom is grounded.

Still, the point I've tried to make here is that although indeterminism needn't take away our freedom, it also could not contribute to the *promotion* of our freedom. Again, all it does is introduce a range of open possibilities about how things could have turned out, without giving us more control over those possibilities. At least, I think that this is a problem that arises for a libertarian model like Bob's, where the open possibilities consist in the fact that our efforts of will could have failed to succeed, simply due to the indeterministic nature of those processes. The mere fact that our efforts of will could have failed to succeed at the time is not something that can boost or enhance our freedom in any significant way. (In his opening statement, Bob briefly discusses other libertarian models that postulate more robust forms of agency or causation. As he notes then—see, e.g., section 1—these models are commonly challenged on the basis that they postulate magical or mysterious forms of agency that clash with the modern scientific picture of the world.)

To sum up the contents of this section: in this section, I took up Bob's challenge that my Reasons-Sensitivity view fails to provide sufficient conditions for free will and his suggestion that another necessary condition for free will is indeterminism or, more precisely, the opportunity to perform SFAs in an indeterministic setting. I argued that Bob's proposal fails because the addition of such an opportunity doesn't enhance our freedom but merely introduces open possibilities that are not within our control.

2. Leeway Compatibilism: The Consequence Argument and "Weak" Abilities

In section 5 of my opening statement, I explained how compatibilists could defend their view from the challenge posed by the

Consequence Argument for Incompatibilism. One of the two answers I discussed in that section was the perspective of *leeway compatibilists*. Recall that these are compatibilists who believe that we can act freely in deterministic scenarios because we can retain the ability to do otherwise in such scenarios. In other words, leeway compatibilists are compatibilists who embrace the following conception of freedom:

> **Leeway Freedom:** The idea that acting freely requires some "leeway" in action, in the sense of having the ability to do otherwise.

Leeway compatibilists, I noted, could respond to the Consequence Argument by refusing to accept the premise that says that we are powerless over the remote past and the laws, because they could argue that *if* we had the ability to do otherwise in a deterministic world (as they believe we do), we would also, *as a result*, have the following ability concerning the past and the laws:

> **Weak Ability:** The ability to act in a way that is such that, had we acted that way, then the past/laws would have been different.

Although this is a "weak" ability, not a "strong" ability (or an ability to directly influence the past or the laws, which we obviously don't have), I noted that such a weak ability might be all that is required to cast doubt on the soundness of the argument. (In reconstructing the argument in this way, I was basically following the philosopher David Lewis [1981], who championed this type of defense.)

In his reply, Bob disagrees. He argues that the weak ability is too weak to ground our freedom. It's too weak because it's an ability that we could never exercise *in the actual world we live in*, with the past and the laws as they really are. We could never exercise such an ability in the actual world (assuming that the actual world is deterministic) because if we were to exercise it, then the past or the laws would have to have been different. Thus, Bob writes:

> [W]hat is really needed for free will at least at some times in our lives is the ability to do otherwise that it is possible for us to *exercise* in the real world in which we live and must act,

with the past as it really is and the laws as they really are. And such an ability cannot be had if determinism is true of that real world. What compatibilists would be giving us instead is an ability that could only be exercised in merely hypothetical or possible worlds that never actually existed.

(Section 2 of Bob's reply)

There are two possible interpretations of this objection. I'll argue that the objection fails on both of them.

According to the first interpretation of the objection, the complaint is that the weak ability that results from the ability to do otherwise in a deterministic world is an ability *that we won't ever exercise in the actual world* and that this is somehow problematic.

I believe that, under this interpretation, the objection can easily be put to rest. Although it seems right to say that the relevant ability is one that we won't ever exercise in the real world, I don't see how this can be grounds for an objection. The weak ability is, by definition, an ability that results from having the ability to do otherwise, or from having the ability to act differently from the way in which we actually act. *Of course* such an ability will never in fact be exercised! After all, it is (again, by definition) an ability that results from the ability to do something that we won't *in fact* ever do. If so, it's hard to see how this could be a reason to think that we lack such an ability.

For example, I didn't go to med school (and imagine that I never will). Leeway compatibilists want to say that I can still have the ability to go to med school, even if we live in a deterministic world, and that such an ability results in the weak ability concerning the past and the laws (because had I gone to med school, then the past or the laws would have to have been slightly different). Neither of these abilities is an ability that I will ever exercise in the actual world. But they're still abilities that I have and that I *could have* exercised, or so they would argue. Plus, when we imagine ourselves exercising such abilities (for example, when we imagine me going to med school), we must thereby imagine that something went differently, given that we're imagining ourselves acting in a way that is different from the actual way. And if the world is deterministic, what we are imagining is a merely hypothetical, nonactualized possibility where the past or the laws are slightly different, too. For example, we might have to imagine that my past experiences were different in some way that led me to want to pursue med school instead of graduate school in philosophy, which was my actual choice.

But there is a second possible interpretation of the objection (in fact, I suspect that this second interpretation better tracks the objection that Bob meant to raise in his reply). According to this alternative interpretation, the complaint is, not that the weak ability is an ability that we won't ever exercise in the real world, but that it is an ability that we can't imagine ourselves exercising *in any hypothetical scenario where the past and the laws are exactly the same as ours*. I take it that the thought is that nonactualized possibilities with a different past or laws are just too different from our world to matter to how free we are in this world.

To illustrate the objection further, imagine, first, that some of our choices are not determined. For example, when my neighbor performed the SFA described in the previous section, it was in fact undetermined that his effort of will would succeed and thus that he would make the choice to become an inconsiderate person. In that case, Bob would say, my neighbor could have failed to become an inconsiderate person, and this is a possibility that concerns a merely hypothetical possibility but one *with exactly the same past and laws as ours*. Whereas his effort of will succeeds in the actual world, it fails in those nonactualized possibilities with the same past and laws. This is what you cannot have if Determinism is true. If Determinism is true, the same past and laws lead to one and only one possible outcome: there isn't such a range of possibilities "branching out" at different points in time. Thus, assuming that an agent acts differently in a deterministic world automatically results in the assumption that the past/laws are different, too.

Now, if this is the objection, then I think it fails, too, but for other reasons. Basically, it fails because (at least as it stands) the objection assumes what it's trying to prove. Under this interpretation, the objection consists in insisting that for us to have the ability to act freely, we must have the capacity to act differently *in a way that is consistent with the same exact past and the laws*. But this amounts to an outright rejection of the idea that we can have the ability to do otherwise if Determinism is true (the leeway compatibilist idea that we are considering), because it amounts to claiming that the ability to do otherwise requires the falsity of Determinism.

It might help to retrace the main steps of the debate between the proponents of the Consequence Argument and the leeway compatibilists who respond to it. In this context, the proponents of the Consequence Argument are the ones making the first move. They argue that if Determinism is true, nobody could have done otherwise, partly on the basis that we are all powerless over the remote past and the laws. In reply, leeway compatibilists refuse to accept that starting point (the assumption that we are, in fact, completely powerless over the past and the laws) on the grounds that if we retain the ability to do otherwise in a deterministic world (which they believe we do), such an ability automatically results in a weak ability concerning the past/laws. In turn, the proponents of the Consequence Argument (at least as I think Bob is imagining them) respond by pointing out that the weak ability is too weak because it's an ability that we cannot exercise in hypothetical scenarios with exactly the same past and laws as ours (we can only exercise it in hypothetical scenarios with a different past or laws). However, the leeway compatibilist counterreplies by noting that it's inappropriate, in this context, to assume that more than such an ability is required, because assuming that more than such an ability is required is, in fact, assuming that Determinism must be *false* in order for us to be able to do otherwise. And this is exactly what the leeway compatibilist denies.

In sum, the dialectic of this debate is quite complex, but I think that, at the end of the day, and regardless of how Bob's objection is interpreted, the objection fails to hit its mark.

Still, I want to emphasize once again that I am *not* a leeway compatibilist. Being a leeway compatibilist requires thinking that it's independently plausible that we can retain the relevant ability to do otherwise in a deterministic world and that our freedom is grounded in such an ability. I'm not convinced of either of these things. In fact, I believe that freedom *isn't* grounded in the ability to do otherwise and, as a result, I'm a *source* compatibilist, not a leeway compatibilist. Still, I'm a source compatibilist who is not convinced that the reasoning behind the Consequence Argument, coupled with the observations made by Bob in his reply, succeed in establishing that the leeway compatibilist view fails or that it's a nonstarter. I'm not convinced that this reasoning shows that it's a nonstarter, and I've tried to explain why. But I still think that source compatibilism is much more promising, as a compatibilist view, than leeway compatibilism. Hence, the remainder of my reply will be specifically concerned with source compatibilism and with Bob's reservations about that form of compatibilism.

To sum up the contents of this section: in this section, I returned to the Consequence Argument for Incompatibilism, in particular, to the leeway compatibilist reply to that argument, and I critically discussed Bob's objection to that reply. I distinguished two different ways of interpreting Bob's objection, and I argued that the objection fails on both of those interpretations.

3. Source Compatibilism and Frankfurt-Style Cases

Again, the form of compatibilism I embrace is *source compatibilism*, and this means that I am committed to the following conception of freedom:

> **Source Freedom:** The idea that acting freely only requires having the right kinds of "sources" or actual causes (and not, in particular, the ability to do otherwise).

As I explained in my opening statement and Bob also notes in his reply, this conception of freedom is typically supported or motivated by "Frankfurt-style" scenarios (named after the philosopher Harry Frankfurt [1969], who introduced them). My example of a Frankfurt-style scenario was a variant on the noncompulsive neighbor case, one that went as follows:

> **Idle Aliens:** The night before my neighbor made the choice to key my car, some evil aliens had sneaked into his house while he was sleeping and implanted a highly sophisticated mechanism in his brain that allowed them to both monitor his thoughts to the very last detail and to manipulate his choices. To their surprise and delight, my neighbor made the choice that they wanted him to make completely on his own. (And they could tell that he would, a few seconds before he did, because they were closely monitoring his thoughts by means of the mechanism.) As a result, the aliens remained completely idle; they never had to intervene in any way.

Idle Aliens suggests that acting freely in the sense required for moral responsibility does not require the ability to do otherwise. My neighbor seems to make his choice to key my car freely and seems to be responsible for making it, despite the fact that (given the presence of the aliens) he couldn't have done otherwise. Intuitively, he acts freely and is responsible because his choice has the right kinds of causes: he acts from his own motives and for his own reasons and not because of any intervention or manipulation by the aliens.

Bob's response to this (in section 5 of his reply) returns to a point that we've encountered before. He thinks that in order for my neighbor to be ultimately responsible for the choice to key my car, he must first be responsible for having *the will* (the character and motives) that he is expressing in that choice. And this means that there must be some earlier point in his life when he performed the relevant self-forming action (SFA), which requires the ability to do otherwise—at least at that time.

Why does Bob think that the agent performing an SFA requires the ability to do otherwise, at least at that time? The reasoning seems to be this. Go back to that point in time when my neighbor is about to perform the relevant SFA. Imagine that we try to take away his ability to do otherwise by reinserting the monitoring aliens into the picture *back then*. That is, we're imagining that the aliens want my neighbor to make the choice to become an inconsiderate person, and they're ready to do whatever it takes to secure that outcome. However, recall that the process involved in an SFA is essentially *indeterministic*. This means that my neighbor's efforts of will at the time could have failed or succeeded. As a result, the aliens cannot be sure which of these will happen before it happens. In order to be sure, then, they have to intervene by forcing him to make the choice. And, if they intervene, this is not really an SFA where my neighbor sets his own will (rather, the aliens set it for him).

In sum, Bob is arguing that the strategy of appealing to Frankfurt-style cases fails because it is impossible to design an SFA with a Frankfurt-style structure (and those are the only times when we need the ability to do otherwise). In other words: SFAs *essentially require* the ability to do otherwise; so, given that on his view freedom requires SFAs, it follows that freedom requires the ability to do otherwise (at least at those key times in our lives).

My reply is twofold. First, I am not convinced that Frankfurt-style cases involving SFAs are impossible (very odd and unusual, yes, but not impossible). Imagine, for example, the following variant on the **Idle Aliens** case:

> **Clairvoyant Idle Aliens:** In addition to being highly resourceful and technologically advanced, the aliens have some clairvoyant abilities that allow them to look into the future: they can know with absolute certainty what will happen before it happens, and this includes undetermined events. They can know ahead of time when some undetermined quantum process will go to completion and, similarly, they can know ahead of time what the outcome of the indeterministic process involving my neighbor's efforts will be. If they foresee that my neighbor won't make the decision to become an inconsiderate person on his own, they'll intervene by forcing him to make it, by activating the mechanism they previously inserted in his brain. But they don't have to intervene because my neighbor makes the decision on his own, and the aliens foresee that he will.

Can't we imagine a scenario of this kind? Isn't this a *possible* scenario (again, a very odd one involving agents with supernatural powers, but at least a possible one)?

Now, maybe the scenario described is really impossible and I have a hyperactive imagination that is playing tricks on me. This is one reply Bob could give.

But there is another reply that Bob could give about this case. He could say that although the scenario described in **Clairvoyant Idle Aliens** *is* in fact possible, it still cannot be used to show what Frankfurt-style cases are designed to show (that there can be freedom without alternative possibilities), because my neighbor *doesn't act freely* in this case. He doesn't act freely because his decision is, in fact, *determined* in this case. What's not determined is whether he will make that decision *on his own* (given that the indeterministic process involving his efforts of will could succeed or fail). But the decision itself is determined, Bob could say, because the presence of the aliens in fact guarantees that he will make that exact decision (if not on his own then by means of the aliens' intervention). So, if (as Bob believes) determined decisions cannot be free, it follows that my neighbor's decision isn't free in **Clairvoyant Idle Aliens**.

This seems like a natural move for Bob to make at this point. But this brings me to the second part of my reply. Imagine that the arguments in section 1 convinced you that the opportunity to perform an SFA in an indeterministic setting doesn't add anything of value to our free will (because all it does is introduce mere randomness or openness, instead of alternatives within our control). In that case, Bob's response to the **Idle Aliens** case won't be effective, because then one could reject Bob's earlier claim that in order for my neighbor to act freely, he must have performed an SFA of the kind we were imagining (one by which he made himself into an inconsiderate person who performs those sorts of acts and where his decision was truly undetermined).

So, in the end, this takes us back to the central issue: Is Bob right in thinking that the indeterminism he imagines can enhance our freedom? Or does it merely introduce randomness or openness that is outside our control? Bob would say that indeterminism can help, as long as it takes the form of an undetermined SFA. In contrast, I have argued that it doesn't, because the SFA doesn't provide us with any real ability to do otherwise but merely an opportunity for our efforts of will to *fail*. (And an opportunity to fail is no genuine ability to *do* otherwise; it's just an opportunity to fail.)

> To sum up the contents of this section: in this section, I returned to the Frankfurt-style scenarios that are typically used to motivate source compatibilism (the type of compatibilism I embrace), and I critically discussed Bob's objection to the use and significance of those scenarios. I argued that Bob's objection fails by examining the relevance of Frankfurt-style scenarios involving self-forming acts (SFAs).

4. Concluding Remarks

In my contributions to this debate with Bob, I have sketched, motivated and defended a compatibilist view of free will. According to this view, acting freely is just a matter of making choices in "normal" ways that exercise our agential capacities—in particular, our capacities to respond to reasons. To have free will, we needn't have magical or supernatural powers of any kind. Also, our choices can be subject to natural influences, which can take the form of deterministic causes that trace back to times before we were born.

As we have seen, Bob agrees with me about some of these claims but not with others. He agrees with me that acting freely doesn't require any mysterious or supernatural powers and that our world could in principle be such that we have free will (at least many of us, at some times in our lives). These are important points of agreement between us. But Bob and I disagree about the relevance of Determinism. The way he sees it, indeterministic contexts of a certain kind (those that provide us with the opportunity to shape our own wills by performing self-forming acts) are essential to our freedom. Thus, in Bob's view, indeterminism of the right kind can make the difference between our being free and our not being free.

I have argued that Bob is wrong about this and that the indeterminism he imagines results in mere "openness" that cannot help promote our freedom. In section 4 of my opening statement, I mentioned this as an important part of the motivation for being a compatibilist: the thought that indeterminism (even if it were true) could not help our freedom, because it could not give us any more control over what we do than we would have if Determinism were true. So, if we are free, we must be free in a way that is already compatible with the truth of Determinism. And, in that case, the "Reasons-Sensitivity" view that I have proposed would arguably provide a plausible account of what our having free will consists in.

As we have seen throughout this book, the free will problem is as fascinating as it is complex. As with any other major philosophical problem, its complexity inevitably results in some intricate debates and some substantial disagreements. Hopefully, by now you have at least some sense of what the main terms of the debate are and of the main motivations for each view—including Compatibilism and Incompatibilism.

Perhaps working your way through this book has helped you make up your own mind about these issues. But even if it hasn't and you're still not sure what to believe, know that you're not alone: many people feel the same way about the free will problem (and about other central philosophical problems). The goal of philosophical discussion is not always to find definite answers but to think through the problems themselves and to get a better understanding of the difficulties and complexities involved in finding those answers. In any case, I hope you've enjoyed the discussion!

Further Readings

Robert Kane and Carolina Sartorio

Further Reading (Robert Kane)

For a more advanced treatment of the libertarian view of free will I defend here, see my book *The Significance of Free Will* (Kane 1996).

For more advanced discussion of competing views of free will considered in this debate and in contemporary philosophy generally, see the essays by different authors collected in *The Oxford Handbook of Free Will* (Kane 2011b).

My Introduction to this *Oxford Handbook of Free Will* collection (Kane 2011a), titled "The Contours of Contemporary Free Will Debates", provides an overview of the essays by different authors in the volume and an overview of current free will debates generally. My essay later in the volume, titled "Rethinking Free Will: New Perspectives on an Ancient Problem" (Kane 2011c), provides a further defense of the libertarian view of free will defended here.

For more works in the libertarian tradition, see, for example, *Free Will as an Open Scientific Problem* (Balaguer 2010); *Libertarian Accounts of Free Will* (Clarke 2003); *Free Will: A Philosophical Study* (Ekstrom 2000); *A Minimal Libertarianism: Free Will and the Promise of Reduction* (Franklin 2018); *On Action* (Ginet 1990); "Agent Causation" (Griffith 2016); *A Pragmatic Approach to Libertarian Free Will* (Lemos 2018); *Personal Agency* (Lowe 2008); *Free Will and Luck* (Mele 2006); *Persons and Causes: The Metaphysics of Free Will* (O'Connor 2000); *A Metaphysics for Freedom* (Steward 2012); and *Free Will: Sourcehood and Its Alternatives* (Timpe 2008).

Further Reading (Carolina Sartorio)

I developed the Reasons–Sensitivity compatibilist view of free will in *Causation and Free Will* (Sartorio 2016). For a compatibilist view that preceded it and is similar to the one developed here (but also different in significant respects), see *The Metaphysics of Free Will* (Fischer 1994) and *Responsibility and Control* (Fischer and Ravizza 1998). See also "Reasons-Responsiveness, Agents, and Mechanisms" (McKenna 2013).

For a general overview of compatibilist views of free will, see "Compatibilism" (McKenna and Coates 2020; https://plato.stanford.edu/archives/sum2020/entries/compatibilism/).

For an overview of Causal Determinism, see "Causal Determinism" (Hoefer 2016).

The most detailed formulation of the Consequence Argument was developed by Peter van Inwagen in *An Essay on Free Will* (1983).

The first compatibilist reply to the Consequence Argument discussed here was originally presented by David Lewis in "Are We Free to Break the Laws?" (1981).

The second compatibilist reply to the Consequence Argument discussed here is based on the source conception of freedom defended by Harry Frankfurt in "Alternate Possibilities and Moral Responsibility" (1969).

For more on the debate between the leeway and source conceptions of freedom, see the Introduction to *Moral Responsibility and Alternative Possibilities* (Widerker and McKenna 2006).

For more on the source conception of freedom, see "Frankfurt Cases: The Moral of the Stories" (Fischer 2010) and "Frankfurt-Style Examples" (Sartorio 2017).

The Design Argument for Incompatibilism was developed by Alfred Mele in *Free Will and Luck* (2006).

A related argument to the Design Argument (the also highly influential "manipulation argument" for Incompatibilism) can be found in *The Significance of Free Will* (Kane 1996) and *Living without Free Will* (Pereboom 2001).

For more on the main compatibilist answer to the Design Argument discussed here, see *Causation and Free Will* (Sartorio 2016), chapter 5, and section 2 of "Replies to Critics" (Sartorio 2018).

For a general overview of the free will problem, see "Free Will" (O'Connor and Franklin 2020; https://plato.stanford.edu/archives/spr2020/entries/freewill/).

For a basic and general introduction to the problem of free will, see *A Contemporary Introduction to Free Will* (Kane 2005) and *Free Will: The Basics* (Griffith 2013).

A more advanced resource on the problem of free will, including a discussion of all of the main contemporary views and arguments, is *Free Will: A Contemporary Introduction* (McKenna and Pereboom 2016).

A compilation of classical articles on the free will problem is *Free Will* (Watson 2003).

For another debate on the free will problem that contains a defense of philosophical positions other than the ones defended here, see *Four Views on Free Will* (Fischer et al. 2007).

Glossary

The glossary was compiled by both authors. Where they provide different definitions, each is listed with the corresponding author's initials.

Acting "of One's Own Free Will": Acting from a will that is "one's own free will" by virtue of the fact that it was formed by other choices or actions in the past (self-forming choices or actions, or SFAs) for which you could have done otherwise.

Alternative Possibilities Condition (or AP): Free agents must at some times have "alternative possibilities" or "open alternatives" for choice or action, which implies that the agents "could have chosen or acted otherwise".

Argument: A series of claims, one of which (the conclusion) is supported by the others (the premises).

Causal Impossibility: An event E occurring at a time t is *causally impossible* just in case the following is true: "If the past prior to t is as it is in the actual world and the laws of nature are as they are in the actual world, then E cannot possibly occur at t".

Classical Compatibilist Strategies: Assert that what we mean when we say that agents were "free or had the power to do otherwise" or "could have done otherwise" is that the agents "would or might have done otherwise, if the past (or the laws of nature) had been different in some way".

Compatibilism: The thesis that Determinism is compatible with free will. [C.S.]

Compatibilists: Believe that free will is compatible with determinism, so that we can have all the free will possible and worth wanting, even if determinism should be true. [R.K.]

Complex Dynamical Systems: Systems (now known to be ubiquitous in nature and which include living things) in which emergent capacities arise as a result of greater complexity. When the emergent capacities arise, the systems as a whole impose novel constraints on the behavior of their parts.

Conclusion: In an argument, the claim that the argument aims to establish and that is supported by the premises.

Contrastive Explanation: An explanation for why one thing occurred *rather than* another. In the case of free choices, it would be an explanation in terms of an agent's prior character, reasons or motives for why the agent made one choice rather than another.

Determinism: Means that given the past at any time and the laws governing the universe, there is only one possible future. Whatever happens cannot but occur, given the past and laws. [R.K.]

Determinism: The thesis that our acts are the necessary consequence of causes in the remote past and the natural laws. [C.S.]

Dimensions of Responsibility: First Dimension: Responsibility for *expressing* in action the will one *has*. Second Dimension: Responsibility for *having* the will one *expresses* in action.

Explanatory Luck Objection: If different free choices could emerge from the same past of an agent, as indeterminism would seem to imply, there would be no explanation for why one choice was made rather than another in terms of the total prior character, motives and purposes of the agent. The difference in choice—that is, the agent choosing one thing rather than another—would therefore be just a matter of luck.

Fair Opportunity Condition: A necessary condition for ascribing responsibility and culpability to agents in legal contexts according to which the agents must have had a "fair opportunity to avoid wrongdoing" or, more generally, a "fair opportunity to have done otherwise" than they have done.

Freedom of Will (in a libertarian sense):   "The power to be the ultimate source and sustainer to some degree of one's own ends or purposes".

Free Will Defense: For why an all-powerful and all-good God might have allowed evil in the world. According to this common defense, God did it because the love of creatures is greater when it is freely given, and if it was to be freely given, God could not determine that creatures would choose to love and follow God's way. It would be up to the creatures to choose this or not. God would therefore allow the possibility of evil for this greater good.

Incompatibilism: The thesis that Determinism is incompatible with free will. [C.S.]

Incompatibilists: Those who deny that every kind of freedom worth wanting is compatible with determinism. [R.K.]

Indeterminism: A technical term that rules out deterministic causation, not causation altogether. Indeterminism is consistent with probabilistic forms of causation, where outcomes are caused, but not inevitably. Being "undetermined" therefore does not necessarily mean or imply being "uncaused".

Intelligibility Question: Is a libertarian free will requiring ultimate responsibility intelligible or possible? Can one make sense of such a free will requiring indeterminism without reducing free will to mere chance, on the one hand, or to mystery, on the other; and can such a free will be reconciled with modern scientific views of the cosmos and of human beings?

Leeway Freedom: The idea that acting freely requires the ability to do otherwise.

Libertarians about Free Will: Those who believe that there is an important kind of freedom of will we can possess that is incompatible with determinism and satisfies the following conditions: (1) at some points in our lives, we face a genuinely open future, with forking paths into that future, either of which we may choose, and (2) at these crucial times, it is "up to us", and no one and nothing else, which of these possible paths into the future will be chosen.

Liberum arbitrium voluntatis (**Latin for "free judgment of the will"**)**:** The medieval designation for free will.

Moral Responsibility: A kind of moral assessment of people that can warrant blaming them or praising them for what they do.

Plurality Conditions: For free will: the power of agents to act voluntarily, intentionally and rationally in more than one way, rather than in only one way, and in other ways merely by accident or mistake, unintentionally, involuntarily, inadvertently or irrationally.

Plural Voluntary Control (PVC): Agents have plural voluntary control over a set of options (e.g., choices or actions) when (1) they are able to bring about either of the options voluntarily (without being coerced or compelled or otherwise controlled by other agents), intentionally (knowingly and on purpose, rather than merely by accident or mistake) and rationally (for reasons that they then and there wish to act upon) and (2) whichever option they do bring about by exercising such plural voluntary control will have been brought about by them voluntarily, intentionally and rationally in these senses.

Premises: In an argument, the claims that are offered in support of the conclusion.

Principle of Alternative Possibilities (PAP) of Frankfurt: Agents are morally responsible for their actions, only if they could have avoided performing them or could have done otherwise when they performed them.

Problem of Free Will and Determinism: The problem that seems to arise for our free will on the assumption that our acts have deterministic causes beyond our control.

Quantum-Level Indeterminism: The thesis that the laws that govern our world at the bottom or fundamental (quantum) level are not deterministic but indeterministic (merely probabilistic).

Reactive Attitudes: Attitudes toward persons associated with ordinary practices of holding persons morally responsible, including attitudes such as blame, resentment, indignation, guilt, moral approval and moral praise.

Satisficing Reasons: Reasons that are good enough to justify a choice or action even though they are not sufficient to render any possible alternative choice or action that might have been made in the circumstances unreasonable or irrational.

Self-forming Actions (SFAs): Those acts by which we form and re-form our wills (our characters, motives and purposes) and for which we could have done otherwise, which must occur at some times in our lives, if we are to be ultimately responsible for having the wills we have and hence for being the kinds of persons we become.

Sensitivity to Reasons: Our capacity to be motivated to act by reasons, including both self-interested reasons (considerations that have to do with the promotion of our self-interest) and moral reasons (considerations that have to do with morality).

Soundness: An argument is sound when it is logically valid *and* its premises are all true.

Source Freedom: The idea that acting freely requires having the right kinds of actual causes (and not, in particular, the ability to do otherwise).

Teleological Guidance Control (TGC): Agents are able to exercise teleological guidance control over some of their own processes, when they are able, through feedback loops and error correction mechanisms, to bring it about that these processes converge on a goal (called an attractor) in the face of perturbations.

Ultimate Responsibility Condition (UR):   To be ultimately responsible for an action, an agent must be responsible to some degree for anything that is a sufficient reason (a sufficient condition, cause or motive) for the action occurring.

Validity: An argument is logically valid when the conclusion logically follows from the premises: *if* the premises were true, *then* the conclusion would also have to be true.

Will-Setting Actions: Actions are "will-setting" when the wills of agents, their motives and purposes are not already "preset" or "set one way" before they act; rather, the agents set their wills one way or another in the performance of the actions themselves.

Will-Setting Condition: Agents are ultimately responsible for having the wills (characters, motives and purposes) they express in action only if at some times in their lives they had the power to willingly (voluntarily and intentionally) perform certain ("will-setting" or "self-forming") actions that they also had the power to have willingly avoided performing.

Will-Settled Actions: Actions are "will-settled" when the wills of agents, their motives and purposes are already "set one way" on doing what they are trying or intending to do before they act.

References

Adams, Douglas. 1979. *The Hitchhiker's Guide to the Galaxy*. New York: Harmony Books.

Balaguer, Mark. 2010. *Free Will as an Open Scientific Problem*. Cambridge, MA: MIT Press.

Bishop, Robert C. 2011. "Chaos, Indeterminism and Free Will." In R. Kane (ed.), *The Oxford Handbook of Free Will*, 2nd ed., 84–100. Oxford: Oxford University Press.

Brembs, B. 2011. "Towards a Scientific Concept of Free Will as a Biological Trait." *Proceedings of the Royal Society B: Biological Sciences* 278: 930–39.

Brink, David, and Dana Nelkin. 2013. "Fairness and the Architecture of Responsibility." In David Shoemaker (ed.), *Oxford Studies in Agency and Responsibility*, Volume 2, 283–87. New York: Oxford University Press.

Caruso, Gregg. 2012. *Free Will and Consciousness: A Determinist Account of the Illusion of Free Will*. Lanham, MD: Lexington Books.

Clarke, Randolph. 2003. *Libertarian Accounts of Free Will*. Oxford: Oxford University Press.

Dennett, Daniel. 1984. *Elbow Room*. Cambridge, MA: MIT Press.

Doris, John. 2015. *Talking to Ourselves: Reflection, Ignorance and Agency*. Oxford: Oxford University Press.

Double, Richard. 1996. *Metaphilosophy and Free Will*. New York: Oxford University Press.

Doyle, Robert. 2011. *Free Will: The Scandal of Philosophy*. Cambridge, MA: I-Phi Press.

Ekstrom, Laura. 2000. *Free Will: A Philosophical Study*. Boulder, CO: Westview Press.

Ellis, G.F.R. 2009. "Top-Down Causation and the Human Brain." In Nancey Murphy, G.F.R. Ellis and Timothy O'Connor (eds.). *Downwards Causation and the Neurobiology of Free Will*, 63–81. Berlin: Springer.

Fischer, John Martin. 1994. *The Metaphysics of Free Will: An Essay on Control*. Malden, MA: Blackwell.

———. 2006. *My Way: Essays on Moral Responsibility*. Oxford: Oxford University Press.

———. 2010. "Frankfurt Cases: The Moral of the Stories." *Philosophical Review* 119: 315–36.

Fischer, John Martin, Robert Kane, Derk Pereboom, and Manuel Vargas. 2007. *Four Views on Free Will*. Oxford: Blackwell Publishers.

Fischer, John Martin, and Mark Ravizza. 1998. *Responsibility and Control*. Cambridge: Cambridge University Press.

Frankfurt, Harry. 1969. "Alternate Possibilities and Moral Responsibility." *Journal of Philosophy* 66: 829–39.

———. 1971. "Freedom of the Will and the Concept of a Person." *Journal of Philosophy* 68: 5–20.

Franklin, Christopher. 2018. *A Minimal Libertarianism: Free Will and the Promise of Reduction*. Oxford: Oxford University Press.

Ginet, C. 1990. *On Action*. Cambridge, UK: Cambridge University Press.

Glimcher, Paul. 2005. "Indeterminacy in Brain and Behavior." *Annual Review of Psychology* 56: 25–56.

Griffith, Meghan. 2010. "Why Agent-Caused Actions Are Not Lucky." *American Philosophical Quarterly* 47: 43–56.

———. 2013. *Free Will: The Basics*. New York: Routledge.

———. 2016. "Agent Causation." In Kevin Time, Meghan Griffith and Neil Levy (eds.), *The Routledge Companion to Free Will*, 72–85. New York: Routledge.

Haji, Ishtiyaque. 2009. *Incompatibilism's Allure*. Toronto: Broadview Press.

Hameroff, Stuart, and Roger Penrose. 1996. "Conscious Events as Orchestrated Space–Time Selections." *Journal of Consciousness Studies* 3: 36–53.

Hart, H.L.A. 1968. *Punishment and Responsibility*. New York: Oxford University Press.

Heisenberg, Martin. 2013. "The Origin of Freedom in Animal Behavior." In A. Suarez and P. Adams (eds.), *Is Science Compatible with Free Will?*, 95–103. Berlin: Springer.

Hoefer, Carl. 2016. "Causal Determinism." In Edward N. Zalta (ed.), *The Stanford Encyclopedia of Philosophy*. https://plato.stanford.edu/archives/spr2016/entries/determinism-causal/.

Jedlicka, Peter. 2014. "Quantum Stochasticity and (the End of) Neurodeterminism." In Antonella Corradini and Uwe Meixner (eds.), *Quantum Physics Meets the Philosophy of Mind*, 183–97. Berlin: Walter de Gruyter.

Kane, Robert. 1985. *Free Will and Values*. Albany: State University of New York Press.

———. 1993. *Through the Moral Maze*. London: North Castle Books.

———. 1996. *The Significance of Free Will*. Oxford: Oxford University Press.

———. 2005. *A Contemporary Introduction to Free Will*. Oxford Fundamentals of Philosophy Series. New York: Oxford University Press.

————. 2010. *Ethics and the Quest for Wisdom*. Cambridge: Cambridge University Press.

————. 2011a. "The Contours of Contemporary Free Will Debates." In Robert Kane (ed.), *The Oxford Handbook of Free Will*, 2nd ed, 3-38. New York: Oxford University Press.

————. 2011b. *The Oxford Handbook of Free Will*, 2nd ed. New York: Oxford University Press.

————. 2011c. "Rethinking Free Will: New Perspectives on an Ancient Problem." In Robert Kane (ed.), *The Oxford Handbook of Free Will*, 2nd ed., 381–404. New York: Oxford University Press.

————. 2014. "New Arguments in Debates on Libertarian Free Will: Responses to Contributors." In David Palmer (ed.), *Libertarian Free Will: Contemporary Debates*, 179–214. Oxford: Oxford University Press.

Koch, Christoph. 2009. "Free Will, Physics, Biology and the Brain." In Nancey Murphy, G.F.R. Ellis and Timothy O'Connor (eds.). *Downwards Causation and the Neurobiology of Free Will*, 31–52. Berlin: Springer.

Lemos, John. 2018. *A Pragmatic Approach to Libertarian Free Will*. New York: Routledge.

Levy, Neil. 2011. *Hard Luck*. Oxford: Oxford University Press.

Lewis, David. 1981. "Are We Free to Break the Laws?" *Theoria* 47 (3): 113–21.

Locke, John. 1975. *An Essay Concerning Human Understanding*. Edited by P. Nidditch. Oxford: Oxford University Press.

Lowe, E.J. 2008. *Personal Agency: The Metaphysics of Mind and Action*. Oxford: Oxford University Press.

Mawson, T.J. 2011. *Free Will: A Guide for the Perplexed*. London: Continuum Books.

McKenna, Michael. 2013. "Reasons-Responsiveness, Agents, and Mechanisms." In David Shoemaker (ed.). *Oxford Studies in Agency and Responsibility*, Volume 1, 151–83. Oxford: Oxford University Press.

McKenna, Michael, and Justin Coates. 2021. "Compatibilism." In Edward N. Zalta (ed.), *The Stanford Encyclopedia of Philosophy*. https://plato. stanford.edu/archives/sum2020/entries/compatibilism/

McKenna, Michael, and Derk Pereboom. 2016. *Free Will: A Contemporary Introduction*. New York: Routledge.

Mele, Alfred. 1998. "Review of Robert Kane's *The Significance of Free Will*." *Journal of Philosophy* 95: 381–84.

————. 2006. *Free Will and Luck*. New York: Oxford University Press.

Miller, E., and J. Cohen. 2001. "An Integrated Theory of Pre-frontal Cortex Function." *Annual Review of Neuroscience* 24: 167–202.

Nichols, Shaun. 2015. *Bound: Essays on Free Will and Responsibility*. Oxford: Oxford University Press.

Nietzsche, Friedrich. 1989. *On the Genealogy of Morals*. Edited by Walter Kauffman. London: Vintage Books.

O'Connor, Timothy. 2000. *Persons and Causes: The Metaphysics of Free Will*. New York: Oxford University Press.

O'Connor, Timothy, and Christopher Franklin. 2020. "Free Will." In Edward N. Zalta (ed.), *The Stanford Encyclopedia of Philosophy.* https://plato.stanford.edu/archives/spr2020/entries/freewill/

Pereboom, Derk. 2001. *Living without Free Will.* Cambridge: Cambridge University Press.

Pink, Thomas. 2011. "Freedom of Action without Causation: Noncausal Theories of Freedom and Purposive Agency." In Robert Kane (ed.), *The Oxford Handbook of Free Will,* 2nd ed., 349–65. New York: Oxford University Press.

Polkinghorne, John. 2009. "Is the Brain Indeterministic?" In *Questions of Truth,* 128–35. Lexington, KY: Westminster John Knox Press.

Rolls, E.T. 2012. "Willed Action, Free Will and the Stochastic Neurodynamics of Decision Making." *Frontiers in Integrative Neuroscience* 6: Art. 68.

Ryle, Gilbert. 1949. *The Concept of Mind.* London: Hutchinson Publishers.

Sartorio, Carolina. 2016. *Causation and Free Will.* Oxford: Oxford University Press.

———. 2017. "Frankfurt-Style Examples." In Kevin Timpe, Meghan Griffith and Neil Levy (eds.), *The Routledge Companion to Free Will,* 179–90. New York: Routledge.

———. 2018. "Replies to Critics." *Philosophical Studies* 175 (6): 1545–56.

Satinover, J. 2001. *The Quantum Brain: The Search for Freedom and the Next Generation of Man.* New York: John Wiley & Sons.

Shadlen, Michael. 2014. "Comments on Adina Roskies: Can Neurosciences Resolve Issues about Free Will?" In W. Sinnott-Armstrong (ed.), *Moral Psychology,* Volume 4, 175–87. Oxford: Oxford University Press.

Simonton, Dean K. 2004. *Creativity in Science: Chance, Logic, Genius and Zeitgeist.* Cambridge: Cambridge University Press.

Speak, Daniel. 2004. "Towards an Axiological Defense of Libertarianism." *Philosophical Topics* 32: 353–69.

Stapp, Henry. 2007. *The Mindful Universe.* Berlin: Springer.

Steward, Helen. 2012. *A Metaphysics for Freedom.* Oxford: Oxford University Press.

Strawson, Galen. 1986. *Freedom and Belief.* Oxford: Clarendon Press.

Strawson, P.F. 1962. "Freedom and Resentment." *Proceedings of the British Academy* 48: 1–25.

Timpe, Kevin. 2008. *Free Will: Sourcehood and Its Alternatives.* New York: Continuum Books.

Tse, Peter Ulric. 2013. *The Neural Basis of Free Will.* Cambridge, MA: MIT Press.

Usher, Marius. 2006. "Control, Choice and the Convergence/Divergence Dynamics." *Journal of Philosophy* 304: 188–214.

Van Inwagen, Peter. 1983. *An Essay on Free Will.* Oxford: Oxford University Press.

Vargas, Manuel. 2009. "Revisionism about Free Will: A Statement and Defense." *Philosophical Studies* 144: 45–62.

Vasiri, A., and M. Plenio. 2010. "Quantum Coherence in Ion Channels: Resonances, Transport and Verification." *New Journal of Physics* 12: 085001.

Waller, Bruce. 1990. *Freedom without Responsibility*. Philadelphia: Temple University Press.

Watson, Gary. 1987. "Responsibility and the Limits of Evil." In F.D. Schoeman (ed.), *Responsibility, Character, and the Emotions*, 256–86. Cambridge: Cambridge University Press.

—— (ed.). 2003. *Free Will*, 2nd ed. Oxford: Oxford University Press.

Widerker, David. 1995. "Libertarianism and Frankfurt's Attack on the Principle of Alternative Possibilities." *Philosophical Review* 104: 247–61.

Widerker, David, and Michael McKenna (eds.). 2006. *Moral Responsibility and Alternative Possibilities*. New York: Ashgate.

Wittgenstein, Ludwig. 1953. *Philosophical Investigations*. Oxford: Blackwell.

Index

Printed in Great Britain
by Amazon

38193828R00129